Working with Children, Young People and Families

Edited by
Graham Brotherton, Helen Davies and Gill McGillivray

SAGE

Los Angeles | London | New Delhi
Singapore | Washington DC

SAGE Publications Ltd
1 Oliver's Yard
55 City Road
London EC1Y 1SP

SAGE Publications Inc.
2455 Teller Road
Thousand Oaks, California 91320

SAGE Publications India Pvt Ltd
B 1/I 1 Mohan Cooperative Industrial Area
Mathura Road
New Delhi 110 044

SAGE Publications Asia-Pacific Pte Ltd
33 Pekin Street #02-01
Far East Square
Singapore 048763

Library of Congress Control Number: 2009943265

British Library Cataloguing in Publication data

A catalogue record for this book is available from
the British Library

ISBN 978-1-84860-988-4
ISBN 978-1-84860-989-1 (pbk)

Typeset by C&M Digitals (P) Ltd, India, Chennai
Printed by CPI Antony Rowe, Chippenham, Wiltshire
Printed on paper from sustainable resources

Working with Children, Young People and Families

To Dennis Brotherton (1927–2009)
For whom family was at the heart of everything.

Contents

1

Working with children, young people and families – the policy context

Graham Brotherton

The aims of this chapter are to:

- Consider what we mean by 'policy' in the context of children, young people and families and how this is shaped by government
- Consider how policy has evolved in recent years
- Explore the implications of current policy for those working with children, young people and families.

Anyone working with children young people and families cannot escape the significance of policy – any workplace will have policies on a wide range of issues, for example on health and safety, safeguarding children and young people or equal opportunities. Policies exist at the local level as described here, but also at a national level, for example the broad sweep of policy ideas and issues which comprise Every Child Matters or Youth Matters. The local policies which govern day-to-day practice are a reflection of the concerns and priorities of national policy.

Policy around children, young people and families is therefore an area of social policy which can be described as the study of the way in which governments seek to influence social life. In this sense anyone working in this area can be said to be working in a political arena. It is therefore one of the central arguments of both this chapter and the book more generally that to understand the role of a practitioner working with children, young people and families, we need to understand the political context in which it takes place. In order to understand the way in which policy is created we need to look briefly at how government operates in the United Kingdom but with specific reference to England.

The structure of government in the United Kingdom

One of the key features of the UK government, particularly in England, is that it is very centralised, even allowing for the recent impact of devolution (see later section in this chapter). This means that the government in general and the Prime Minister in particular has considerable power and the ability to exert considerable influence on policy. There are a number of overlapping reasons for this. In part this stems from the way in which the government is elected. The 'first past the post' system in which Members of Parliament (MPs) are elected on the basis of who gets the greatest number of votes in a geographical constituency means that effectively government will almost always come from one of two parties; Labour or Conservative. This gives the leaders of these two parties considerable power within the party, as, effectively, political careers are dependent upon being successful within party hierarchies. This is reinforced especially in government by the fact that the Leader/Prime Minister (with close colleagues/advisers) has considerable power of patronage, that is the ability to appoint people to positions both within government and in government agencies (see below).

Governments of all political persuasions have been accused of appointing people to significant roles in 'agencies' whose views support theirs, though in the last few years there has been a move to a more open selection process, through advertising for suitable applicants.

Activity: Government Agencies

This is a term used to refer to a range of organisations that are linked to government (often by funding) but are not technically part of government. Perhaps the most important for those working with children, young people and families is Ofsted which despite officially being called the Office for Standards in Education actually regulates not just education but also social care and related services for children and young people.

Whilst you may already have a basic understanding, find out more about the role of Ofsted, for example:

- How does it regulate settings working with children and young people?
- Who does it employ to carry out its inspections?

The use of agencies to implement policy is not without its critics, who highlight the fact that they are not directly accountable to either local or national electorates in the way that governments or local authorities are.

The structure of government in England

There are three main elements to central government: the Executive, the Legislature and the Judiciary. The Executive consists of those who have decision-making power; that is the Prime Minister, Cabinet Ministers and those who

Working with children, young people and families

advise them. In policy terms this is where policy tends to be initiated, that is, where, 'ideas' about new policy tend to come from.

The Legislature consists of the two Houses of Parliament, the Commons and the Lords. This is where policy – especially that which requires changes in the law – is discussed or 'debated' and sometimes amended. All potential legislation has to go through a series of readings in the two Houses and also through a series of committee stages where it is scrutinised in more detail by committees of MPs. Whilst this process does lead to some changes, it is important to note that the government can still exert considerable influence as it chooses the timetable for the readings and the composition of the committees which scrutinise the legislation.

The Judiciary is comprised of the senior Judges who play a role in terms of defining the way in which legislation 'works' in practice, by the creation of 'case law' which is the process by which judgements, made in test cases, create a framework for later judgements. The Fraser Guidelines (sometimes called Gillick Competence) referred to later in the chapter provide an example of this.

It is important to note that to a very considerable extent a government's ability to initiate and push through legislation is dependent upon the size of its majority in Parliament. The larger the majority, the easier it is to maintain control of the process outlined above. Over the past 30 years or so, governments have for most of the time enjoyed sizeable majorities and have therefore been able to push through radical change if they have wished to. We now move on to consider the way in which governments actually develop policy.

The policy process

The 'traditional' view of the policy process is that governments start the process by putting out a consultation document in the form of a Green Paper which organisations are then able to respond to. Green Papers often include a range of options that are then either proceeded with or dropped on the basis of the response from interested parties. This is followed by a White Paper that tends to set out more definite proposals. After the consultation on the White Paper the government will produce draft legislation, a 'bill' that then enters the process described previously. At the end of this process the bill becomes a new piece of legislation or Act. To give one recent example of this process which applies in the context of working with children, young people and families, in 2003 the government issued a Green Paper on the future of services for children in the light of the Laming report into the death of Victoria Climbié (discussed more fully in Chapter 7). This was Every Child Matters. After going through the process described above this became the basis for the Children Act 2004.

3

Current consultation documents can be found on the relevant government departments' websites (Department of Health, Department for Children, Schools and
Families, Scottish Executive, Welsh Assembly). Have a look at any relevant consultation documents.

If there are any that are particularly relevant to your area of interest, think about
whether and how you might want to respond, either individually, as a student group
or as a group of work colleagues.

It is important to highlight that not all new policy follows this route, as some
changes do not require changes in the law and are brought about by government
changing the advice or 'instructions' it gives to local authorities in the form of
policy guidance. A change in the way funding is provided or targeted can also be
used to change the direction of policy. There is a good summary of how the process of introducing legislation works, as well as useful information on many other
aspects of government at http://www.parliament.uk/works/works.cfm

Whilst the role of local authorities in direct service provision is declining,
they remain significant as commissioners of services. This process of utilising the
mixed economy as a basis for policy and using non-governmental agencies as a
key element of policy implementation has been described as a shift away from
government to a broader framework of governance.

The mixed economy of welfare

One of the key changes in the way in which the services provided for children, young
people and families have changed over the past 20 years or so has been a move away
from the state (through the NHS or local authorities) as the main provider of services
to a situation where services are provided by a range of private and non-profit organisations (charities, voluntary organisations, etc.) who are contracted by the state to
provide specific services through a process of 'commissioning'.

Devolution

One of the key changes of the last few years has been the introduction of devolution, which has led to the creation of a Scottish Parliament and Welsh Assembly
and the transfer of powers to this 'new' tier of government. In the case of the
Scottish Parliament this includes full responsibility for children's services issues.

In the case of the Welsh Assembly there is a greater overlap with the UK Parliament but policy in Wales is clearly diverging in some areas.

From a policy point of view, one of the most interesting implications of devolution is the emergence of different emphases and approaches to children's services policy within the different parts of the United Kingdom.

At present, in the area of policy around children and young people for example, this is most pronounced in the differing roles of the Children's Commissioners in England, Scotland, Wales and Northern Ireland. There are also a range of other issues relating to, for example, testing and the structure of the curriculum especially in the early years.

Activity

Explore the four Children's Commissioners' websites which can be easily found through any search engine. Look at the differences in roles and emphases between the different Commissioners. What might explain the differences in emphasis between the roles in each country?

Local government

In Scotland and Wales, the structure of local authorities is quite straightforward with a system of 'unitary' authorities: a single layer of local government in which all authorities have the same roles and responsibilities. In the case of England, the system (largely for historical reasons as reform has been incremental) is more complex; some areas of England (mainly the large urban areas) have unitary authorities, whereas other areas have a two-tier system of district and county councils. In this case responsibility for children's services lies with the county authority. The role of local authorities in the provision of services for children, young people and families has changed significantly in a number of ways.

Firstly there has been a move to Children's Trusts in which there is integrated management of education, social care and other children and young peoples' services. Secondly, in many services, for example early years provision, family support or children's social care, there has been a move away from direct provision towards a purchasing and co-ordination role (the mixed economy as described earlier), with services provided by voluntary and private organisations, though there are still considerable variations in the amount of direct provision between local authorities. Thirdly, in education, there has been a move towards academy schools in which private or charitable organisations take a much greater role in the running of state education.

Implementing policy

In actually implementing policy, governments have a number of powerful levers in seeking to ensure that policy 'works' in the way that was intended. The first is finance. Central government provides the bulk of the money (which is raised through national taxes; income tax, Value Added Tax and National Insurance and then redistributed locally) which local authorities use to provide services, and often this is given in ways which mean that it has to be used in particular ways through targeted funding, which can only be used for specific purposes. A second way in which central government is able to control policy is through using legislation to create 'statutory duties', which are duties that local authorities must do, for example providing a child protection service.

A third option open to central government is to give local authorities powers to undertake particular functions. Much of the Community Care legislation works in this way and it gives local authorities greater discretion. However, in many cases the use of 'powers' is clarified by the production of guidance or standards, which may in itself create a fairly tight framework within which agencies have to operate (see, for example the Every Child Matters outcomes framework). This links to the final major 'tool' available to government which is the use of inspectorates such as Ofsted to scrutinise services, and this is discussed in more detail in a later section.

The development of services for children, young people and families

The nineteenth century can be seen as the point at which there emerged a recognisable pattern or system of services for children, young people and families. Key elements of this came from within the charitable movement through organisations like Barnardos which grew very rapidly in the second half of the nineteenth century, providing residential childcare in orphanages (though only a relatively small proportion of the children in them were technically 'orphans'). From 1906 onwards the emphasis switches to increased state intervention as the new Liberal government introduced a series of measures which are still recognisable as key elements of our existing system; school meals, legislation against child neglect, the introduction of school nurses and health visitors and education reform to try to ensure universal primary education. In particular, for the purposes of this chapter, the 1908 Children Act was passed which, for the first time, can be seen as trying to define in a general sense the role of parents in bringing up children.

During the Second World War the government commissioned a senior civil servant, William Beveridge, to look at the technical workings of the benefit system. Beveridge's report somewhat exceeded his brief and called for wholesale reform of the welfare system, arguing that the interconnected nature of the problems associated with poverty and unemployment, for example, required an interconnected response. The Beveridge report *Social Insurance and Allied Services* published in 1942 was effectively a blueprint for a welfare state and formed the basis for the general election at the end of the Second World War with the Labour party promising to implement Beveridge's recommendations in full but with the Conservatives largely opposed. The only aspect of the Beveridge report which was implemented before the election was its proposals for education which formed the basis for the 1944 Education Act with its introduction of a unified system of grammar and secondary modern schools that have shaped all subsequent education policy.

The post-war election resulted in a landslide victory for Labour, the first time the party had enjoyed an overall majority in Parliament, and the Beveridge proposals now became the basis of far reaching social reform in health, benefits and personal social services, thereby creating the framework of services which, it can be argued, still largely pertains today. In part, the National Health Service (NHS) had already come into existence as the Wartime Health Service, a co-ordinated system set up to meet the demands of war. When the NHS was formally set up in 1948 it marked a decisive shift, giving women and children full access to healthcare for the first time, setting up a proper primary care system through the general practitioner system and integrating the various strands of hospital provision.

In terms of social care, the government set up both the Welfare Department for Adults and the Children's Department, marking the first time that the state had become significantly involved in social care provision. Many of the services which now form the mainstream of social care provision such as residential care and child protection were introduced at this time. The Children Act of 1948 was introduced, as many of its successors, in direct response to a tragedy. In this case it was the death of 13-year-old Dennis O'Neill killed by his foster parents. The 1948 Children Act led to each local authority being required to appoint a Children's Officer and also led to the development of children's services in each local authority. The Children's and Welfare Departments were merged into generic Social Services Departments in 1970, but almost immediately were criticised by the report into the death of Maria Colwell (discussed more fully in Chapter 7).

Another significant aspect of the Beveridge proposals was his plans for the restructuring of the benefit system, which have proved to have ramifications and influence over subsequent policy development. Beveridge proposed a contributory system based on National Insurance which workers would pay whilst in work and receive whilst not working (providing that they had paid sufficient contributions). Women would pay contributions whilst working, but as women left the workforce upon marriage they would then receive access to benefits through their husband. Beveridge anticipated that as there was a return to near full employment after the war, the system would become largely self-funding.

For those who were unable to access the contributory scheme, a safety net scheme called National Assistance was introduced. This was intended to be a

The policy context

minor part of the system, but for a complex variety of reasons, for example the fact that there was no return to full employment and later that this was the only benefit women not living with their husbands could claim, this soon became the larger element of the benefit system. Efforts to control National Assistance and its successors, Supplementary Benefit and Income Support have been a major feature of social policy right through to New Labour and the 'welfare to work' initiative. There has been a debate for many years about the links between the operation of the benefit system and its impact on poverty and social exclusion in general, and on child poverty in particular. Recent research (for example that funded by the Joseph Rowntree Foundation in 2008) highlights that this is an issue of ongoing importance and it is discussed more fully in Chapter 4.

It is also worth highlighting that a central element of the Beveridge plan in the years immediately after the war was housing provision. In the decade immediately after the war, two-thirds of all house building was undertaken by local authorities and social housing became a significant part of provision. Whilst there were some attempts at reform and reorganisation over the next 20 years, the basis of the Beveridge system remained in place until the late 1970s, though after the recession of the early 1970s, spending on house building fell sharply. However, as outlined in the next section, the availability of social housing has fallen markedly since then as a direct result of government policy. The impact of this is important for a variety of reasons. Firstly, there is a shortage of good quality social housing. Shelter (2006) suggest that at the end of 2006 around 1 million children in the UK were living in bad housing and around 130,000 were homeless or in temporary accommodation. Secondly, where social housing does exist, there tends to be an increased concentration of families who are experiencing difficulty, causing a process sometimes referred to as 'ghettoisation' where there is a concentration of disadvantaged groups in disadvantaged areas. This point is developed later in this chapter.

The New Right reforms

The period after 1979 saw a process of radical reform in a number of areas. In housing there was the end of local authority house building and the introduction of the opportunity for local authority tenants to buy the house they lived in.

In terms of benefits, there was the introduction of the Income Support System based around fixed levels of payment for people who fall into specific categories, which still exists in amended form. For children's services, the significant changes were in the implementation of the Children Act 1989 and to a lesser, but not insignificant extent, the National Health Service and Community Care Act 1990. In order to explore these changes fully it is important to place them in the context of the debate about the ideological context of children's services.

Working with children, young people and families

The ideological context of children's services

Children's services, as with other areas of welfare, take place in an ideological context: they are heavily influenced by the political views of the government of the day. The expansion of 'Welfare' between 1945 and 1951 took place in the context of a government committed to social democracy whereas the reforms of the 1980s and early 1990s took place in the context of a New Right approach (sometimes referred to as 'Thatcherite' after the Prime Minister for most of this period).

The basis of social democracy is that the state has a positive role to play in the provision of services. This is because in a 'market' context (see below), services (in this case health and education, etc.) will be allocated on the basis of ability to pay rather than need. This is what social democrats refer to as 'market failure'. In order to ensure fairness, the state needs to get involved to ensure all citizens receive adequate support. This is sometimes called 'positive freedom': the idea that people need positive support from the state in order to be able to take advantage of the opportunities that might be available to them. The money needed to provide for these services is raised through taxation. Taxation is also related to income and the ability to pay, so higher earners pay tax at a higher rate. This is referred to as progressive taxation and is linked to a belief that the system should be redistributive, giving on the basis of need.

New Right thinking emerged as a reaction to this. It argued that the inevitable consequence of social democracy was bureaucracy and inefficiency and that the welfare system had a tendency to trap people in dependency on the state. The solution was to reduce the role of the state by reducing its role as a service provider through the privatisation of services. This would also introduce competition between service providers leading to greater choice and efficiency, and free up money which could be used to reduce taxes giving people the opportunity to take greater responsibility for themselves. Of particular significance to the 'New Right' critique has been the way in which public services, it is argued, tend to be inflexible and unresponsive and to deliver a 'one size fits all' service, rather than one tailored to the specific needs of children, young people and families. Whilst in practice even most New Right governments have retained some element of progressive taxation, most are critical of the principle, arguing for a move towards a 'flatter' tax system in which everyone pays the same rate on all income.

Central to New Right thinking is a belief in a 'free market' system, which in this context is a belief that market principles of supply and demand apply even to welfare services, that is that if someone 'supplies' a good or service at an appropriate price there will be demand for it. The better the price and quality, the greater the demand. If goods or services are of poor quality or priced too high for their market, demand will fall and the supplier will need to adjust price, quality or both in order to become competitive. This leads to the best goods or services being available at the most competitive prices, so called 'market discipline'. It also leads to flexibility and choice, as there

(Cont'd)

The policy context

are likely to be a range of providers competing to provide appropriate services. In this model the NHS and social care services could and should be provided in the same way as any other good or service.

There are however two key problems in the area of welfare. One was how to introduce market forces into an area where the state was the only or most dominant provider of services. The second is the problem of free services, as, in a market model, providing a service for free is likely to lead to an excess of demand – of which more later.

New Labour emerged in the 1990s as an attempt to reconcile a commitment to social justice with a belief in markets. Its adherents claimed that it encompassed key features of both social democracy and the New Right, hence the claim to be a new approach – the 'third way'. New Labour in government have retained, in a modified way, most of the market reforms of the 1980s and 1990s but have also developed some distinctively new elements which are explored in the next section.

The Children Act 1989

It can be argued that the Children Act 1989 remains the most important piece of legislation around children, young people and families as it covers both the broad framework of child protection (though some of the structures which surround this and the associated guidance have changed, and this is discussed more fully in Chapter 7) and the framework for state intervention into family life in the context of relationship breakdown. It is a large and complex piece of legislation and a full description is beyond the scope of this book. Suggestions for reading, giving a fuller picture, are at the end of the chapter.

Whether the 1989 Children Act can be described as a 'New Right' piece of legislation is contentious. It certainly enjoyed all-party support during its passage through Parliament and like so many other pieces of legislation in this area it arose from perceived failings in practice. At this point though, there were countervailing pressures, firstly from a series of high-profile child protection 'failures' of which the most notorious were the deaths of Jasmine Beckford in 1985 and Kimberley Carlile in 1987, and secondly as a result of perceived overreaction by social workers in the context of the 'Cleveland' case (which is discussed more fully in Chapter 7). In the light of this tension, the legislation is built around a number of key principles:

1   The child's interests are paramount – all decisions should focus on what is in the best interests of the child.
2   Minimum intervention – that is, that any intervention into a child or young person's life should take place at the lowest level possible to secure the child or young person's safety or well-being. In court cases the test is that the court has to decide whether making an order is likely to lead to a better outcome than not making an order.

Working with children, young people and families

3   Speedy decision making – where decisions about whether, and how, to intervene need to be made, these should be taken as quickly as possible to secure the child's best interests. In many cases there are specific timescales built into the legislation.

4   The welfare checklist – in court cases, the court shall have regard in particular to a number of matters set out in the welfare checklist, and in particular:

- the ascertainable wishes and feelings of the child concerned
- the child's physical, emotional and educational needs
- the likely effect on the child of any change in circumstances
- the child's age, sex, background and any relevant characteristics
- any harm which the child has suffered or is at risk of suffering
- how capable each of his parents and any other relevant person are in meeting the child's needs
- the range of powers available to the court.

5   Partnership with parents – where possible it is better for children to live with their natural family, and parents should continue to be involved in terms of both decision making and contact as long as this is in the child's best interests.

An example – Section 8 Orders

Section 8 is the part of the 1989 Children Act which deals with intervention in family life in the context of relationship breakdown. It is important to highlight that Section 8 only applies where families (and in this context mainly parents) have been unable to reach an informal agreement themselves which is what happens in the majority of cases. There are four Section 8 Orders; Residence, Contact, Specific Issue and Prohibited Steps.

- Residence Orders – these orders specify who a child will live with and under what circumstances. They can be unconditional or have specific conditions attached, e.g. the requirement to live in a particular area.
- Contact Orders – cover contact arrangements between the child/young person and named people (usually the other parent but can include extended family or others who have had a significant role in the child's life). Again these can be general or very specific.
- Specific Issue Orders – allow courts to make an order around a particular issue, e.g. where a child or young person is to be educated.
- Prohibited Steps Orders – allow the courts to prevent something happening, e.g. contact with a named individual.

In any situation the court has to decide which Order/combination of Orders is the most appropriate taking into account all the factors described previously.

Alongside the family Orders and the child protection framework, the 1989 Children Act also gave local authorities considerable discretionary powers to

The policy context

provide information, advice and support to a range of families and to support young people leaving the care system. As these were discretionary, there were wide variations in the pattern that emerged and especially in relation to the leaving care provision, evidence that the system has not always been successful.

New Labour reforms

Children (Leaving Care) Act 2000

This was the first attempt by New Labour to deal with the issues highlighted in the previous section and focuses on giving young people leaving care ongoing support in terms of accommodation, financial support and access to further education. This legislation is to be superseded by the Children and Young Persons Act 2008.

Every Child Matters and the Children Act 2004

The context of Every Child Matters is usually seen as that of child protection. In many senses this is true and this dimension of Every Child Matters is discussed more fully in Chapter 7. However, it also needs to be seen as a specifically New Labour response which incorporates other New Labour themes around employ-ability, inclusion and joined-up services as well as an emphasis on the use of computer systems to support policy; each of these issues will now be considered.

Central to any understanding of the Every Child Matters agenda is the emphasis on employability on two levels: firstly through provision of services which support parental employment such as early years childcare and extended provision within schools; secondly through the emphasis on early intervention aimed at ensuring that children 'succeed' within education such as Sure Start and the 'personalisation' emphasis within education. Related to this has been the continued emphasis on the inclusion of children with additional needs in 'mainstream' education.

In terms of 'joined-up services' these are most pronounced in the context of child protection, but it is worth highlighting the role of Children's Trusts. According to the DCSF:

> Children's Trusts are local partnerships which bring together the organisations responsible for services for children, young people and families in a shared commitment to improving children's lives. It is local authorities – through their Directors of Children's Services and Lead Members for Children's Services – which lead Children's Trusts, but they work closely with the other local agencies with a legal duty to be part of the Trust: strategic health authorities, primary care trusts (PCTs), police authorities, local probation boards, youth offending teams, Connexions partnerships, the Learning and Skills Council for England and district councils. We recommend that Children's Trusts also include other important local partners like schools, colleges and third sector organisations, as well as other local authority services like adult social care and housing. (DCSF, 2008a)

Working with children, young people and families

The Children's Trusts represent a key initiative but are as yet relatively new and untested and in particular the extent of full involvement of the organisations identified in the quote above is still variable.

This raises a key issue: the past few years since the Laming Report and subsequent publication of Every Child Matters have seen a period of unprecedented change in a whole range of issues related to policy and practice with children, young people and families which are discussed in the rest of this book. It is, in practice, too early to see whether the changes are 'working' and indeed any judgement is dependent upon the criteria for success given the broad sweep of policy change. For example, do we make judgements on 'improvement' in terms of child protection, or greater parental employment, or indeed on whether overall parenting 'quality' changes? All of these are not only ambitious changes in their own right but raise complex issues of judgement in terms of how they can be measured.

Managerialism and surveillance

One way in which the changes of the past 20 years or so can be explained is through the emergence of managerial approaches to children's services. Managerialism is a set of ideas that emerged from the New Right critique of welfare services more generally and is based on the idea that public services need to be managed in the same way as commercial organisations. It has been at the heart of both the Conservative reforms in the 1980s and 1990s and more recently key aspects of the Every Child Matters reforms. There are tensions in managerialism as an approach in that it has tended to both highlight the need for flexibility in service delivery and also the need for targets to assess performance and service delivery with critics suggesting the latter approach has proved dominant. Linked to managerialism has been a distrust of professional autonomy which has led to increased surveillance through the various inspection bodies such as Ofsted. This has been particularly pronounced in the area of child protection where a number of high-profile cases since the implementation of the Every Child Matters agenda, notably the 'Baby P' case in 2008, have led to an intensification of the inspectorial approach.

Children's services under Labour – changed direction or the New Right continued?

One of the central issues when trying to consider the way in which children's services have developed under New Labour is to what extent is policy a continuation of the New Right reforms of the 1980s and to what extent it represents a new phase. There is, in some senses, evidence for both. There is certainly more private sector involvement in the children and young people's sector, whether in

The policy context

the form of academy schools, private childcare provision in children's centres or the contracting out of family support services (and a strong commitment from government for this to be extended). Furthermore, the way in which market 'choice' has become the mantra for change across this sector has shades of the New Right critique, for example in the context of parental choice of schools.

However, there has also been a real increase in spending on a number of major initiatives though this highlights two further aspects of Labour reforms which warrant discussion: firstly, the use of targeted services to tackle deep-rooted disadvantage and secondly the central importance of work as an aspect of welfare. In terms of targeted services perhaps the most prominent has been the Sure Start programme where areas of particular disadvantage with a high concentration of families have received additional funding to provide appropriate services, for example childcare or a greater health visitor presence. Other examples are the 'action zone'/'challenge' approach in health and education. Sure Start also provides an example of the emphasis on employment, as one function of the projects has been to provide childcare and training in order to help parents find work.

Linked to this is the other element of the surveillance debate. Some commentators (see, e.g. Anderson et al., 2009) have highlighted the way in which the combination of greater contact with some groups of children and parents, for example through Sure Start, greater emphasis on recording and assessing information through the Common Assessment Framework (described in Chapter 7) and greater reliance on electronic recording of information, has a number of consequences. Firstly it can be argued that more parents and children are likely to be formally assessed; secondly that this information will be more carefully recorded, and thirdly that this information will be shared more widely. This can have both positive consequences in terms of rational allocation of resources to those whose needs are greatest, but also raises the danger of children and families with regular or complex needs becoming inappropriately labelled simply as a result of ongoing contact with services.

What does the future hold?

At the point of writing there appears to be a broad political consensus around the shape of children's services, though it remains uncertain how the changed climate around greater public spending will have an impact over the next few years. Nonetheless the model of a mixed economy of services working in an integrated way appears to be the dominant policy discourse for the foreseeable future.

Further reading

One of the main difficulties with policy is that the rapidly changing context means that books tend to date quickly. Using journals is therefore important in maintaining a clear view of the current position. The following journals are likely to be particularly helpful:

Journal of Social Policy
Social Policy and Administration
Social Policy and Society

For a historical perspective see:
Fraser, D. (2002) *The Evolution of the British Welfare State*. London: Palgrave Macmillan, is a clear and highly readable account, as is:
Timmins, N. (2001) *The Five Giants: A Biography of the Welfare State*. London: Harper Collins.

For a fuller exploration of ideological perspectives and how they link to policy see:
Lavallette, M. and Pratt, A. (2006) *Social Policy: Theories, Concepts and Issues*. London: Sage.

For a clear overview of policy on a more general level see:
Bochel, C. et al. (2005) *Social Policy: Issues and Developments*. London: Prentice Hall.
Hendrick, H. (2005) *Social Policy and Child Welfare*. Bristol: Policy Press.
Robert Gordon University provide an excellent social policy site with lots of useful content at: http://www2.rgu.ac.uk/publicpolicy/introduction/contents.htm

The policy context

2

Changing childhoods,
changing families

Graham Brotherton and Gill McGillivray

The aims of this chapter are to:

- Explore ways in which the notions of childhood and family are changing, and to explore the implications that this might have for those working with children, young people and families
- Examine constructs of 'childhood' and 'family' and how these are influenced by broader social changes such as technology, global migration, changing patterns of work and the economy.

In this chapter we will use case studies of children of different ages and backgrounds to explore, in a practical way, issues such as attachment experiences, changes through separation from parents/carers, time in childcare, chaotic childhoods and multiple transitions. We will also consider where power is exerted on and by children and the consequences for children themselves as well as for those who work with them. Finally we will examine temperament and resilience, and the influence of parents and childhood experiences.

The central argument of this chapter is that the 'meaning' of childhood and how it is experienced changes over space and time and in understanding childhoods we should recognise this. Indeed it can be argued that we need to talk about 'childhoods' in its plural form to acknowledge the range of social, cultural, economic and psychological factors which influence the experience of 'growing up'. The term childhood is at risk of obscuring difference to a greater extent than it highlights similarities. In order to start our discussion of the range of differences, we start by taking a historical perspective.

A very brief history of childhood(s)

In a chapter such as this it is only possible to give a very brief overview and for more detail you are advised to look at the excellent discussions which can be found in Buckingham (2000), Cunningham (2006) and Wyness (2006).

Activity

As you start this chapter, think about your own experience of growing up. How was your childhood different to that of your parents and grandparents? If you're not sure, you might want to take the opportunity to ask them in the near future and/or talk to carers and close relations about their experiences.

If you have any children or close family/friends with children, how is their experience of growing up different to yours?

There is some discussion as to when the contemporary concept of a child emerged. According to one influential view proposed by the French historian Philippe Ariès (1962), childhood did not exist in medieval society. By the age of around seven years, children were treated as 'mini' adults and dressed and treated in some ways as adults. Ariès' work has been widely challenged and in some senses discredited (for example by highlighting the fact that he relied on portraits to show how children were represented when this might in fact have been a very formal representation rather than a picture of 'everyday life'). However, Ariès did draw attention to the fact that childhood is the product of particular societies at particular points in time, rather than a universal state which applies in all societies at any given time.

We can argue that, at least in the western industrialised world, childhood emerges as a direct consequence of the process of industrialisation. Putting this in oversimplified terms to illustrate some general points, it is because industrialisation had a number of important social consequences. It led to the separation of 'home' from 'work', as in most pre-industrial societies work consisted of agricultural production which took place in the vicinity of home and within extended family networks. Industrialisation changed this with the separation of the 'home' from the place of work, thus leading to the 'need' for someone to 'look after' children which created both our notion of the traditional family in which the mother was (or is?) perceived as the person primarily responsible for caring for children, and the need for a separate space to cater for children as parents worked. At first, this need was filled by the then emerging school system which served two other key purposes: firstly that of educating the next generation of workers and secondly that of providing appropriate 'moral' education.

By the turn of the century in the UK most of the population lived in urban areas. As described in Chapter 1, this was when the pattern of services which constitute modern welfare services began to emerge. In this chapter however, we want to consider the *context* in which these services emerged and to argue that, to some extent, the services sought to universalise childhood by treating all children in a coherent and similar way. One way of thinking about this is to use the notion of Fordism (Burrows and Loader, 1994) which highlights the fact that in the early part of the twentieth century many people's lives followed similar patterns.

Changing childhoods, changing families

For a 'working-class' boy this might be to receive an elementary (primary) education and then go to work in a particular job or industry which was often defined by where he lived and by family history (for example, following his father down the pit in South Wales or into the motor industry in Birmingham). For girls from similar backgrounds, the pattern tended to be school, work and then upon marriage to be expected to assume the roles of wife and in time, mother. People's lives followed similar patterns, and these are what Lyotard (1984) calls grand narratives: stories that can be applied to whole groups of people. Once in adult occupations, either in work or the home, it was usual to stay in the same role until retirement (and perhaps beyond for most women). It is therefore possible to argue that many childhoods had similar 'patterns', although it is dangerous to oversimplify the range of influencing factors in terms of family relationships. It is inappropriate to talk in universal terms.

After the Second World War, a number of key changes started to occur which make Universalist models even more problematic. Three of these; migration, changing patterns of employment and changing family structures are now considered in more detail.

Over the last 50 years, the UK has become an increasingly diverse society with migrants arriving from all over the world. Many of these groups bring a range of cultural perspectives on family 'values', family structure and family roles, reinforcing the difficulty of talking in general terms about 'the family'. In addition, when the changing role of women in terms of employment is taken into account, as well as the changes in family life associated with divorce, single parenthood and the increasing prevalence of reconstituted families (families where children are the offspring of one parent living with other children who are the offspring of the parent's partner), it can be seen that, as with childhoods, it may not be helpful to talk of family in the singular, but instead to talk in terms of families.

The four case studies below illustrate how economic, cultural and sociological factors contribute to diversity across and within families. We will ask you to consider how such influences may impact on the experiences and identities of Jay, Andrew, Saleem and Lucy after you have read them through.

Case study 1: Jay

Jay is 15 years old and an only child. His father whom he sees only intermittently arrived in the UK from Nigeria a couple of years before Jay was born. His mother grew up in the city where they now live though her parents were from Jamaica. At school he thinks he gets a rough time from the teachers whom he accuses of being racist and as a result his attendance is poor and he is not predicted to do well in his exams next year. His mother is increasingly concerned that he is becoming more

---

involved in 'gang' culture and also that he is taking part in petty crime, though as yet he has no formal convictions. A number of agencies are involved with Jay and his mother, but Jay is very reluctant to talk to 'professionals' whom he sees as being just like the teachers he doesn't get on with. His mother just says he is out of control, that she can't do anything with him and that his father should 'take him in hand before it's too late'.

Case study 2: Andrew

Andrew, aged 1 year and 2 months, is the youngest of four children: the oldest is Kylie (12 years), then Donna (10 years), then Paul (3 years). Andrew's mother, Catherine, is 30 years old and Andrew's father (also Paul's father) has returned to Poland. Kylie and Donna have the same father, and they see him regularly. Catherine works part-time as a dinner supervisor and her mother looks after Andrew and Paul in her own home (round the corner from Catherine's home) when Catherine is at work.

Catherine has been diagnosed with depression and she relies on her mother to take care of all the children when she is feeling particularly low. Kylie and Donna also help Catherine with household chores and childcare when they are not at school.

Andrew was born prematurely (at 35 weeks) by Caesarean section due to Catherine suffering pre-eclampsia. The family has had regular visits from the local health visitor, to monitor Andrew's development and check on Paul. When Andrew is older and Paul is at school, Catherine intends to seek alternative employment to increase her income. In the meantime, Andrew is undergoing assessment for partial hearing loss as his language development appears delayed.

Case study 3: Saleem

Saleem, aged 4 years and 5 months, is about to make the transition into school when he starts reception class. He has an older brother, Mahmood, aged 7 years and 8 months. Mahmood attends the school where Saleem will be starting in September, and they will probably stay there until Year 6. Saleem has not attended any form of childcare as his mother has not worked. His father works long hours at a local

(Cont'd)

Changing childhoods, changing families

restaurant. Saleem's life experiences so far have revolved around his immediate and extended family. He has spent many hours with his grandparents who visit the family home nearly every day. They take Saleem out to the local park and he also accompanies them to the shops. Saleem has several friends in the neighbourhood. They play at each other's houses and in the park under the supervision of extended family members. Saleem's best friend, Mushtaq, will also start school (the same school as Saleem) in September.

Saleem's grandparents have spent time with him, encouraging him to read and write English and Urdu. Saleem also learns Arabic at Mosque school. Mahmood reads to his mother daily and Saleem likes to join in and talk to his brother about his homework.

Case study 4: Lucy

Lucy is 17 and at sixth form college in a prosperous suburb. She did very well in her GCSEs as a day pupil in the local public school and is taking 4 A' levels with a view to getting into a 'proper' university. She has a close group of friends and regularly goes out with them drinking and clubbing. She was on one occasion brought home in an ambulance after collapsing in the street after a drinking game at a friend's house and her parents suspect that she has experimented with drugs. Her parents who are both solicitors see her behaviour as nothing but youthful exuberance and as her 'rebellious phase'.

The case studies are intended to highlight the argument already made: it is very difficult to talk about 'childhood' or 'family' in any generic or universal sense.

Activity

At this point think about each of the case studies: how might each of the children and young people concerned think about themselves and their family?

How might their early experiences, through childcare arrangements, interaction with family members, cultural expectations and the well-being of those around them impact on each child/young person?

How might the various professionals involved perceive them? What might be the practical consequences of these differences? For example, both Jay and Lucy are likely to have been involved in behaviour that can be thought of as illegal or criminal. Would the police or other agencies be likely to respond in similar ways to the two young people and their behaviour, or is one more likely to be dealt with as 'criminal' or at least potentially 'criminal'?

Before we move on to other aspects of change, another way in which childhoods for each of the children and young people may be different is how they might 'succeed' in formal education. Given their various backgrounds, can we be confident that they will all experience education in positive ways and therefore be able to gain the qualifications which will 'help' in terms of their future educational and career success? Aspects of education and experience as influenced by family and the home are returned to later in the chapter.

Intergenerational change

So far we have focused on the differing experiences of children within the same generation. We also need to consider the notion of intergenerational change in the experience of childhood. To start with a technological example, what impact have mobile phones had on the experience of 'growing up'? What have been the benefits, and have they created new problems?

Perhaps the most significant effect has been the way in which mobile phones facilitate 24-hour communication. This creates both the possibility of constant communication, of always being in touch, but also makes it difficult to 'escape' and develop a sense of separateness and being able to possess a private realm of personal experience. Does this make the lives of today's children and young people easier or more difficult than that of previous generations? On one hand, mobile phones may make parents feel more secure in their children's safety, but on the other, they are perceived to promote the possibility of 'cyber bullying'. The limited research that there is in this area suggests that all of these competing factors apply differently in relation to factors including age, gender, class, ethnicity and whether children and young people live in urban or rural areas (Pain et al., 2005).

Nonetheless, it is apparent that mobile phones make the experience of being a child or young person now different to that for any preceding generation. It is perhaps not possible to say that any generations' experience is better or worse than that of other generations, but a range of factors are likely to make the experience different. Also, intergenerational change is not a one-way process. For example, we (the authors) find it difficult to understand the experience of growing up in a city during wartime in the way that our parents did; yet there will be children growing up now who will have much greater common ground with our parents in sharing this aspect of their lives (but with very considerable

21
Changing childhoods, changing families

differences in other areas). Intergenerational change therefore cuts across time, culture and class and between generations.

The death of childhood

A view that has emerged in recent years is that childhood has changed to such a fundamental extent that it can no longer be thought of as a safe and secure process of growing up. Many writers have pointed to the effect of 'commercialisation' of childhood through direct advertising to children, the growing influence of electronic media and games, and the sexualisation of children through fashion. Children are now exposed to such influences through modern technology and media at a younger age, it is argued, and therefore before they have the maturity to understand. Some writers, for example Postman (1994), talk about the move to a 'post literate' society, as new media can be visual or aural and are therefore accessed without the mediating influence of literacy. It can be suggested that the notion of a 'golden age' of childhood is a culturally, historically and geographically specific construct, and as Buckingham (2000) highlights, it is a construct which has considerable symbolic power. However, a difficulty with this view is that it assumes a specific set of characteristics which are universal, transferable and definable (in practice, definable by adults) whereas one of the central arguments of this chapter is that childhoods are multiple, complex and fluid. There is a long history of each generation defining at least some elements of its successor generation as problematic (numerous examples of this can be found in Cohen et al. (2004)) and we would argue that to see changes as a linear decline in the experiences of childhoods is a limited and partial view.

Activity

Think about the lives of the children in each of the case studies. How might their lives be different from those of their parents and their grandparents?

What implications might this have for both children and parents? You may want to consider some of the ways in which different generations in each case study will have perceptions and experiences that bear on how they interact with children and grandchildren.

The economic status of children and childhood

Perhaps the most common way in which the economic status of childhood is currently discussed is through periodic media stories about the use of child labour in the production of goods for the UK market. Wyness (2006) highlights

Working with children, young people and families

the way in which the issue is constructed, with children seen as passive victims of economic circumstances. This can lead us to fail to recognise the way in which child labourers may, from their own perspective, be active agents in improving their own and their families' circumstances. This is not to say that child labour is not a major social issue on a global level, but it does highlight how we need to recognise that a multiplicity of perspectives is possible. It also highlights that in the more economically developed countries there is a tendency to construct childhood as a period of economic dependence in which children and young people are seen as the 'responsibility' of varying combinations of their family and the state for quite long periods of time, typically until the end of statutory education. In an influential model, Esping-Andersen (1990) suggested that the relationship between the individual and the state in 'developed' economies could be divided into three models, which are outlined below.

Esping-Andersen's three worlds of welfare capitalism (1990)

The starting point of Esping-Andersen's model is the extent to which welfare has become 'de-commodified', that is not seen as something that has to be purchased by individuals and families but as something that should be provided free at the point of delivery by the state. From that position, he develops a model with three groupings.

In **social democratic** systems, the state is the main provider of free (or largely free) welfare services: healthcare, education, early years, social care and so on. These services tend to be directly provided by state agencies or by third sector organisations mainly funded by the state. The Nordic countries, Sweden and Finland, for example, are often seen as the best examples of this model.

In **conservative (or corporatist)** systems, the emphasis is on family responsibility and access to services, and this is often through social insurance linked to employment. This means there may be differential access to services dependent upon parental employment, though in many cases education is free and universal, and operates outside the social insurance system. Germany and France are usually considered to be examples of this model.

In **liberal (or residual)** systems, the prime way of accessing services is through the market, either by direct payment for services or through private insurance. The role of the state is to be a 'safety net' provider of a basic level of services for those unable to access market-based provision. The most commonly cited example of this model is the United States.

In Esping-Andersen's view, central to understanding this model is the attitude of the middle classes to state provision. In social democratic systems, there tends to be a high level of middle-class satisfaction with, and therefore participation in, the state system. As a specific example of this, the proportion of children who attend private schools is generally very low in Scandinavia. Likewise, middle-class

Changing childhoods, changing families

participation in public services in the United States is generally low, and this is perhaps best exemplified by the healthcare system. Esping-Andersen goes on to argue that keeping middle-class involvement in public services is vital to the survival of public services in an increasingly commercialised and globalised world where there tends to be pressure for lower taxes and hence a move to the residual model. It can thus be argued that in the UK there has been a drift to a more residual model over the past 30 years and that one of the 'New Labour' justifications for public service reform in the context of education has been the desire to keep middle-class voters engaged with public services.

Activity

Using placement or other work-based experiences, reflect on families you have worked with, and/or the services provided by the state and other organisations. How useful are the three systems in helping us understand the perceptions we hold, or the perceptions held by others, of welfare services?
In applying aspects of Esping-Andersen's model to our perceptions of the role of the welfare state, what is your initial response to how the families in the case studies may benefit (or not) from one or more of the three models.

The Esping-Andersen model has been developed and criticised by a number of writers who argue that it is too broad to accommodate all of the possible variations in terms of the relationships between the state and individuals or families. It is also argued that it excludes other models and fails to acknowledge the central role of gender and women's roles in the workforce (see Bambra (2004) for a summary of the arguments). However it remains a useful way of attempting to understand the differing bases of welfare systems and how these affect children and families.

Fox Harding and value positions

To understand further the relationship between the state and families, a model developed by Fox Harding (1996) is helpful. She suggests that there are four basic 'value positions' in relation to the provision of welfare services for children, young people and families: laissez-faire, state paternalist, birth family defender and children's rights.

The *laissez-faire* approach emphasises the idea of family as a private realm beyond the 'interference' of the state. The state may send messages through legal and social policy about desirable family forms (such as 'the nuclear family') or behaviour (such as the issue of corporal punishment). However, it tends only to

Working with children, young people and families

intervene as a last resort in extreme situations. Fox Harding makes the link here to traditional models of the family with a strong patriarchal presence.

State paternalism is associated with a limited but authoritative role for the state. Intervention is carried out by 'experts' who seek to either remedy the 'problems' in families or provide high quality substitute care. It tends to have an optimistic view of the possibilities of limited positive intervention.

The *birth family defender* perspective identifies a positive role in intervention of a more proactive kind through supportive intervention to either provide welfare services or promote the rights and well-being of families. It is often associated with relatively high levels of welfare provision and notions of 'early intervention'.

The final perspective, that of *children's rights*, identifies the separate interests of children as being a key issue which needs to be seen as potentially different from the broader interests of families as highlighted through the UN Convention on the Rights of the Child or the growing international move towards having Children's Commissioners and advocates.

In Table 2.1 there is an attempt to link Esping-Andersen's model with Fox Harding's perspectives to highlight the link between the broader economic context and the types of services which are likely to be found in practice. Note that the children's rights perspective can be said to exist slightly outside this framework as some elements of it are found in a variety of systems such as the almost universal signing of the UNCRC (United Nations Convention on the Rights of the Child). However, it must be acknowledged that this is a rather 'rough and ready' model. For example, it could be argued that the UK has aspects of both the social democratic approach (such as Every Child Matters and early intervention) and the liberal residual approach (such as some of the philosophical underpinnings of the 1989 Children Act in terms of decisions about intervention in family life). However, it does begin to provide us with a way of thinking about similarities and differences in approaches to child and family welfare.

Activity

Using Table 2.1 try to think about how child welfare is organised both in the UK (England) and if possible in another country. (The European Union website has some useful resources for this activity.) What conclusions could you draw from your comparisons in terms of outcomes and support for children and families?

Table 2.1 Links between the Esping-Andersen and Fox Harding models

Esping-Andersen's 'World'	liberal residual	conservative corporatist	social democratic
Fox Harding's Perspective	laissez-faire	state paternalist	birth family defender
		children's rights	

This debate could be extended into exploring aspects of the two models and policy changes in England over recent decades and their impact on childhoods and families. You may choose to develop the responses to this activity in order to come to a view relating the models to recent changes.

The changing role of gender

Perhaps the greatest change in most industrialised societies has been the changing opportunities available to girls and young women. For example, in England girls now outperform boys at every level within education and also outnumber boys in many forms of professional training within higher education. This pattern is seen in many other countries. Whilst this is not as yet fully reflected in women's career trajectories or earnings it does challenge many of the assumptions about families and roles implicit in the models discussed in the previous section.

Interlinked with this is the complex area of cultural and religious assumptions around gender roles and the impact that these might have in complex and diverse societies like the UK in the twenty-first century, which again may not be fully reflected in the models.

Activity

Consider gender and other aspects of the individual experiences or circumstance of each of the children and young people in the case studies. How do you anticipate each of their trajectories might be determined by such experiences or circumstance and why?

Psychological aspects of childhood

It is worth taking account of some psychological perspectives in the context of changing childhoods, although this chapter offers just a brief consideration. Readers can consult Browne (2008), Harwood et al. (1995), Mayall (2002), Prout (2005) and for example, for both psychological and sociological perspectives on childhood and the impact of dominant discourses. Neither do we attempt to explore or challenge the traditional theories of child development, such as those of Piaget or Bruner. Again, the reader can consult Barron (2005) or Penn (2005) for helpful reflections on legacies and philosophies. We therefore aim to provide students with space to reflect on how children and young people may be making sense of the experiences around them and responding to them, drawing on research and some theoretical perspectives.

Working with children, young people and families

From birth, there is a multiplicity of ways in which children acquire a sense of identity: who they are and how they perceive themselves to 'be', as well as how they interact with, and act on, their environment, in their day-to-day lives. Bronfenbrenner's ecological model of child development (Bronfenbrenner, 1979) illustrates how global change and policy exerts influence at the level of the individual child. At the 'micro' and possibly 'meso' level, each individual child or young person we encounter in our professional practice has had experiences and significant relationships that have underpinned the child's life-course prior to that point. In the UK, children will probably have the opportunity to develop an attachment with a main carer, but increasingly, as already stated, it is becoming more likely that both parents will not be living in the same home. Research (David et al., 2002; Layard and Dunn, 2009) suggests that the nature of attachments, if it is agreed that the establishment of at least one secure attachment is a significant feature of optimum well-being for children, is complex and needs to be understood in the broadest context of family circumstances. Sociological influences of poverty, migration, disability and family unit structure may cause significant change for children, and thus their potential for attachment or detachment. Secure attachments, for example, have been shown to be disrupted by divorce (Lewis et al., 2000) and for those working with children, young people and families who are experiencing change and disruption, the need to foster attachments in a sensitive, respectful manner may be part of their work role.

Activity

The case studies illustrate how four children have had different attachment opportunities. Take time to consider to whom each child may be attached, and why they may have formed such attachments. Also, reflect on the implications for parents, family members and professionals (specialist support services, health visitors and teachers) who are likely to be working with these families.

We also need to be sensitive to how the fragmentation of childcare provision in the UK exacerbates the potential multiplicity of spaces, places, people and attachments that young children can experience if their main carer is employed to work away from the family home. The needs for different forms of childcare have changed over recent years, primarily as more mothers return to work. The marketisation and mixed economy of childcare have also contributed to there being a variety of experiences for children, often determined by funding sources. Also, children who are looked after, either in residential care, or who are fostered or adopted, may also have fragmented attachment opportunities, sometimes exacerbated by multiple placements (David et al., 2002). Research indicates that

Changing childhoods, changing families

attachment experiences are significant in how early childhood experiences can influence later resilience to cope with transitions and life experiences (Lewis et al., 2000; Waters et al., 2000), and the potential implications of such findings are explored later in the chapter.

Taking a social constructivist perspective, children construct identity through interaction with people around them, again, with reference to Bronfenbrenner's (1979) ecological model, with varying levels of influence. Thus children will construct an identity through interaction with their immediate family, but their identity will also be influenced by media (children as consumers, for example), the national economy (their parents' employment opportunities, for example) and policy (childcare provision). Vygotsky acknowledged how children make sense of their social and cultural experiences through socialisation and the inter-nalisation of what it means to be part of cultures through participation in activities with others (Prout, 2005). Cultural specific practices in child-rearing are likely to influence aspects of a child's identity, specifically their construc-tion and interpretation of relationships. Brooker (2002) and Browne (2008) note ways in which children's self esteem is shaped by those around them: by the ethos of a setting, by the ways in which relationships are nurtured and how the well-being of the child is promoted so they feel included and valued. Brooker (2002) takes the debate further: how *do* settings (and the same argu-ment can be posed with regard to government policy) promote well-being? In her research in a primary school, Brooker (2002) interrogates the 'regulative discourse' and the 'instructional discourses' within a reception classroom. Currently, discourse prevails relating to 'well-being', but it could be contested that it takes more than tools and interventionist structures to promote well-being. It is the quality of relationships between children, young people, fami-lies and those who care for them or work with them that is the pivot point for better outcomes.

Activity

Consider the children in the case studies and their experiences within their immediate families, neighbourhoods, care and education settings. What may be influencing each child's construction of their individual identities? You may wish to start by reflect-ing on cultural, gender, relationship and economic aspects, before moving to others.

Resilience and transitions

Research (Layard and Dunn, 2009; Reading and Reynolds, 2001) highlights the link between poverty and post-natal depression (and other mental health difficulties for parents) in the UK. Other statistics portray the levels of poverty, unhappiness and poor mental health of children in the UK (CAMHS, 2008; UNICEF, 2007).The impact on children of their mother having post-natal depression can be long term. Research has indicated that effects of post-natal depression can, in some cases, last into adolescence, and can also be exacerbated by gender and socio-economic status (Murray et al., 2006). Family break-up and mental health difficulties for parents affect children, and can do so from an early age (David et al., 2002; Griggs and Walker, 2008) and so illustrate aspects of childhood children may have to cope with. Supporting transitions is one of the six areas of skill and knowledge in the Common Core (DfES, 2005a). Transitions cited are 'family illness or the death of a close relative; divorce and family break-up; issues related to sexuality; adoption; the process of asylum; disability; parental mental health; and the consequences of crime' (DfES, 2005a: 16).

Children are increasingly likely to encounter multiple transitions as childcare provision for working parents tends to be fragmented and determined by geography and economy (McGillivray, 2007). Sensitive and informed practitioners can offer support when children and young people experience such transitions, but it is also apparent that the potential for trauma and disruption can arise if transitions are mismanaged or even ignored. How can children and young people become resilient and able to cope with transitions and disruption in their lives? Seaman et al. (2006) investigated parent–child relationships in areas of deprivation in Glasgow and found that parents were strategic in how they fostered resilience in their children. For example, parents recognised the need for planned activities, and for democratic parenting styles.

Activity

Returning to the four children and young people illustrated in the case studies, consider the multiple transitions that each have made so far in their lives, on a regular or irregular basis. What might be the implications of these, for the children and young people themselves as well as the people close to them and professionals who work with them and their families?

Newman and Blackburn (2002: 1) propose that 'Resilient children are better equipped to resist stress and adversity, cope with change and uncertainty, and to recover faster and more completely from traumatic events or episodes' and from their research, identified the resilience factors shown in Table 2.2.

Changing childhoods, changing families

Table 2.2 Resilience factors

The Child	The Family	The Environment
Temperament (active, good-natured)	Warm supportive parents	Supportive extended family
Female prior to and male during adolescence	Good parent–child relationships	Successful school experiences
Age (being younger)	Parental harmony	Friendship networks
Higher IQ	Valued social role (e.g. care of siblings)	Valued social role (e.g. a job, volunteering, helping neighbours)
Social skills	Close relationship with one parent	Close relationship with unrelated mentor
Personal awareness		Member of religious or faith community
Feelings of empathy		

Source: Newman and Blackburn, 2002: 3

Activity

(a) Select an individual who you work with in your placement or employment, and, if you consider the factors in Table 2.2 as contributing to the person's resilience, do they allow a deeper understanding of that person's ability to cope with stress, upset and day-to-day life? How useful is the collation of resilience factors when reflecting on our own ability to cope with work and life demands?

(b) From the information provided about the children in the case studies, who may be in a stronger position to develop resilience? What factors have you taken into account and what are the implications for the other children in the case studies?

Policy that promotes well-being and positive relationships is becoming increasingly visible. However, a tension emerges if we contemplate the conflict identified by Wyness (2006) between allowing families to nurture relationships privately within themselves, facilitating attachments between parents and their children, and the implications of the growth of state agencies, their intervention, and thus increased 'responsibility for maintaining family relations' (Wyness, 2006: 98). As the Early Years Commission cites a range of research that reinforces how outcomes for children are influenced by parenting styles and behaviours (and we need to be critical of the position of the authors of the report), the challenge for practitioners who work with children, young people and families is to develop an understanding of the intentions and motivations that underpin interventionist policy. The debate about intentions, motivations, the role of the state and how practitioners, parents and families interpret and interact with children leads into an examination of power relationships and their implications.

Relationships, power and practice

Who is powerful in children's lives, and have there been changes in those who have a powerful role to play? As already acknowledged, some may argue that the media is now more powerful, with children being part of the consumer target market for clothes, gadgets and food items and encouraged to make choices on behalf of their parents, families or carers as to what should be bought. What has created such shifts? Aspects of the digital age and their impact on children have already been considered, and James et al. (1998) suggest that now there is a sociology *for* the child as well as *of* the child, and that this leads to 'the universal child becoming a minority group with demands that have to be heard' (James et al., 1998: 31). Again, there is a shift in expectation that children must be heard in terms of research, policy and reports. Consultation with children and young people is now often accepted as 'good practice' and children's and young people's involvement in decision making, such as job selection for example, is not uncommon. Research that embraces children's and young people's participation in a variety of contexts has emerged from the Mosaic Approach (see Clark and Moss, 2008). How such approaches are said to 'empower' children and young people is contentious. It is arguably a different normalisation, as opposed to liberation, and contributes to the regimes of truth perpetuated by dominant discourses (Foucault, 1980).

To add to the dominant discourses of participation, consultation, well-being and outcomes is that of record-keeping and information sharing. Surveillance of children is as prevalent as surveillance of practitioners, as highlighted elsewhere in this book. It is apparent when we consider the Contactpoint database (DCSF, 2009a) for example, or the introduction of closed circuit television cameras in early years settings for parents to observe what their child is doing. The dilemma for practitioners is grappling with the 'traditional' perspectives on childhood of supervisory, regulatory normalisation of children in schools, for example, set against the newer forms of normalisation, or dominant discourses, such as children participating in decision making. In Foucauldian terms, such dominant discourses create the regimes of truth, or what is accepted at any point in time (Dahlberg and Moss, 2005). It is *a* truth, not *the* truth, and such discourses shape what we do and what we think, and thus exert power over what we do. The point for examination here is to acknowledge that change which some might see as emancipatory for children, young people and families (participation, consultation, partnership) may in fact be argued to be another regime of truth, and that we need to be critical and questioning of the underlying continuation of subjectification (constructing ourselves as a child, as a parent, as a practitioner, and therefore as a subject (Dahlberg and Moss, 2005)) which in turn perpetuates power being exerted by those who create dominant discourses. To return to Brooker's research (2002), she examines how the child's and their family's social and cultural capital influence their transition into the reception class. She found that some of the children in her research adapted to the behaviours expected of a pupil in a reception class ('learning to be a pupil') more easily than others.

Changing childhoods, changing families

Children whose families understood the 'subtext' of playing with the resources provided adapted more quickly than those who did not. This is attributed by Brooker to concepts of social and cultural capital identified by Bourdieu (1997) and illustrates the power of institutions to implicitly convey what is expected, and that all those who work, play, live and interact within it are expected to conform. Adults who work with children, young people and families, across the spectrum of settings where they interact (youth clubs, family centres, schools and children's centres, for example), may report changes in policy and practice to reflect contemporary values and new thinking.

Conclusion

In summary, issues raised in this chapter relating to families and childhoods are intended to promote debate and discussion, as well as reflections on the complexities and challenges for those who work with families, children and young people. There are many other aspects of experience, policy and practice that have not been included here, but the multi-disciplinary nature of childhoods and families has informed those themes that have been presented.

Further reading

Several texts provide critical consideration of childhood, from global, anthropological, psychological and sociological/political perspectives. In addition to those referenced, other examples include:

Jenks, C. (2005) *Childhood*, 2nd edn. London: Routledge.
Penn, H. (2005) *Unequal Childhoods*. London: Routledge.
Thomas, N. (2000) *Children, Family and the State*. Bristol: Policy Press.

3

Working with parents

Graham Brotherton

> **The aims of this chapter are to:**
> - explore the current policy context in terms for work with parents
> - look at some of the possible difficulties and tensions around work with parents
> - explore some models of good practice in working with parents and families.

To understand the way in which practitioners are expected to work with parents, we intend to use the idea of policy discourses. For the purposes of this chapter, this can be defined as the way in which language is used in both policy and practice documentation and the way in which this shapes practitioner attitudes. In other words, the ways in which policy and practice are described influence the way we think about and therefore construct our role. In seeking to explore the ways in which these policy discourses construct the role of parents and how these influence the practice of 'frontline' professionals, we need firstly to consider the nature of current policy discourses and the way in which they emerged.

Constructing capable parents

Within present government policy in the area of children and families the role of parents is constructed as central to ensuring that children make successful transitions through the various 'stages' to adulthood. With younger children parents are frequently described as a child's 'first educators' within the various documents associated with Every Child Matters, the National Primary Strategy and most recently in the Children's Plan (DCSF, 2007a). Here the first of the five key principles which the Department for Children, Schools and Families has said will form the basis for future services for children, young people and families is, 'Government does not bring up children – parents do – so government needs to do more to back parents and families' (DCSF, 2007a: 4) . This is developed later in the plan;

> A modern family policy starts from what helps family life to flourish. Our vision is of all families being confident in their ability to achieve the best for their child. Parents and carers expect to be responsible for every aspect of their child's development, prepared to trust the judgement of professionals, who consult and engage them on the way. They want information, advice and support to be easily accessible and available when they need it. (DCSF, 2007a: 18)

Of course, superficially, it is difficult to argue with this, but beneath the rhetoric it can be argued that there is a clear normative dimension to this view of family policy.

Activity

How does this statement from the plan compare with your own views and parents within your own setting or work placement? What assumptions are made in the statement?

A second key document can be used to illustrate assumptions about families. *Every Parent Matters* (DfES, 2007) produced by the then Department for Education and Skills (and the change of title to the Department for Children, Schools and Families is interesting in itself) elaborates further on this in the introduction. The then minister Alan Johnson suggests;

> Parents and the home environment they create are the single most important factor in shaping their children's well-being, achievements and prospects. We know that the overwhelming majority of parents want to do the very best for their children. We know that the majority say they expect to need advice or help at some time or another. And we know that mainstream services are not as good as they should be at recognising and responding to parents' needs. Being a parent is – and should be – an intensely personal experience and parents can be effective in very different ways. However, we also have a growing understanding, evidenced from research, about the characteristics of effective parenting. (DfES, 2007: 1)

Activity

'Parents and the home environment they create are the single most important factor in shaping their children's well-being, achievements and prospects' (DfES, 2007: 1). Discuss to what extent you feel this is the case.

A number of key points emerge from this: firstly the assertion of the absolute centrality of the parents' role; secondly the suggestion that parents will need to work in partnership with services in order to promote their children's development; and thirdly the claim that there is an empirical evidence base which enables us to identify the characteristics of effective parenting. Each of these points is central to the New Labour discourse on effective parenting which suggests that it is possible to identify the characteristics of good parenting. Again a quote from Every Parent Matters can be used to illustrate:

> Parents' influence is important throughout childhood and adolescence. At different times parents guide, encourage and teach. Children learn from the example set by their parents. The support parents give for their children's cognitive development is important, as is instilling of values, aspirations and support for the development of wider interpersonal and social skills. Recent research has shown the importance of parental warmth, stability, consistency and boundary setting in helping children develop such skills:
>
> • In the early years, parental aspirations and encouragement have a significant impact on children's cognitive development and literacy and numeracy skills;
> • Parental involvement in a child's schooling between the ages of 7 and 16 is a more powerful force than family background, size of family and level of parental education;
> • Educational failure is increased by lack of parental interest in schooling; in particular, a father's interest in a child's schooling is strongly linked to educational outcomes for the child. (DfES, 2007: 6)

What the quotes reveal is a discourse which constructs parents in a very particular way.

Activity

What is a 'good' parent? Is it possible to accurately define this?

'Good' parents take the responsibility of parenting seriously and are actively engaged as consumers of children's services, seeking to choose the 'best' school or nursery for their child or children. They are the 'concerned parents' seeking to further their children's interests in a competitive world. Ball (1990) sees this as stemming from a central component of the New Right critique of comprehensive education and indeed all universal state services, which he calls the 'discourse of derision'. This is the view that public services have been run by self-interested professional groups in their own interests and that children, young people and families have been expected to 'fit in' to services rather than being treated as individuals. As Ball highlights, this conception of the concerned parent whose sole focus is their own child is linked to 'Thatcherite' or New Right notions of individualism and individual responsibility.

A number of authors, perhaps most notably Gewirtz (2001), have highlighted that within current government policy there is a clear normative dimension to

Working with parents

the way in which parents are both represented and constructed. Central to this is the notion of parental involvement or parental partnership.

Activity

What is meant by parental partnership? Might there be varying interpretations and understandings of parental partnership? If so, why, and by whom? Is there a difference between parental partnership and parental involvement?

Bakker and Denessen (2007) summarise the literature as suggesting that this encompasses a range of activities:

> Most authors (e.g. Epstein & Dauber, 1991; Epstein, 1992; Reynolds, 1992; Grolnick & Slowiaczek, 1994; Lareau, 2000) distinguish three aspects of parental involvement: (a) participation in schools, which can vary from volunteering for school activities to participation in decision-making processes; (b) communication between parents and schools, which can vary from attendance of parent–teacher conferences to the reading of school newsletters; and (c) educational activities in the home, which can vary from joint reading to the discussion of daily school activities. (2007: 178)

Furthermore, it has been regularly claimed that parental involvement is, to some extent at least, linked to socio-economic status with the view that middle-class parents are more likely to be active partners in a child's education than working-class ones. Again the literature is summarised by Bakker and Denessen:

> Among others, Finders and Lewis (1994) have asserted that high SES (socio economic status) parents tend to be specifically more involved in school activities and parent–teacher contacts than low SES parents. This assertion has received some clear empirical support (e.g. McGrath & Kuriloff, 1999; Denessen et al., 2001). Nevertheless, a lack of parent–school contact does not automatically mean that lower SES parents are not involved in the education of their children. Lower SES parents, for example, evaluate the importance of education for their children similarly to higher SES parents (Chavkin & Williams, 1993; Hyson & DeCsipkes, 1993; Serpell et al., 1997). Moreover, most parents – irrespective of their social background – have been shown to be involved in such home-based learning activities as reading to the child, helping with homework, showing an interest, providing encouragement, etc. (Reynolds, 1992; Shun-Wing, 2000; Tett, 2004). In fact, the home-based involvement of lower SES parents has even been shown to be higher than the home-based involvement of higher SES parents (Stoep et al., 2002). (Bakker and Denessen, 2007: 179)

In other words, this assumption about the link between class or social status and involvement is a questionable one, but it is a questionable assumption with important practical consequences. Within the UK this notion of involvement has been framed within the notion of parents as consumers of education on behalf of their children, through the introduction of an at least 'official' policy of parental choice. Furthermore it is often translated as being about active engagement with the frontline practitioners, both through conversations at the school or nursery 'gate' and through active involvement in parent–teacher activity. In a different but equally significant context it has been argued that one of the reasons the professionals working with the mother of 'Baby P' failed to act sooner was that she was viewed as a compliant parent who sought to work with the various practitioners who were involved in the case (Munro, 2008).

Activity

Does it matter what type of involvement parents have? How do you involve parents in your setting, or how have you seen parents being involved in your placement setting? How do parents participate in the setting, and contribute to aspects of provision? How are they consulted?

Up to this point we have focused on the impact of parental involvement, but now we need to provide a definition. One of the most widely used definitions comes from Desforges and Abouchaar (2003) who define parental involvement in the following way:

> Parental involvement takes many forms including good parenting in the home, including the provision of a secure and stable environment, intellectual stimulation, parent–child discussion, good models of constructive social and educational values and high aspirations relating to personal fulfilment and good citizenship; contact with schools to share information; participation in school events; participation in the work of the school; and participation in school governance. (2003: 4)

This immediately raises a number of issues in terms of 'capacity' for involvement, for example Tett (2001) highlights the complex relationship between parents' experiences of education and their subsequent 'confidence' in interaction with education professionals. Similar issues may well exist in terms of the complex relationships between social workers and multi-generational involvement with families. It can of course be argued that these tensions and difficulties have always existed but it is our contention that recent changes in policy mean that practitioners have to consider the issues more explicitly in the current context. To give two particularly significant current examples we will now consider the Common Assessment Framework (CAF) and Home School Agreements. As discussed in Chapter 7, the CAF is a central element of the move from a responsive to a proactive approach to safeguarding children and young people. As such it inevitably means a move to greater surveillance by practitioners charged with identifying 'early signs' and hence a changed relationship with parents. At

Working with parents

the time of writing this chapter both of the major political parties are proposing that the current system of home school agreements, in which both school and parent sign a form which sets out their obligations in relation to a child's education, is placed on a contractual basis with fines for either party should the agreement not be upheld. This, it is argued, will make those parents who don't take their parental responsibilities seriously, accountable for their actions.

Activity

What might be the factors that limit the capacity for parental involvement?
How do changing images of childhood impact on perceptions of parental roles?

For practitioners these changes raise a number of questions around the nature of professional judgement, and particularly as these judgements now have to be explicitly stated as the basis for action. This brings us to a consideration of the work of Michael Lipsky (1980) who highlights the complex position of frontline workers in health, social care, education and related areas (for example housing or benefits staff). On the one hand they are there to implement formal policies and procedures, but on the other hand the nature of their role, which often involves individual contact in unsupervised contexts, gives them an element of discretion in the way they choose to interpret their role. For Lipsky this discretion is a 'dilemma' for practitioners, the organisations they work within and for policy makers in government.

Activity

Think about the contacts that practitioners might have with parents in 'work' situations that you are familiar with. How much discretion do you or they have? How might preconceived ideas about their 'capacity' as parents influence how this discretion is used?

For practitioners the dilemma relates to how to approach practice. The nature of work with parents means that much of it takes place unsupervised in private or semi-public space (e.g. the doorway or playground conversation as a child is dropped off/collected), thus giving practitioners considerable room to interpret their task in ways which may not reflect those intended by policy makers and indeed managers. In particular, Lipsky (1980) highlights the way in which the pressures often associated with being a 'frontline' worker in health, social care or

Working with children, young people and families

education, for example the pressure to provide services which in reality are scarce resources, can lead to workers responding to service users in routine and stereotypical ways (Hill, 2005). One potential danger here is that these responses become formalised and recorded, for example through the Common Assessment process.

Practice with parents therefore requires an understanding of the social, cultural and economic context within which parenting takes place. In Chapter 4 we discuss the effect of poverty on children and young peoples' lives and of course the same issues impact upon parents, which in turn may impact on their capacity to be, or equally importantly, be perceived as 'capable' parents in the context of the current discourse. At this point we need to consider another element of the discourse, the role of child development theory. Again this is discussed more fully in Chapter 9 and in the context of the 'natural' child in Chapter 2. The influence of this aspect of the discourse and the way it overlaps with other elements is summarised by Barron et al. (2007) who argue that:

> While constructions of the child in need of services have changed over time, all have relied to some extent on a notion of 'insufficiency'. In western societies, the labels we learn to associate with the idea of childhood tend to define children as incompetent, unstable, credulous, unreliable, and emotional (Mayall, 2002), and these are very often the same notions that lead agencies within and beyond the school into contact with children. For much of the twentieth century and beyond, developmental psychology has dominated the ways in which children (and provision for them) have been conceived. Lawyers, doctors, social workers, educationalists and academics have all come to depend on child development theory as a basis for their work on, for, and with children. Whilst, within sociology, there is a growing awareness of the different ways in which agencies construct children, the image of the child as an 'incomplete' or 'inadequate' being often persists within the agencies themselves and within schools. (Barron et al., 2007: 6)

It is our contention that the view of children as insufficient and incomplete also applies to parents who are deemed to not be 'capable' of bringing up children 'adequately'. There is therefore a significant issue in terms of professional judgements about parenting having long-term implications for both parent and child. We are not of course arguing against the notion that on occasions difficult decisions might have to made, but do wish to highlight the complex context in which these decisions have to be made.

The ethics of care

Dahlberg and Moss (2005) attempt to define an ethical basis for early years practice which we would argue can be broadened to give a basis for practice with children, young people and families more generally. In seeking to do this they make a distinction between 'universal' ethics which they define as, 'a categorical distinction between right and wrong applicable to and by everyone irrespective of social or historical context or circumstances ... Ethics here is the "should" question: from a universalist perspective, how should we think and act' (Dahlberg and Moss, 2005: 66). They argue that this model of ethics creates a 'subject' who is constructed as able to apply moral principles by dealing with situations in an objective autonomous way and who as a result of satisfying moral obligations by acting in this way becomes the bearer of 'rights'. In other words, in this context the 'right' to be a parent is contingent on supporting the developing child or young person in the 'correct' way.

This is contrasted with a relativist or post-modern ethics which starts from a critique of the universalist position based on Bauman's suggestion (1992) that the consequence of this approach is to morally paralyse individuals who therefore tend to follow rules rather than making objective decisions. For Bauman this is accentuated by the process of modernity with its emphasis on the creation of a rational and ordered world. We will return to this discussion after looking at some specific practice examples.

Activity

As you will be aware there have been a number of television programmes about parenting in recent years, for example *Supernanny* or *The House of Tiny Terrors*. Any bookshop will also sell a range of books about parenting. Why do you think this is and how does it relate to the discussion in this chapter?

For practitioners a number of potential issues stem from this. Firstly the danger that this creates a position in which power and decision making become detached from the consequences of the decision ('I was only following the agreed procedures') and in which this instrumental rationality can lead to moral indifference to the particular needs of people living in often complex situations.

If this argument is accepted then moral relativism becomes not, as is sometimes argued, an abdication of moral responsibility, but an attempt to reclaim moral decision making at a local level and a way of seeking to empower both parents and practitioners. In order to explore this in practice we will now seek to consider three specific issues as examples: working with fathers; working with cultural difference; and responding to potential neglect. All of these are complex and difficult issues and the demands of space mean that they can only be dealt with in a brief illustrative way.

Working with fathers

A number of authors have argued from a variety of perspectives that in practice parental partnership means partnership with mothers, both from a

Working with children, young people and families

feminist perspective which has highlighted the ways in which responsibility for caring with children and young people is predominantly seen as a mother's responsibility and from some of the groups who take a 'fathers' rights' perspective and argue that policy discourses and their practical consequences have tended to marginalise even those fathers who wish to take an active role, especially non-resident fathers. Of course the term 'father' can itself be problematic as children may live with a person who acts as a 'father figure' to them, whether or not they are the biological father and who may be additional to or in some cases a 'replacement' for the 'natural' father. In attempting to define each of the highlighted terms in the previous sentence we immediately become aware of the depth of this complexity. Whilst similar complications can and do exist in respect of 'mothers' they are much less common simply because children are very likely to remain living with their 'natural' mother.

Activity

Why might fathers find it difficult to get involved in their children's education? What strategies might schools or other organisations adopt to deal with this?

Most of the literature produced in recent years has tended to focus on fathers' involvement in their children's education (e.g. Goldman, 2005; Welsh et al., 2004) rather than on their broader involvement in children's lives and has highlighted a number of features, though it has to be said that many of these findings are both controversial and disputed:

- Resident fathers are more likely to play an active role than non-resident ones.
- More 'educated' fathers are more likely to play an active role in their children's education.
- Non-resident fathers are more likely to play an active role if there is a low level of conflict with their former partner.
- Fathers are more likely to play an active role where the mother also plays an active role.
- Fathers are more likely to be involved in certain types of activity: practical tasks, physical play, maths and IT. In these areas their role may be greater than that of mothers.
- Fathers may also see their role as 'provider' in an economic context as being their primary one.

A crucial finding though, and it can be argued one of the major reasons for the interest of policy makers, is that children seem to do better in terms of educational outcomes when both parents are involved and also that fathers' and mothers' roles are not interchangeable – children it is argued need the involvement of both parents, hence the emphasis on engaging fathers.

Working with parents

According to the DfES (2004a) in the publication *Engaging Fathers* there are a number of strategies which have been successful in promoting the involvement of fathers:

- Activities which are specifically marketed to fathers, as there is some evidence that fathers respond less well to activities marketed to 'parents'
- Activities which prioritise practical skills, IT, etc. and are active without involving too much discussion
- Activities which take place outside school hours are also more successful in attracting fathers.

You might conclude that much of what has been said in the last couple of paragraphs is a statement of the fairly obvious, and on one level it clearly is, nonetheless it conflates a number of issues, for example resident status, educational background and nature of parental relationship whilst saying nothing about others, such as the role of social class or ethnicity. It also provides an illustration of the sort of normative discourses around parenting and the roles that parents should be undertaking as discussed previously. Nonetheless it also shows how practice can be structured often in unintentional ways and for historic reasons, in this case the school day, which have the effect of excluding some or all of a particular group, in this case fathers.

Working with cultural difference

Activity

Moving on to a second example of ways in which practitioners work with parents, in many situations practitioners increasingly find themselves working with parents from a variety of cultural backgrounds. What issues might arise from this? How can/should practitioners respond?

This is an increasingly significant complex area which has a number of dimensions, firstly in terms of practitioners' perceptions of parents from different cultural backgrounds and vice versa, and secondly, as there is an increasing emphasis on parental education and parental support programmes, how can we ensure that these programmes are culturally sensitive and aware. A third dimension is that increasing numbers of children are being brought up by parents/carers in situations where parents or carers may have a different cultural heritage from each other or from some or all of the children. All of these dimensions mean that it is crucial that practitioners seeking to build partnerships with parents have a sound understanding of the issues, yet there is an absence of both research and resources in this area and most of the little that there is comes from the United States and may not transfer easily to UK settings. A key issue therefore remains unresolved in

Working with children, young people and families

terms of providing ways for practitioners and others to explore these issues and respond in safe non-judgemental and creative ways, and the challenge of doing this will need to be embraced in the next few years.

Responding to neglect

The final example we wish to consider at this stage is that of working with neglect or suspected neglect. Again this is a complex area and, as Horwath (2007) highlights, there are a number of challenges here, firstly around definition, as neglect is complex and multi-faceted. For example, does it have to be a failure of parenting, or can it be just circumstantial (perhaps as a result of poverty as discussed in Chapter 4)? Secondly, challenges exist around deciding when to intervene, when 'inadequate' parenting becomes 'neglectful' parenting and at what point intervention is required, and thirdly there are issues relating to how decisions are made, and the role of class or culture in this debate.

For the purposes of this discussion we wish to focus not on those situations where neglect is clear, such as significant malnutrition or failure to provide adequate clothing, and where neglect becomes identified as a formal child protection issue, but on those situations where neglect is less clear-cut and where practitioners do feel that there are concerns. Here a number of issues arise: how real or accurate are practitioners' concerns or are there misunderstandings based on different understandings of parenting? Secondly, what are the realistic options in terms of intervening and are they likely to 'improve' parents' capacity for effective parenting? Thirdly, given that there is often perceived to be a shortage of resources available for child protection, at what point does parenting become sufficiently poor to warrant intervention? And how do we strike a balance between controlling and supportive interventions?

Each of these questions has both practical and political dimensions which are inextricably linked – particular definitions of what constitutes effective parenting, such as those set out in *Every Parent Matters*, as discussed earlier in the chapter, become the definitions which practitioners use in their day-to-day work with parents. Therefore the construction of parents in policy discourses plays a crucial role in defining the way in which practitioners are encouraged to act in terms of practical decision making.

At this point it is useful to return to the role played by values and ethics in shaping practice and in particular to what different value positions highlight as being the purpose of practice. To start with, the utilitarian model highlights the role of practice in bringing about the broadest possible benefits for society. From this position what matters is overall social benefit rather than the benefits to particular individuals and groups, and it is possible to suggest that relative 'harm' to some groups of people may be inevitable or at least acceptable if the overall impact of policy is to benefit the majority. The purpose of policy then is to seek to impose overall benefit to the majority by seeking to ensure a high standard of parenting through the identification of and support or control of those parents

Working with parents

who are not able to bring up children in a way which enables them to thrive and ultimately become responsible adults, citizens and future parents.

The opposite ethical position is that of Kantian or de-ontological ethics which takes a more individualistic position and argues that everyone has an inherent moral worth and the right to equal treatment, together with the right for their own perspective on a situation to be recognised and worked with. It can of course be immediately recognised that both of these perspectives are problematic – in terms of utilitarian perspectives how far is it reasonable to go in overriding the rights of any individual family, even one defined as a 'problem', in order to create broader social order; on the other hand to what extent can individual rights be allowed to override concerns about the quality of parenting being provided?

It can be seen that these debates link to the models of intervention in family life suggested by Fox Harding which are discussed in Chapter 2 and reflect real tensions in terms of developing effective models of working with parents. A number of writers have attempted to develop models which seek to find a balance and support practitioners in finding an appropriate balance. We return at this point to the way in which Dahlberg and Moss (2005) use Bauman's (1992) notion of the paralysing impact of universal ethics and the way practitioners need to respond. If we accept that there is no universal failsafe then we need to take responsibility in terms of negotiating the 'rules of engagement' for our interaction with parents. Banks (2000, in Parker 2007) has suggested that in social care work these rules of engagements should be based upon

- Respect for and promotion of individual rights to self determination
- Promotion of welfare or well-being
- Equality
- Distributive justice.

We need here to highlight a very significant complicating factor when we are talking about children, young people and their parents. This is that these issues might apply quite differently to different family members and whilst the focus of this chapter is parents it is important to highlight that the interests of parents in terms of welfare or self determination, etc. may at times be in active conflict with the needs of children and young people, for example in the cases of possible neglect.

One possible solution to this, according to Husband (1995, in Parker 2007), is the notion of becoming a morally active practitioner. This links to both the notion of the reflective practitioner discussed in Chapter 11 and the notion of street-level bureaucracy as mentioned earlier in this chapter (p. 38). Husband argues that practitioners have to take personal responsibility for their own actions and are not simply agents of the state (either directly or indirectly). In doing this they need to develop a personal ethical framework for practice which leads to well thought out interventions. It is immediately apparent that there are some real dangers in this approach: practitioners can take this too far and it would not be appropriate to permit excessively anarchic or individualistic practice, nor is it desirable to have completely different patterns of intervention in similar situations based on the personal proclivities of different practitioners. A further potential complication as we move to more integrated and multi-agency approaches is that different practitioners may come from differing personal, professional and cultural backgrounds which will inevitably have an influence on personal ethical or value positions.

How then can we develop this notion of being personally responsible in the light of the caveats expressed previously without descending into a morass of messy relativism? In order to attempt to answer this we now return to the model of morality proposed by Bauman which was briefly introduced earlier in the chapter. Central to understanding Bauman's model is his idea of the shift from what he calls 'heavy capitalism' in which most people lived ordered structured lives governed by a fairly fixed set of roles and relationships (rather like the 'Fordist' model described in Chapter 2) and in which the state played a clearly defined regulatory role identifying the normal and the abnormal or the moral and the immoral and policing this through the role of state institutions – sometimes quite literally as in the role of the institutions for those defined as 'abnormal' or 'immoral'.

This is contrasted with what Bauman calls 'light capitalism' – modern fluid capitalism in which money, jobs and resources move quickly from place to place in order to maximise profit. The consequences of this are many and complex but here we will highlight two of particular relevance for our concerns. Firstly, for individuals and families it means a loss of certainty about roles and identity and a need to be able to adjust and adapt to circumstances which change in ways beyond their control. For the state it means greater contestation about its role. Bauman argues that the move to light capitalism is associated with privatisation and the rolling back of the policing function of the state and an emphasis on self regulation and self surveillance. So how does all of this relate to our discussion about the ethics of practice? For Bauman, a Jew brought up in Poland, a key element in understanding the modern world is to understand the holocaust, which he sees as a logical if extreme example of rational modernity, where industrialised technologies were used systematically and rationally to deal with the problem of an unwanted and stigmatised 'other'. Modern states in seeking to create order become 'gardening states' (Bauman, 1992) seeking to impose order on the wild. Intrinsic in this process is the need for categorisation and, if appropriate, removal of that which is not in the right place. In particular Bauman makes links to the influence of the eugenics movement and its calls for purity and selective breeding across most of the western world and across the political spectrum during the late nineteenth and first part of the twentieth centuries. A crucial aspect of the operationalisation of the holocaust was the social distance between the perpetrators and the victims, while the command and control structures meant that there was a division of labour which in some senses limited the sense of responsibility of individuals. For Bauman the danger of bureaucratic rationality lies in its tendency to reduce decisions, even complex moral decisions, into simply

Working with parents

implementing rules and procedures. A further concept from Bauman, the idea of liquid modernity, says that as a result of social, political, cultural and economic change (as, for example, in the discussion of changing family structures in Chapter 2), life has become more complex fluid and shifting – a difficult situation for traditional rationalist approaches to deal with.

For Bauman it is this complexity and the ambivalence that it provokes which need to be addressed, hence his notion of post-modern ethics, which argues on the one hand that we have a responsibility for 'the Other' and secondly that as real life is complex, messy and ambivalent then moral decisions need to be both specific and contingent.

As an example of the practical consequences of this it is worth having a look at a concrete example, that of the Common Assessment Framework – one of the key policy initiatives in terms of the framework for work with parents (see Chapter 7). The CAF can in many senses be seen as a rationalist attempt to develop a systematic approach to the identification of need and the allocation of resources. It creates a clear framework, supported by extensive guidance, and has been criticised for bringing a far greater number of parents under the formal surveillance of practitioners, in particular those deemed to not be succeeding when judged against the dominant discourses discussed earlier in this chapter. On the other hand though, the process of completing the Common Assessment Framework requires an encounter with others and potentially provides the opportunity for morally active practice.

In conclusion then working with parents requires us to acknowledge explicitly elements of difference, power and control. Bauman (1993) himself puts this very clearly:

> Human reality is messy and ambiguous – and so moral decisions, unlike abstract ethical prin-
> ciples, are ambivalent. It is in this sort of world that we must live … The illusions in question
> boil down to the belief that the 'messiness' of the human world is but a temporary and repair-
> able state, sooner or later to be replaced by the orderly and systematic rule of reason. The
> truth in question is that the 'messiness' will stay whatever we do or know, that the little
> orders and 'systems' we carve out in the world are … as arbitrary and in the end contingent
> as their alternatives. (32–3)

Activity

If we accept Bauman's view that reality is 'messy and ambiguous', what are the implications for us in seeking to build partnerships with parents?

This is clearly a difficult question but we would argue it means a number of things, firstly that practice is contextual and contingent and has to be based upon negotiating a shared perception of the situation, whilst recognising the power

Working with children, young people and families

dynamics that inevitably apply. This requires practitioners to be open to multiple perspectives about situations and aware of the complex social, economic and cultural perspectives which affect the way both parents and practitioners make sense of situations. This in turn requires an understanding of the political context in which practice takes place and the discourses stemming from this which affect the way in which policy 'becomes' practice. This represents a very considerable challenge but it does provide a means of attempting to respond to ways of working with parents which seek to move beyond a contractual and instrumental notion of partnership.

Further reading

Bakker, J. and Denessen, E. (2007) 'The concept of parent involvement. Some theoretical and empirical considerations', *International Journal about Parents in Education*, 1(0): 188–99. Available at: http://www.ernape.net/ejournal/index. php/IJPE/article/view/42/32

Dahlberg, G. and Moss, P. (2005) *Ethics and Politics in Early Childhood Education*. Abingdon: Routledge Falmer.

DfES (2007) *Every Parent Matters*. Nottingham: DfES Publications.

Working with parents

4

The meaning of poverty: issues and policy development

Hilary Dunphy and Terry Potter

The aims of this chapter are to:

- Explore the meaning of poverty
- Define and distinguish between 'relative' and 'absolute' poverty
- Examine ways in which successive British governments have attempted to address poverty and disadvantage
- Describe how policy development has evolved over the past three decades.

In this chapter we will be exploring the issues of 'poverty' and what it really means. We will begin by offering definitions of two much used terms, *absolute poverty* and *relative poverty*. We will refer to other countries in an attempt to explain what poverty means for different sections of our global community. This will lead into how poverty affects children in our society, particularly in relation to education. We will then focus on the impact that poverty has in our communities in Britain and the various initiatives that have been introduced in attempts to tackle poverty, particularly child poverty, through the building of multi-agency partnerships, often initiated at a national or local government level.

The eradication of poverty is arguably the greatest global challenge of the twenty-first century. Charities such as Oxfam, CAFOD (Catholic Fund for Overseas Development), Islamic Relief, Christian Aid, the British Red Cross, the Islamic Red Crescent, Child Poverty Action Group, Shelter and many others have been tackling this challenge for many years. You will have seen many, many images on television and in newspapers of people, mostly from countries in the continents of Africa and Asia, suffering from malnutrition, homelessness and disease brought on by poverty resulting from famine due to failed crops, massive debt, lack of water or war. These images have been responded to by many well-publicised campaigns such as regular and on-going projects like Comic Relief and Children in Need. There have also been very large 'one-off' events such as Live Aid (London and Philadelphia, 1985), and Live8 (2005) which developed out of the 'Make Poverty History' campaign, when music concerts took place in the UK,

France, Germany, Italy, USA, Canada, Japan, South Africa and Russia. The laudable aims of raising awareness of world poverty, encouraging the eradication of the insurmountable debts with which many poor nations are encumbered and raising millions of pounds with which to make a difference to people's lives lay behind these campaigns.

The '8' in Live8 comes from the meetings, or summits, held annually by the leaders of the world's eight wealthiest countries – Canada, France, Germany, Italy, Japan, Russia, the United Kingdom and the United States of America. Established by France in 1975, this group is now known as the G8. The Chair of the G8 changes annually and the Chair for 2009 is Prime Minister Silvio Berlusconi of Italy.

Activity

Look at this map of the world, on which the G8 countries are shaded. What strikes you about their position in the world?

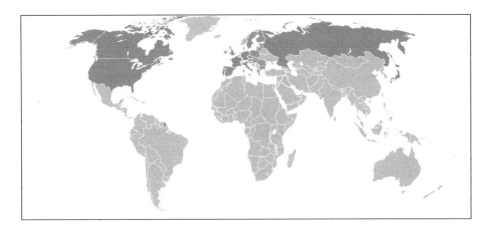

(Group of Eight, 2009)

What do you think the reasons for these countries being identified as the wealthiest might be?

Tackling the issue of world poverty is not a new challenge, but despite many attempts by some to make changes, the leaders of the G8 have collectively and continually failed to make any real progress. Add to this the fact that, within this century's first decade, those same countries are facing, what some have called, the greatest ever world recession, then what hope is there for people living in poverty?

What does 'poverty' mean?

This is a very difficult question to answer, as it depends on the context in which it is being measured. The terms *absolute poverty* and *relative poverty* are used by politicians, sociologists and statisticians when referring to figures related to percentages of people experiencing differing levels of deprivation.

Absolute poverty

This is the term used to describe the position of people living below what is determined as the 'poverty line' or a stated minimum income for that society. Absolute poverty is also defined as:

> the lack of sufficient resources with which to keep body and soul together ... and tends to be associated with developing countries –

- Over 1 billion people – 1 in 6 people around the world – live in extreme poverty, defined as living on less than $1 US a day.
- At least 80% of humanity lives on less than $10 US a day.
- The poorest 40 percent of the world's population accounts for 5 percent of global income. The richest 20 percent accounts for three-quarters of world income. (Shah, 2009)

An additional source of information is provided by UNICEF (United Nations International Children's Emergency Fund) and the Townsend Centre for International Poverty Research. These bodies use the human rights framework to develop a deprivation index where they identify poverty measured against access to seven basic needs:

- clean water
- sanitation
- shelter
- education
- information
- food
- health.

Using these criteria, if a household or individual person does not have access to a particular basic need, they are defined as 'deprived'. Those who are deprived of two or more of the seven basic need indicators are defined as being in *absolute poverty*.

Relative poverty

This term refers to people who have considerably less wealth than others around them. Relative poverty defines income or resources in relation to the average of

Working with children, young people and families

the society, or country, in which the person lives. Townsend (1979) defined poverty thus:

> Individuals, families and groups in the population can be said to be in poverty when they lack the resources to obtain the types of diet, participate in the activities, and have the living conditions and amenities which are customary, or are at least widely encouraged and approved, in the societies in which they belong. (Townsend, 1979: 31)

What Townsend, who we will return to later in this chapter, described then has come to serve as a better definition of what we now know as *relative poverty*; it is concerned with the inability to obtain material needs, opportunities and access to services that enable an individual to participate fully in 'normal' daily life. The widely accepted explanation of what relative poverty means is having an income which is less than 60 per cent of the national average (also frequently referred to as 60 per cent of the median). On this measure, at the present time, the proportion of the UK population defined as in poverty is roughly one in five.

As our expectations change with time and progress in areas such as technology, we also need to constantly reconsider what we expect to have in our households as the 'norm'. Forty years ago not all households would have expected to have a television or automatic washing-machine or a car. Now, not only are these things considered in a household with even a modest income to be the norm, there is also an expectation that children will have their own TV, computer, DVD player, etc. Such things are considered to be the sort of possessions an individual will have, not just a family. In addition to hi-tech goods, we have to consider all the other things which go towards what we have come to expect of a normal, happy childhood in our society – parties, school trips, holidays, new clothes and the latest toys and music. Whether we, as adults, endorse these things or not, they all play a large part in the identity of a young person as they grow up. The ability to 'fit in' and not to be singled-out for negative reasons is all-important to the maturing young person.

Activity

Take time to discuss with friends, family and colleagues the suggestions here about what items contribute to being in relative poverty if we do not have access to them. How helpful are these suggestions? Is there consensus amongst those you talk to about what relative poverty might be? What do your friends', family's and colleagues' responses suggest about society's perceptions of poverty?

What all this means, in terms of facts about poverty is that in 2005/06, 12.7 million people in the UK (22 per cent of the population) were income poor, living in households with below 60 per cent of the median income after housing

The meaning of poverty

costs. There is some evidence to suggest that in recent years this has been falling, but in 2005/06 it increased. In 1999, the Poverty and Social Exclusion in Britain survey showed that 14.5 million people in Great Britain (26 per cent) were living in poverty (defined as lacking two or more 'socially perceived necessities', like those referred to in the previous paragraph, because they could not afford them). A related survey showed that in 2003, 29.6 per cent of households in Northern Ireland were poor (lacking three or more 'socially perceived necessities' because they could not afford them and having a low household income). And finally, in 2004, the Families and Children Study found that eight per cent of lone-parent families and two per cent of couple families could not afford to eat vegetables most days (the same numbers were also found for fruit and cakes/biscuits most days). Twenty-one per cent of lone-parent families and six per cent of couple families reported that they could not afford new clothes when these were needed (Flaherty et al., 2007).

In this publication we are most concerned with the lives and experiences of children and young people, so how does living in poverty affect them? If one looks at the many sources that have addressed this question, it is generally agreed that the experience of poverty in the early years of children's lives can increase the likelihood of:

- experiencing poor health and limited life expectancy
- gaining lower educational attainment
- having reduced access to information through books and computers
- an increased exposure to drugs and crime
- having reduced quality of social interaction
- being trapped in cycles of deprivation
- having limited life aspirations.

The statistics surrounding a child's health and life expectancy in our society, when related to their family's financial circumstances, make shocking reading. Even the H.M. Treasury's own statistical evidence, which presented data from the Family Resources Survey in the Child Poverty Review of 2004, shows that 2.6 million children were living in low-income households. The main focus of the report was 'workless households' and whether these were 'couple' or 'single-parent' households. The data included in the report identifies worklessness as a key risk factor (HMSO, 2004).

Research carried out by Dunphy on behalf of the Catholic Education Service (Catholic Bishops' Conference, 1999), focused upon primary schools in areas of economic disadvantage in England and Wales. Headteachers of schools in the study identified their main concerns for their schools as: under-funding due to a lack of recognition of their circumstances; the added pressures that league tables put upon them; difficulties in attracting and retaining skilled staff to these disad-vantaged areas; support for literacy and numeracy for adults as well as children; support for families in general; and lastly, agencies not working effectively together. Ironically, this last point, during the last 10 years, has been seen as one of the most crucial challenges to be addressed in attempts to 'fix' the issues brought about by poverty.

The headteachers and other staff in these schools had become all things to the parents and children who made up their school communities. Breakfast and after-school clubs were common (and much needed to enable mothers to undertake two or three part-time jobs), as were attendance at Child Protection meetings and sorting out fuel bills or other non-educational needs of the community. The headteachers, many of whom described themselves and their staff as social workers and housing officers as well as educators, were very specific when it came to identifying the impact of poverty on the children in their care. Their concerns could be categorised under the following headings, in no particular order, and not all these conditions were present in all 146 schools that took part in the study:

- Lack of books
- Poor language development
- Low expectations of children and parents
- Lack of parental support
- Lack of positive male role models
- Racism

- Poor punctuality
- Tiredness
- Inadequate nourishment
- Poor health
- Alcohol
- Drugs
- Violence

As many of these concerns lead to issues of safeguarding children, the most common, and overriding, concern was that of child protection. It is true to say that schools in these circumstances, not just those in this particular study, face daily challenges that more affluent schools face only occasionally. This means, of course, that children experiencing the daily disadvantages of living in poverty constantly face an uphill struggle to achieve what other children would expect as a right.

There have been numerous initiatives put into place to tackle the issue of child poverty. By the late 1990s and the start of the new millennium poverty, and the effects of poverty, were seen as key issues which had an impact on all aspects of social policy. This included initiatives, which we will return to in greater detail later, such as:

- Better support for children, young people and families in schools and communities
- Support for parents through changes in employment law and parenting initiatives
- Changes in the fiscal programme – better benefit levels
- Working families tax credit (WFTC), which came into force in October 1999 and is designed to ensure low-income families do not lose out by working
- An increase in child benefit
- A minimum wage
- A new deal for lone parents.

Successive British governments have made pledges to improve income levels in this country and made even more specific pledges to take children out of poverty. This was one of the targets set by the Labour government of Tony Blair in

The meaning of poverty

1997 and later taken up by Gordon Brown, when he became Prime Minister in 2008, stating that:

> For me, the fairer future starts with putting children first – with the biggest investment in children this country has ever seen. It means delivering the best possible start in life with services tailored to the needs of every single precious child.
>
> In 1997 there were no Sure Start centres and nursery education for only the few. Today, thanks to the work of Beverley Hughes, there are children's centres opening in every community to serve 3 million children who a few years ago had nothing, and free nursery education for every three and four year old.
>
> But our ambitions must be greater still. I want Britain to take its place among the leading nations in pre-school services, and so I pledge here today in Manchester starting in over 30 communities, and then over 60, we will, stage by stage, extend free nursery places for two year olds for every parent who wants them in every part of the country backed by high quality, affordable childcare for all.
>
> That's the fairness parents want – and that's the fairness every Labour party member will go out and fight for.
>
> And because child poverty demeans Britain, we have committed our party to tackle and to end it. The measures we have taken this year alone will help lift two hundred and fifty thousand children out of poverty. The economic times are tough of course that makes things harder – but we are in this for the long haul – the complete elimination of child poverty by 2020. And so today I announce my intention to introduce ground-breaking legislation to enshrine in law Labour's pledge to end child poverty. (Labour Party Autumn Conference, 2008)

However, the situation has worsened since 1997; the interim targets set then have not been reached, making these pledges even harder to achieve. The number of children in poverty in Britain actually increased by 100,000 according to the 2005/06 Households Below Average Income (HBAI figures released March 2007). The End Child Poverty campaign estimated that Blair's target for 2010 would be missed unless a further £3 billion was spent. Britain's position amongst the wealthier nations on earth was bottom of the UNICEF league on child well-being and 21st out of 24 countries on child poverty (UNICEF, 2007). The picture across the United Kingdom, and specifically the West Midlands and London is shown in Figure 4.1.

The very latest (as this publication goes to press) national statistics on Households Below Average Income (HBAI) produced by the Department for Work and Pensions were released on 7 May 2009 for the period up to the end of the financial year 2007/08. They show that on what are termed 'relative' low-income indicators there were 2.9 million children living in UK households with below 60 per cent of contemporary median net disposable household income before housing costs (BHC) and 4.0 million after housing costs (AHC). This represents no change from the previous year and a fall of only 0.5m (BHC) and 0.4m (AFC) since 1998/99. Targets to tackle child poverty may have been

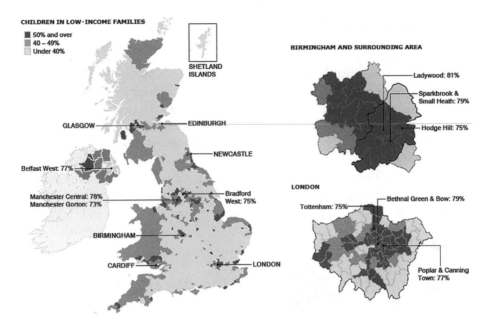

CHILDREN IN LOW-INCOME FAMILIES

- 50% and over
- 40 – 49%
- Under 40%

SHETLAND ISLANDS

GLASGOW

EDINBURGH

NEWCASTLE

Belfast West: 77%

Manchester Central: 78%
Manchester Gorton: 73%

Bradford West: 75%

BIRMINGHAM

CARDIFF

LONDON

BIRMINGHAM AND SURROUNDING AREA

Ladywood: 81%

Sparkbrook & Small Heath: 79%

Hodge Hill: 75%

LONDON

Bethnal Green & Bow: 79%

Tottenham: 75%

Poplar & Canning Town: 77%

Figure 4.1   Children in low-income families (CESI, 2009)

established with good intentions, but the gap between the richest and poorest continues to grow. The targets will also keep moving. As any economy grows and its population as a whole becomes richer, the income you need to get out of 'poverty' moves upwards.

Activity

Before this section ends, review the data and statistics that have been set out above. Whether the information was previously known to you or not, what are some of the implications of such variations nationally? Depending on where you live and/or work, what are the implications for you and others working with children, young people and families in terms of their needs?

As we have indicated, poverty is a complex, multi-dimensional issue that involves more than the crude measure of low income alone. As a result, responding effectively to the problems of poverty requires sophisticated policy development and subtle and nuanced implementation. In the next section we turn to look at how national and local government have headed and co-ordinated a range of responses involving a multiplicity of different agencies seeking to tackle poverty at the neighbourhood level.

The meaning of poverty

Developing policy interventions to tackle poverty and disadvantage

Over the past three decades there have been numerous attempts to build effective anti-poverty policies and bodies of practice that address the problems faced by individuals and specific vulnerable groups. It would be outside the scope of this chapter to undertake a full review of all of these initiatives: instead, the focus will be on the development of what we might call integrated, multi-agency strategies which are designed to tackle the role that poverty plays in the process of social exclusion. The history of how these multi-agency approaches have emerged and how this history has helped shape current policy will form the core of this section and, by way of conclusion, we will look at how individuals and communities are now seen as key 'partners' in making these strategies efficacious.

Re-discovering poverty and the development of the multi-agency response

In their pioneering study of comparative poverty in the years between 1953 and 1960, *The Poor and the Poorest*, Brian Able-Smith and Peter Townsend (1965) invited their readers to ask whether the assumption that the creation of the post-war universal welfare state had 'abolished' poverty was in fact true. Alongside the work of Able-Smith and Townsend, evidence from a range of studies in the early years of the 1960s, including the work of Audrey Harvey (1960) and Dorothy Wedderburn (1963), suggested that poverty and its impact had remained, despite significant improvements at the lower end of the income scale, a structural part of the social policy environment. Indeed, as Glennerster et al. (2004: 7) noted, Townsend's work led him to develop a different way of thinking about poverty:

> His central point was that we cannot determine a level of adequacy simply by virtue of some expert calculation of dietary or health needs. Social custom requires that we share cups of tea with neighbours or buy presents for our children at Christmas, even have the occasional pint ... To be income poor, in Townsend's terms was to be excluded, by virtue of one's income, from the normal activities of social life. (Glennerster et al., 2004: 87)

Townsend's development of the idea of *relative poverty* had an important impact on the casting of policies designed to tackle the issues his work was highlighting. Relative poverty as a concept underscored the view that poverty could not be tackled solely by dealing with levels of income. What was needed in addition to this was an approach that would address the quality of the social infrastructure within which people lived and the kind and quality of services they could access.

The idea that poverty could only be effectively tackled by a significant change in the way we conceptualised the problem was picked up in the work of Coates and Silburn (1973) who built their review of the poverty debate around a study of a specific neighbourhood, St Ann's in Nottingham. They concluded that the problems facing the people of St Ann's could only be effectively tackled by what we might now call a 'multi-agency' response:

> Clearly what is required is a systematic, simultaneous and integrated assault upon all these areas of deprivation. All the social policies mentioned have an essential role, not as alternatives to one another, but as essential complements to one another; and for any one policy to succeed there must be a parallel success in all others. Piece-meal reforms by bureaucratically separate agencies can contribute little; the commitment that is required is a whole-hearted and comprehensive one ... (Coates and Silburn, 1973: 229)

Pockets of poverty – tackling deprivation at the neighbourhood level

The rediscovery of poverty in the 1960s had an impact on government policy and rhetoric. In an attempt to explain the findings of researchers like Coates, Silburn and Townsend, political strategists argued that the problem was not the lack of an adequate structural response by the state in creating appropriate services or benefits but the inability of some people to access those services. Alcock (2006) puts it this way:

> Implicit ... is a perception that poverty is caused not so much by the failings of social and economic policy planning, but rather by the inability of people living in poverty to take advantage of the opportunities that such planning already offers. (Coates and Silburn, 2006: 226)

This idea – that the causes of poverty might be the failure of some people to understand what they are entitled to or the support structures that have been designed to help them – created the template for a generation of central and local government action based on 'targeted' or small area and neighbourhood initiatives.

Thus, in policy terms, the problem was presented as one of 'pockets of poverty' that needed to be tackled at a local level. This would enable the issues to be addressed in a targeted way, focusing on how to encourage the take-up of benefits and support services. This approach would also be advantageous to central and local government agencies in that it obviated the need to undertake what might be a lengthy and expensive review of the relevance of those services and the inevitable bureaucratic disruption that would follow from restructuring them accordingly. An analysis that located the continuing problem of poverty as being, in some way, the fault of the poor themselves was clearly attractive to policy makers at this time. As a result, dedicated funds were made available through initiatives such as Urban Aid, Educational Priority Areas or the Community Development Programme (CDP) to establish anti-poverty programmes built around improving access to services, grants and welfare benefits. However, the

The meaning of poverty

impact of this approach failed, by and large, to live up to expectations. The key assumption that lay behind the programmes – that the services needed to move people out of poverty were there but not being accessed – was simply wrong. As Alcock (2006) quite rightly points out:

> ... they also quickly realised that much of this [deprivation] was the product not of individual inadequacy or service malfunctioning, but of wider social and economic policies leading to industrial decline, rising unemployment and deprived local environments. A handful of professionals with a few resources to support local activities could do little or nothing to counteract these wider forces. (Alcock, 2004: 231)

Local government takes a lead

By the end of the 1970s a new political environment had emerged. The Conservative Government elected in 1979 and led by Margaret Thatcher had very little sympathy with the concept of anti-poverty action. The economic recession of the early 1980s and the major industrial restructuring promoted by the government resulted in a dramatic rise in unemployment and tough constraints on the value of welfare benefits. But this was characterised as a necessary, short-term readjustment of the economic base which would ultimately see everyone benefiting from a newly invigorated and modernised economy.

Indeed, John Moore, Minister for Social Security, said in a speech made in St Stephen's Club on 11 May 1989 that the critics of his government's policies were:

> not concerned with the real living standards of real people but with pursuing the political goal of equality ... We reject their claims about poverty in the UK, and we do so knowing their motive is not compassion for the less well off, it is an attempt to discredit our real economic achievement in protecting and improving the living standards of our people. Their purpose in calling 'poverty' what is in reality simply inequality, is so they can call Western capitalism a failure. We must expose this for what it is ... utterly false. (Gordon and Townsend, n.d.)

Despite the reluctance of the Thatcher-led Conservative Government, elected in 1979, to acknowledge the perception that poverty had once again become a key social policy concern, a new and solid body of evidence was emerging that would articulate the nature and scale of the problem. Peter Townsend's major new study of poverty – *Poverty in the United Kingdom* (Townsend, 1979) – was published and the findings of Douglas Black (1992), who had been charged with looking at the nature and scale of inequalities in healthcare, emerged despite attempts by the government to distance themselves from the damning conclusions.

Documents such as these became the rallying-points for an emerging political struggle between local government, which was increasingly under the control of the opposition Labour Party, and central government in the hands of the Conservative Party.

Working with children, young people and families

There are links to explore here with some of the political ideologies considered in Chapter 1. What are the tensions that are apparent in the context of poverty, political ideologies and who holds authority and power to influence inequalities for children, young people and families?

By the second half of the 1980s a new emphasis on anti-poverty action began to emerge, led specifically by a confederation of local authorities who were seeking to capitalise on their experiences of neighbourhood action in delivering the CDP some years earlier. Although local authorities seemed well positioned to lead a fight against poverty, this was more problematic than might have been thought. As Balloch and Jones (1990) observed:

> Thus local authorities can contribute in many ways to supporting the poor although it is undoubtedly central government with whom the final responsibility must rest ... There is, however, evidence to suggest that currently it is not the poor but the better off who benefit most from local authority services. (Balloch and Jones, 1990: 3)

The message from this was clear – the design of local government services would not axiomatically benefit those people trapped in the so-called pockets of poverty. To make a real difference services would have to be specifically designed and delivered in a way that was most relevant to their intended users. To enable this, the local authorities would need to have:

- Good quality demographic information
- A strategy document to ensure the effective targeting of resources
- Agreed short-, medium- and long-term goals
- A multi-agency, multi-disciplinary mechanism for implementation.

In many ways the local authority-led anti-poverty action of the late 1980s and early 1990s was more successful in its political campaigning objectives than it was in significantly changing the scale and nature of poverty. Although the objective was to redirect or 'bend' mainstream local authority spending towards the programme outlined in the anti-poverty profiles and action programmes that were drawn up, success on this front was minimal and the resources available to support significant, sustainable initiatives were very limited.

As Alcock (2006: 233) notes, by the early 1990s the political landscape was beginning to shift and the Conservative Government now led by John Major began to develop its own range of local, integrated and targeted neighbourhood renewal initiatives – most notably the Single Regeneration Budget (SRB), which followed the earlier City Challenge and put a premium on tackling poverty at the small-area level. In this environment it was easy for local authorities to subsume their anti-poverty strategies into these types of central government driven renewal programmes – because that is where the funding was now being directed.

It is worth noting at this point that the willingness to talk about poverty as a reality of everyday life in some neighbourhoods began to decline noticeably. Local authorities looking to promote their towns and cities as potential leisure or business destinations were reluctant to be seen competing for money associated with the alleviation of poverty, and local communities were also unwilling to have their localities stigmatised as 'poor'. The emergence of the linguistics of 'social exclusion' came along at an opportune time in this respect and began to replace the use of terms like poverty and anti-poverty. Although, as Percy-Smith (2000) points out, social exclusion is a wider construct than poverty, 'the term social exclusion is sometimes taken as being more or less synonymous with poverty and disadvantage' (Percy-Smith, 2000: 4).

However, as previously noted, poverty had always been a difficult word for successive governments to accept at an ideological level, but exclusion – driven by the notion that some individuals were not able or willing to access otherwise adequate welfare and support structures – was more palatable. The problem of poverty and exclusion was not one created by the *system* but by *individuals* lacking, at some level, the capacity to use the system properly.

If people are the problem they should also be the solution

The idea that poverty arises from a failure of existing services to reach those most in need had been a constant in local and central government initiatives to end poverty. However, despite considerable expenditure and seemingly endless reorganisations of the delivery agencies, there was little evidence that targeted local area regeneration was having the kind of long-term and long lasting impact that was needed. Indeed, there was significant evidence that the public felt that the gap between those on the lowest incomes and those with even moderate or median levels of earnings was becoming unsustainable. In 1992, John Smith, then leader of the Labour Party, captured this mood when he established the Commission on Social Justice which launched a wide-ranging investigation into why the various multi-agency initiatives to tackle poverty had failed to make a significant impact. The conclusions of that report (Commission for Social Justice, 1994) include the view that some of the answers to the problems of social exclusion and social injustice lie with the people themselves being given the remit to rebuild their own communities, and to do so in the context of a renewed and revived local democratic environment. The report of the Commission also notes that: 'A Government that wishes to unleash the energy of the people in their own communities

Working with children, young people and families

must also be willing to devolve some of its own power' (Commission for Social Justice, 1994: 370).

By the time of the election of the Labour Government of 1997, the notion of community *empowerment* as the key missing component in the multi-agency (or now, 'joined-up government') response to poverty and social exclusion had become firmly established. It can be argued that this realisation was a little late in coming given that Coates and Silburn (1973: 229) had argued three decades earlier that:

> ... the commitment that is required is a whole-hearted and comprehensive one involving traditional social-welfare measures, a properly conceived and heavily redistributive incomes policy, a housing programme, and equally crucial but only recently acknowledged, the active encouragement of community-action programmes, which reactivate grass-roots democratic and collective participation in decision-making at all levels.

The in-coming Labour Government of 1997 was also strongly influenced by research on issues of community cohesion undertaken in the United States. They drew heavily on the work of Robert Putnam, whose study of the decline of community in the USA – *Bowling Alone* (Putnam, 2000) – led him to develop a view of social capital as the key component of community cohesion. His study, which shows that isolation, mistrust and fear of crime rises as evidence for collective, community membership declines, was highly influential in encouraging policy makers to think about how social exclusion might be tackled through the building of what Putnam called 'bridging social capital'. This added to the work of Amitai Etzioni (1993) who, from a centre Right political perspective, developed the ideas of communitarianism in the language of rights and responsibilities and proposed the redrawing of the social contract between the individual and the state.

From the neighbourhood to the client group

The 1997 Labour Government, despite its new and stronger emphasis on the role of the individual or 'community' as a key partner in the multi-agency response to poverty, did not abandon the idea of targeted renewal as a key element in their strategy (as the reworking of SRB into New Deal for Communities evidenced in 1998). However, the focus did begin to shift from regeneration plans funded directly by central government to local renewal devised and delivered by local partnerships of service deliverers from the statutory, voluntary and private sector – co-ordinated through local authorities. Local Strategic Partnerships were created to devise community plans that would reflect the aspirations of local people and local service providers but which would be driven by the priorities identified by central government.

The government also prioritised the issue of child poverty as their key indicator of success. The then Prime Minister, Tony Blair, committed his government to a specific target:

> In March 1999, the Prime Minister responded ... by pledging to eradicate child poverty within a generation. This pledge was underpinned by ambitious targets – to reduce child poverty by a quarter by 2004/05, by a half by 2010/11 and to eradicate it by 2020. (Department of Work and Pensions, 2007: 7)

There have been a number of claims and counter-claims about the progress that has been made towards this goal and there are considerable doubts about whether the 2010 or 2020 targets can be met without significant and major investment. However, a more telling criticism of the government's child poverty programme lies in the fact that the evidence suggests that one of the key mechanisms for delivering on the child poverty promise, the multi-agency approach typified by the Sure Start project, has not been the success that many had hoped. A number of separate reports (Belsky and Melhuish, 2007; Malin and Morrow, 2008) have questioned the value of the Sure Start approach and these concerns were captured in a recent article on *The Independent* Education website:

> According to critics, the programme is ill-targeted, poorly implemented and a colossal waste of money. 'Three billion pounds have been spent in the past nine years,' says Maria Miller, shadow minister for the family, 'and they are still not hitting seven out of 14 of their key indicators. You need to have a much more focused approach.'
>
> Gary Craig, professor of social justice at Hull University, who has scrutinised how well Sure Start supports minority families, agrees. 'When you look at the sums of money involved, it's a missed opportunity for ethnic and minority children of historic proportions. This was the one chance they had to be put on a level playing field, and it's been missed. Sure Start is a national disaster.' (Wilce, 2008)

However well the government is able to target additional money in the form of benefits and tax credits towards children and their families, the issue of poverty cannot be solved in the long term without successfully addressing the improvements needed in the wide range of services and support infrastructure that is also so vital in order to address persistent deprivation.

Why has the multi-agency approach failed to effectively combat poverty?

So, if we accept that successfully tackling poverty, deprivation and exclusion needs, at its heart, a complex strategy that looks not simply at income maximisation but at how a wide range of key services can be made accessible and appropriate to the needs of the poorest members of the community, it also follows that mechanisms to deliver on this have to reflect those needs. Why, therefore, have attempts to produce a viable multi-agency response been met with relatively little success?

Working with children, young people and families

The first question we need to ask is whether we have in fact seen any genuine examples of multi-agency working in this area. It is hard to find examples of where statutory agencies – local or national – have been prepared to *plan and deliver* services in a shared and integrated way. The best we can say for them is they have tried to co-operate or collaborate but all sorts of pressures, ranging from legal commitments to professional jealousies, mitigate against genuine joint strategic planning. Where those statutory sector bodies then have to work with the voluntary or private sectors as well – as all of them do – the notion that all of these competing interests and views can be harnessed into a single vision for tackling poverty seems a distant and unobtainable objective.

Activity

As this chapter approaches its conclusion, take time to reflect on your experiences in any capacity that relate to the multi-agency approaches to tackle aspects of poverty as set out here. What is your view in terms of how strategies have been developed and implemented to support children, young people and families in the local areas you are familiar with?

Conclusion

We advocate that involving local people in these multi-agency partnerships is a crucial component to tackling poverty amongst children, young people and families and that through this approach some degree of power passes from the service provider to the community itself, resulting in still more significant challenges being thrown up. The end result of attempts to bring local people into the strategic planning and delivery of services has, more often than not, focused much more on consultation around delivery and much less on throwing open the planning process. Increasingly, statutory agencies (as well as some of the larger voluntary organisations) see themselves as commissioning agents – often seeking to outsource the service delivery through contracts with voluntary sector or community organisations – and by so doing retain the more powerful and influential role of service planning. The consequence of this is that the involvement of local people is not a partnership of ideas but a utilitarian solution to the difficulties of getting services to those deemed 'hard to reach'. In reality, talk of partnership between service providers and the community is largely tokenistic while it remains structured in this way.

The other issue that has constantly undermined the multi-agency approach to anti-poverty is the chronic underfunding of the process. By comparison with the amounts of money spent on the capital infrastructure of neighbourhoods and city centres, the expenditure on anti-poverty action has been very small. Quite often the rationale for this has been that relatively small amounts of 'seed-corn' funding

The meaning of poverty

should be sufficient to trigger a 'bending' of the much larger mainstream budgets. But as we have already seen, this has largely failed to materialise. However, over and above these substantial failures to make good on the potential of multi-agency working, there is a more fundamental issue to address. In reality, policy makers have consistently failed to create what Ruth Lister (2004) refers to as an 'inclusive' approach to tackling poverty – changing the structure and delivery of services for everyone, rather than treating 'the poor' as others with specific deficit needs and in some way outside the social support networks accepted as normal by everyone else.

This kind of 'inclusive' approach requires us to move beyond the idea that poverty persists because those most in need of services are incapable of under-standing or accessing them and to confront the possibility that poverty persists as a function of the way we sustain our macro social and economic structures.

Further reading

For a classic study see:

Runciman, W.G. (1966) *Relative Deprivation and Social Justice*. London: Routledge & Keegan Paul.

For a comparative study see:

Bradbury, B., Jenkins, S.P. and Micklewright, J. (2001) *The Dynamics of Child Poverty in Industrialised Countries*. Cambridge: CUP.

From the perspective of the community worker see:

Hare, B. (2005) *Urban Grimshaw and the Shed Crew*. London: Sceptre.

Working with children, young people and families

5

Children and young people's health and well-being

Graham Brotherton and Terry Potter

The aims of this chapter are to:

- Look at different ways in which health and well-being can be conceptualised and the contested nature of some of these definitions
- Examine evidence on the impact of a range of factors on health and well-being
- Consider current policy responses and their implications.

In recent years there has been a growing interest in the issues relating to children and young people's health and well-being. In this chapter we seek to look at the development of this debate, current policy and practice and to present a critique of current approaches.

Children and young people's health and well-being

In trying to build up a full picture of health and well-being we need to address both the specific issue of health but also the broader and more complex question of well-being. In other words as well as acknowledging the absence of 'illness' in the broadest sense of the word, in thinking about well-being we need to consider a number of broader questions about what is meant by positive health and well-being. We start with two very different takes on this. According to the UNICEF report, *Report Card 7, Child Poverty in Perspective: An Overview of Child Well-being in Rich Countries* (2007) the UK does very badly in terms of international comparisons of children's well-being. The UK was ranked at the bottom of a list of 21 'developed' countries and it is suggested that children in the UK are less happy than in any of the other countries surveyed and are more likely to be involved in risky behaviour including alcohol consumption, taking illegal drugs and underage sex. It also suggests that children and young people do less well in education overall and are more likely to feel lonely and report poor relationships with family. Here well-being encompasses access to services and resources as well as to supportive family and peer relationships.

At least partly in response to the UNICEF report, the DCSF produced a report in late 2007 which presents a rather different picture. *Children and Young People Today* starts with the following paragraph:

> Most children and young people say that they are happy, healthy and cared for by their families. They are enjoying life, achieving good results at school and in college and are making a positive contribution to society. Children and young people, more than almost any other group, have grasped the potential of new technologies. The majority of children enjoy taking regular part in a variety of cultural and sporting activities. More young people than ever are seizing the opportunity of going into further and higher education. However, across a range of outcomes there are some children and young people whose potential is not fulfilled. The effects of poverty and disadvantage can be seen in the evidence on health, safety and educational attainment. And the effects of economic, social and technological change create risks and challenges for all children and young people growing up in England today. (DCSF, 2007b)

Are these two pictures as incompatible as they first appear? In fact the DCSF report acknowledges many of the same problems as the UNICEF one, but makes much more explicit links back to the notion of poverty and social exclusion. In so doing this makes a helpful point which is often lost in the context of the debate about children and young people's lives, which is that a very substantial number of children and young people have reasonably happy childhoods and enjoy good health and a sense of well-being. Nonetheless, it also highlights that some of the key concerns of policy in this area are complex and contested and as a result policy responses need to be subtle and differentiated. Furthermore, in a context of reducing levels of overall spending on welfare, which appears the likeliest future, giving more to those who have less may mean coming to terms with giving less to those who have more – a politically very sensitive decision. To give one excellent example of this, in 2007 the City of Brighton decided to allocate places in some over-subscribed schools on a lottery basis to give children from disadvantaged backgrounds a greater possibility of a place. There was (and to some extent still is) an outcry from some parents about this. Leaving aside at this stage some of the arguments about the unfairness and impracticability of lotteries and focusing simply on the 'well-being' dimension of the argument, it can be argued this is a very effective way of dealing with the problems identified in this paragraph. Nonetheless, its political contentiousness means other local authorities have been slow to follow Brighton's example. We return to the links between well-being and broader social issues later in the chapter, but will now move on to considering what we mean by health and then to exploring current policy.

Activity

Spend a few minutes thinking about the following questions.

What do you need in order to be healthy? Is health the same as well-being? If not how do they differ? Are there differences for children and young people and for different stages of 'growing up'?

We will present a model which attempts to answer these questions shortly, however in order to make sense of the model, we need first to consider how views on health have developed. Our starting point for this is a report produced by the Working Group on Inequalities and Health which has become known as *The Black Report* (1992), named after the Working Group's Chair, Sir Douglas Black. This was a government report commissioned by the Department of Health in 1977 as a direct response to an article by Richard Wilkinson (whose work we return to later) in *New Society* magazine which highlighted the massive impact of poverty and social class on individual health. *The Black Report* was, however, not completed until after the General Election of 1979 which saw the Labour Government which had commissioned it defeated and replaced by the Conservative Government of Margaret Thatcher. The incoming government saw the policies being proposed by the report as unpalatable and, as a result, the report was effectively hidden, being published in small numbers over a bank holiday weekend in 1980. However, the report was subsequently published as a Penguin paperback book (Black, 1992) and has had a profound impact on thinking about health – though perhaps a less significant impact on policy.

The Black Report concluded that whilst there had been a general improvement in health since the introduction of the National Health Service in 1948 this had not been even across social classes and that there were significant differences in both mortality (death rates) and morbidity (levels of ill health) across the social classes, with those in social class 5 of the Registrar General's classification in particular enjoying much poorer health outcomes. The report suggested four possible explanations, two of which – the materialist (or structural) and the cultural–behavioural – have continued to frame the subsequent debate.

However, before discussing these in detail it is worth mentioning briefly the other explanations which have been posited to account for unequal health outcomes. The first, the *artefact* explanation, focuses on problems in measuring health and highlights the possibility that the differences are explained by flaws in this process. However, the sheer weight of the evidence over the last 30 years suggests the differences are real and significant. The second explanation, *social or natural selection* suggests that people move up or down the class system as a result of their health status. There is limited evidence of this so-called 'social drift' in a small number of very specific situations, for example in relation to some chronic mental health conditions, but very little evidence of 'healthy' people being significantly socially advantaged. Again, as an overall explanation this can be largely discounted.

We now return to the main explanations in *The Black Report. Cultural-behavioural* explanations focus on differences in behaviour between different groups and suggest that differences in behaviour between those in 'higher' social classes and those in 'lower' social classes in respect of eating habits, exercise and smoking are the main explanation. There are variations in emphasis in different accounts in that some writers have suggested that these differences are mainly based upon individual lifestyle choices whereas others highlight the role of a range of other factors such as where people live and access to resources and services.

Materialist (or structural) explanations focus on the impact of structural factors such as living in poverty or poor housing or working in more risky or hazardous occupations. *The Black Report* highlights that all of these things are much more likely to happen to disadvantaged groups and its recommendation of significant investment to attempt to reduce these inequalities explains its sidelining by the then government.

As previously suggested, the immediate impact of the report was limited but after its publication as a paperback and subsequent research, notably by Margaret Whitehead (1992) the ideas really began to have an impact on the health debate. However not until the election of the Labour Government in 1997 do they explicitly become a feature of policy.

The Acheson Report

This report, produced under the auspices of Sir Donald Acheson, was commissioned as an independent inquiry into health inequalities in much the same way as *The Black Report* had been at the end of the 1970s. It was published in 1998 and effectively revisits the issues dealt with in *The Black Report* and concludes that health inequalities had actually increased over the intervening period. It attempted to produce a holistic model to explain inequalities, which is reproduced in Figure 5.1.

Activity

Looking back now at your answers to the activity at the start of the chapter, how well do your suggestions fit with the model proposed by Acheson?

It can immediately be seen that the Acheson model, which has been the basis for policy around health for the last 10 years or so, at least on a philosophical

Working with children, young people and families

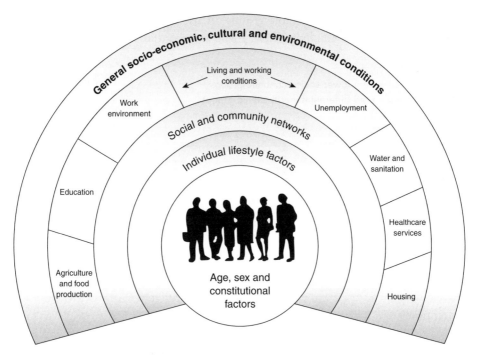

Figure 5.1   The main determinants of health (Department of Health, 1998)

level recognises the link between broader socio-economic issues and health and attempts to take account of both structural and cultural factors.

We will attempt to evaluate the current policy position after looking in more detail at the issues around the evidence for the view that health and well-being are intrinsically linked to the socio-economic context in which particular individuals and families live. Before doing this it is important to establish the current framework in which practitioners are expected to operate. In the context of work with children, young people and families it can be argued that perhaps the best way of exploring where policy stands is through the Every Child Matters outcomes, one of which is to 'be healthy' and which is further subdivided into five areas:

- Physically healthy
- Mentally and emotionally healthy
- Sexually healthy
- Healthy lifestyles
- Choosing not to take illegal drugs (DCSF, 2007b).

However, it has to be noted that whilst the approach is universal in terms of applying to all children, young people and their families, there is an emphasis on

Health and well-being

the particular needs of 'vulnerable groups'. A useful working definition of such groups is provided by Waldman (2007) who suggest that they include:

- looked after children
- young people from lower socio-economic groups
- young people from different minority ethnic groups
- young carers
- young offenders
- young mothers
- mobile children
- asylum-seekers/refugees
- children with disabilities
- children at risk from significant harm
- children living with 'vulnerable' adults
- children of service families
- pupils not fluent in English
- children in unsatisfactory housing.

Activity

Select one of the groups of children identified in the previous list. What factors need to be considered when thinking about their health and well-being? To what extent might the needs of these different groups overlap and to what extent do they need to be considered separately?

Of course this is a very broad (and overlapping) range of children and young people who may be living in very different situations and this immediately raises a number of issues in terms of trying to talk about health and well-being in a general way. It is also important to highlight that the needs of the children in this list, and hence the appropriate responses, are going to be complex and varied. However with these caveats in mind, at this point it is useful to survey the evidence about the role of various factors in promoting or inhibiting health and well-being.

The impact of poverty and inequality on health outcomes

We know what makes us ill.
When we are ill we are told
That it's you who will heal us.
When we come to you
Our rags are torn off us and you listen all over our naked body.
As to the cause of our illness one glance at our rags would tell you more.
It is the same cause that wears out our bodies and our clothes.

From Bertolt Brecht, 'A Worker's Speech to a Doctor' (1938) (Socialist Health Association, 2009)

Working with children, young people and families

Health inequalities: a multi-faceted problem

Poverty kills. The evidence for this is not to be found in one set of indicators or attributed to any specific cause or lifestyle choice. Health and well-being are influenced by social circumstances throughout life and, unless we are able to understand the impact of these social circumstances in their appropriate time and place, we will struggle to understand the dynamic that creates differential outcomes. Mary Shaw et al. (1999) noted it in this way:

> The independent influences of social circumstances in childhood and in later life on ill-health and the risk of dying in adulthood indicate that a search for the causes of inequalities in health must be a broad-based one and must include all stages of the life-course. (1999: 73)

In other words, ill-health and early death are frequently the result of structural inequalities between different groups of people which are evident from the moment they are born to when they die. Differences in life circumstances, such as occupational and social class, income, education, housing and employment prospects all contribute to the picture. As Shaw et al. (1999) observe:

> From infancy to old age, across the country and between different groups in society, life chances are unequal and becoming more unequal as people's lives progress. At the root of the differences observed are differences in the degree of poverty experienced by different people, groups of people and in different areas. (1999: 61)

The impact of inequalities in health outcomes is not only observed as the result of detailed academic analysis; it is also evident to the wider public at large who live with a perception of these inequalities on a daily basis. When asked, an awareness of this fundamental inequality is reflected in their attitudes. The 2004 Public Health White Paper, *Choosing Health*, set out, in uncompromising terms, how the public see the impact of poverty and inequality. It reported that '76% of people in the higher income groups expect to be in good health in 10 years time compared to 53% in the lowest groups' (Department of Health, 2004: 10).

Health and child poverty

If, therefore, inequalities in health outcomes are the consequence of poverty that can last from the cradle to the grave, it follows that the need to tackle child poverty is pivotal to improving health and well-being. Even by the age of three there are significant differences in health status between children from richer or poorer backgrounds, a situation that is illustrated by the *Millennium Cohort Study* (Hansen and Joshi, 2007):

> While the variations in health between groups as measured by social disadvantage are striking, this confirms well-established evidence. A striking finding has been that of marked variations in a range of health outcomes ... according to the characteristics of the communities in which the children live. Thus, children starting out in disadvantaged areas are more likely to experience disability and

ill-health in the form of problems with vision, hearing and longstanding conditions, asthma, chronic infections and injuries and are more likely to be obese or overweight. (2007: 90)

Although infant death rates overall have been on the decline, the gap between those from manual and non-manual backgrounds has not narrowed. 'Infant deaths are still 50% more common among those from manual backgrounds than among those from non-manual backgrounds' (*The Poverty Site*, 2009).

Evidence suggests that the impact of socio-economic differentials on child health and well-being outcomes are widespread and can be manifested in a range of indicators. For example, children from disadvantaged and poor backgrounds are:

- Less likely to be breast-fed
- More likely to be exposed to cigarette smoke
- More likely to be involved in a road accident
- More likely to die before the age of one (Ferguson et al., 2006: 37).

Disadvantaged within the disadvantaged

Given the strong evidence cited above that early death and ill-health have their roots in childhood disadvantage and poverty, it is also the case that there are certain population characteristics that are likely to deepen and intensify the chances of inequality in health outcomes. The work of Nazroo (1997) clearly demonstrated that the health of minority ethnic groups was worse than that of the white population and that within those groups we apply the 'ethnic minority' label to, some did significantly worse than others. Nazroo (1997: 33) summarises it thus: 'Limiting long-standing illness was almost 50 per cent greater amongst Pakistani/Bangladeshis compared to whites, about a quarter greater for Caribbeans and Indian/African Asians and almost a quarter lower for Chinese respondents'.

These findings are supported by Randhawa (2007) whose study on health inequalities for The Race Equality Foundation concluded that:

> There is a plethora of evidence highlighting that people from minority ethnic groups experience poorer health than the overall UK population. Some examples include the observation of higher rates of diabetes, cardiovascular disease and mental illness among certain minority ethnic groups. Furthermore, the data suggests that patterns of poor health vary *within* ethnic groups. (Randhawa, 2007: 4)

There is, in addition, a broad consensus about the issues that are driving this inequality within certain ethnic minority groups. A rich mix of poverty, disadvantage, discrimination and racism enhances the kind of differentials that might be expected to arise from individual lifestyle factors and cultural diversity. This idea of a complex matrix of health inequality is cited by the report of the Parliamentary Office of Science and Technology, *Ethnicity and Health* (2007). It says:

> Many BME groups experience higher rates of poverty than the White British, in terms of income, benefits use, worklessness, lacking basic necessities and area deprivation. Much of the

variation in self-reported health between and within BME groups can be explained by differences in socio-economic status. However, there is a complex interplay of factors affecting ethnic health, such as the long-term impact of migration, racism and discrimination, poor delivery and take-up of health care, differences in culture and lifestyles, and biological susceptibility. (*Ethnicity and Health*, 2007)

In addition to ethnicity, *gender* also plays a determining factor in health outcomes. Arber and Cooper (2000) argue very strongly for looking at gender-based health inequalities 'across the life-course' (Arber and Cooper, 2000: 123). This is very much in line with the view expressed earlier that we cannot take 'snapshots' of an individual's health as a way of expressing or explaining the impact of inequality. Instead we have to look at the individual in their 'whole life' context and consider what societal pressures are combining to create unequal outcomes. In the case of women, Arber and Cooper argue that by looking at childhood, working life and later life it is much easier to see how the social construction of gender roles within these three contexts has a differential impact on health outcomes. They conclude that:

> The nature of inequalities in women's and men's health is likely to differ over time and between societies in concert with the way in which gender roles vary historically and cross-nationally … although class remains an important indicator of inequalities in health, the current emphasis on social class may be masking other important dimensions of inequality relating to an individual's structural position and family circumstance. (Arber and Cooper, 2000: 146)

Mental health

Although the numbers of people deemed to be at high risk of developing mental illness has been declining over the past decade, adults from the poorest fifth of the population are much more likely to develop a mental illness than those on average income. And, the picture is much worse for women than men (*The Poverty Site*, 2009).

Data linking poverty and deprivation indicators to recorded instances of mental illness do not, however, explain why there might be a causal link between the two. Whitehead (1992: 256) notes that there is a strong correlation, for example, between unemployment and ill-health and identifies a range of studies dating back to the 1980s which seem to support the connection, but she concludes that whilst unemployment may contribute to a deterioration in mental health, 'the evidence that unemployment *causes* physical ill-health and suicide is less conclusive'.

Analysis by Payne (n.d.) of the 1999 PSE Survey suggests that we are still lacking definitive research which would link social exclusion and mental health outcomes in a causal relationship:

> There is less research as yet which explores the impact of social exclusion on mental health and well-being. However, again it might be expected that being excluded from mainstream society, for whatever reason, might impact negatively on mental health just as one might

Health and well-being

hypothesise that being part of a community of friends, neighbours or family might have positive effects on mental well-being. (Payne, n.d.)

So, although the weight of evidence would lead us to believe that poverty, deprivation and social exclusion have an impact on differential mental health outcomes, we cannot necessarily say they are the root cause. However, it may be possible to address this seeming conundrum by looking at the work of Richard Wilkinson (1996). In his pioneering work, *Unhealthy Societies*, Wilkinson suggested that in advanced western societies there is a link between health – mental or physical – and the concepts of social justice, fairness and inequality. It is this idea that we look at in more detail in the next section.

Health and perceptions of inequality

Shaw et al. (1999: 65) were firm in their belief that health differentials are primarily the result of the *material* status of individuals throughout their life-span. They were clear they did not want to ascribe differences in health outcomes 'to the psychological effects of position within hierarchies'. Wilkinson, however, disagrees and talks of what he calls the 'psychosocial' causes of illness (Wilkinson, 1996: 175): 'Fortunately, there is now a great deal of epidemiological and experimental evidence which removes any doubt that psychosocial factors can exert very powerful influences on physical health'. Wilkinson's study suggests that there is a direct link between ideas of social equality, perceptions of social justice and health status. At a certain point (already reached by advanced western economies) it is not possible to close the health gap between the rich and the poor simply by spending more money. What counts, he argues, is that we close the gap between the rich and poor and seek to address how society views notions of equality. Wilkinson suggests that the evidence supports the view that the more egalitarian a society is, the better the health outcomes for its citizens. Issues such as stress, alienation, lack of personal control and low self esteem all combine to have a negative impact on health and these are circumstances that are not necessarily susceptible to direct health-led interventions but need a wider political and policy commitment to improving social justice. His argument is that it is not poverty per se that has such a significant impact but the extent of relative inequality, and using five key indicators (Wilkinson, 1996) he seeks to compare a range of societies. The five dimensions considered are;

- Interpersonal violence
- Health inequalities
- Interpersonal trust
- Overall levels of child welfare
- The existence (or otherwise) of social mobility.

Wilkinson's key conclusion based on a very extensive survey of both so-called 'developed' and 'developing' economies is that more equal societies scored better on all indicators.

Working with children, young people and families

This is an important and still fairly controversial suggestion which has important policy ramifications. As discued in Chapter 4, child poverty (however we choose to define this) is still a major issue, but if Wilkinson's argument is accepted then simply dealing with the issue of low income alone is not a sufficient response and a strategy is needed which seeks to address both health and broader considerations of 'well-being'.

Wilkinson and Pickett (2009) develop this theme and seek to draw together the available evidence for the impact of 'psychosocial' influence on health differentials. Their conclusion is that lifestyle and personal choices cannot, in themselves, explain the differentially bad health outcomes of the poorest within our communities. The conclusion of Wilkinson and Pickett is that 'position in society matters' (Wilkinson and Pickett, 2009: 87) and it matters because of the physical and mental impact of stress and low self regard.

Looking for solutions

In this section we have argued for the issue of health inequalities to be seen in a number of ways:

- The problem of poor health outcomes stems from poverty and inequality. The impact of poverty is likely to be multi-dimensional and as a result the health inequalities that follow are also complex. They can only be properly understood as a combination of issues that can follow people from the cradle to the grave. It is the social circumstances of people in key parts of their whole life cycle that can conspire together to create these inequalities.
- If health inequalities are a function of poverty and inequality then it is also the case that within this cohort of disadvantage some groups suffer more than others. Within the black and minority ethnic (BME) population there are those who are particularly susceptible to differentially poor health outcomes and if we look at the impact on gender then we see very poor outcomes for women compared to men.
- Although we sometimes lack the direct causal evidence, there is a substantial body of research that strongly suggests that it is mental as well as physical health that is adversely affected by poverty and disadvantage.
- Inequalities in material wealth and income may well be only part of the health inequalities picture. There is compelling, albeit contested, evidence to support the view that our own sense of self and how that relates to issues of social justice and equality may well have a significant part to play.

We are then left with the question of how policy can be made to better respond to these issues. Black (1992) suggested that the starting point needed to be better data and research and this, surely, remains a constant. In a fast moving global economy the impact of poverty and inequality on health outcomes will always be a moveable feast requiring continual monitoring and information updating. Black's other priorities – tackling child poverty, and better disability awareness and health education – have in many ways become familiar territory. Whitehead (1992) picked up Black's recommendations and added a further priority – tackling poverty at the community level through better education, housing and social infrastructure. Shaw et al. (1999) in turn built on what had gone before, but, alongside calls for a more equitable redistribution of wealth, they introduce the idea of better, more responsive service delivery as a key element. They point out the fact that relatively little work has been done on the impact of equity in service provision and they characterise this as one of the key missing elements. They do, however, concede that this in itself will not be enough:

> However, even if good practice on equitable service delivery was adopted by the NHS and local authorities, these changes alone would not be sufficient to end inequalities in health. Other policies designed to raise the incomes of poor families with children, sick and disabled people and elderly people will also be needed. (Shaw et al., 1999: 199)

Wilkinson and Pickett (2009) offer to take us still further. What they call for is a complete rethinking of our ideas about how we structure society and more 'investment' in ideas around collective decision making, worker control and more commitment to political as well as social equality. 'What is essential if we are to bring a better society into being is to develop a sustained movement committed to doing that' (Wilkinson and Pickett, 2009: 261).

There is undoubtedly now a consensus amongst policy makers that poverty and inequality are the key driving forces behind differential health outcomes. That the poor suffer worse health throughout their lives and die before their richer compatriots is now clearly established. However, picking up on the evidence from Wilkinson's research, poverty alone does not account for all of the difference nor will its alleviation solve the problem. Creating greater equality is not just alleviating poverty as measured by low income but also about reducing the advantages that some groups enjoy in claiming the best of the resources available in health, education, etc. Making a change to this order of things is the bigger challenge and one our public policy makers have yet to deliver on. Improving individual and family incomes, providing more accessible services and better information about lifestyle choices have a part to play and there is a wide consensus that the necessary starting point is a commitment to ending child poverty as a matter of urgency. However, radical as all this might be as a programme, it may still not be enough to close the health inequality gap. What also has to be considered is that differential health outcomes are a product of systemic problems within competitive, market-based societies and that only by challenging the values at the heart of this kind of economic system can we hope to find solutions to fundamental health inequalities.

Children, families and healthy lifestyles: where are we now?

As was suggested earlier in the chapter the issue of children's health and well-being has become a significant one again in policy terms in recent years. Indeed

Working with children, young people and families

as highlighted previously, one of the five outcomes of Every Child Matters is that children and young people should 'be healthy' and there have been a range of initiatives, perhaps most notably the introduction of the national healthy schools standard, which are designed to support this. It is possible in the light of the broader evidence considered previously though to suggest that the range of initiatives which have been introduced take a very particular view of both the 'problem' of health inequalities and the possible range of solutions which are required. In policy terms recent responses have focused upon:

- Healthy eating, for example through the reintroduction of nutritional standards for school meals or the introduction of healthy eating/lifestyles into the national curriculum
- The promotion of active lifestyles through greater emphasis on physical activity within the school day or in out-of-school activities
- Strategies to persuade parents to cook healthy food, for example through classes in schools and children's centres.

Activity

Look back at the section of the chapter that deals with the explanations for health inequalities proposed in *The Black Report*. Which category of explanation are these responses drawing upon? Why do you think this is?

We would argue that a clear link can be seen to the cultural-behavioural models with their emphasis on changing individual and family lifestyles in terms of responsibility for 'healthy' behaviour. As suggested earlier in this chapter one of the central difficulties is that risk factors for health and well-being are not evenly distributed amongst all children, young people and families. The groups identified as being particularly vulnerable are very disparate. To give an oversimplified example to illustrate, the needs of children or families living in unsatisfactory housing are clearly different to, though they may overlap with, the needs of children who are not fluent in English (to use the NFER categories). In the case of the former it can be argued that the 'cause' is largely structural, the absence of a decent supply of affordable housing, whereas in the latter case a range of factors both structural (e.g. poverty) or cultural-behavioural (e.g. parenting 'capacity', difficulties in learning, or the possible consequences of migration) could all be playing a role and any appropriate response needs to be sensitive to the particular facts of any individual situation.

Situations such as the one discussed above, whilst oversimplified, do highlight real tensions for practitioners. We are not arguing that practitioners are not aware of these tensions, but that the 'broad brush' responses which can characterise responses to the Every Child Matters outcomes can hide the need for more sophisticated targeted work with particular groups and individuals. Furthermore, practice and practitioners can only go so far in addressing the fundamental issues identified by Wilkinson and Pickett (2009). Responding to their critique requires action, not just at a practice level but at a societal and political level.

In the light of this, whilst it is of course clearly important to promote healthy lifestyles, it must be argued that if this is not matched by a similar emphasis on tackling the structural dimensions outlined in this chapter then any general improvement in children and young people's health and well-being is likely to prove elusive.

Further reading

Bartley, M. (2004) *Health Inequality: An Introduction to Concepts, Theories and Methods*. Cambridge: Polity Press.

Graham, H. (ed.) (2009) *Understanding Health Inequalities*. Berkshire: Open University Press.

Pilgrim, D. and Rogers, A. (2003) *Mental Health and Inequality*. Basingstoke: Palgrave Macmillan.

Spencer, N.J. (2000) *Poverty and Child Health*. Oxford: Radcliffe Publishing.

6

Listening to children's voices – in educational settings

John Ryan and Stephen Griffin

> **The aims of this chapter are to:**
> - Consider the importance of children's voices
> - Look at citizenship provision in educational settings
> - Provide a clearer understanding of the functions of School Councils or similar forums
> - Contribute to the ongoing debate on the importance of pupil active participation
> - Consider 'Character Education'
> - Explore child protection issues in relation to listening to children
> - Understand more about the five outcomes of the Every Child Matters agenda
> - Promote a range of strategies to encourage effective strategies for listening to young people.

This chapter will encompass the validity of listening to young people and although mainly concerned with schools, the examples and suggestions discussed could be transferred to any environment involved with the development of children and young people.

The chapter aims to provide material such as case studies to promote analysis, reflection and critique in order to encourage a considered and practical approach to strategies for listening to young people in your work settings. It is true to say that adults working with children, at one level, are always consulting with youngsters, such as to ascertain whether they have a clear understanding of tasks, need assistance or have completed work, etc. This chapter outlines something more sustained as it explores the notion of consulting with children, regarding education, curriculum and personal matters.

The content of this chapter draws on government legislation that has been implemented in recent years to ensure that the voice of the child as an individual is heard and more importantly acted upon. Links to citizenship education have also been referenced, as, with 'pupil voice', it is a contentious topic yet they are both intrinsically linked.

The historical construction of childhood

It is perhaps easy to forget that it is only relatively recently that the idea of child-hood, as distinct to adulthood, was formed. Historically speaking 'childhood' is a social construction. In medieval times 'there was a distinct lack of sentiment, an indifference to children as a separate sector of the population' (Wyness, 2006). Consequently, children were seen as apprentice adults who required little more than 'correction', often physical, to mend their ways. It was not until 1693 when John Locke published *Some Thoughts Concerning Education* that this approach was questioned:

> Beating them, and all other sorts of slavish and corporal punishments, are not the discipline fit to be used in the education of those we would have wise, good, and ingenuous men; and therefore very rarely to be applied, and that only in great occasions, and cases of extremity. (Locke, 1693: 50)

Later, in 1762, Jean Jaques Rousseau's *Emile* was published in England. Whilst it did not impact greatly upon the country, many had sympathy with his ideas and in particular the idea of childhood as a worthy state in itself that has 'its own ways of seeing, thinking and feeling' (Rousseau, 1979: 54). The idea that the child has a 'voice' was born and yet it took a long time before this was formally rec-ognised within the education system. Recent thinking and reform has led to a significant change in the way the 'child' is viewed by society and educational institutions in particular. As Wyness concludes: '… a key characteristic of modern childhood is its future orientation, the idea that children are nascent individuals with personalities and social and moral dispositions that need to be harnessed and moulded in preparation for adulthood' (Wyness, 2006: 13).

The degree to which this is tokenistic rhetoric or actual ideological change is to be questioned, but it is fair to say that increasingly childhood, as a distinct state of being, is an accepted construction across many areas of society (see Chapter 2 for further consideration of childhoods).

When considering the relationship between listening to children's voices and educational practice we should consider:

1　The United Nations Convention on the Rights of the Child (UNCRC)
2　Contemporary citizenship educational policy
3　The nature of education for personal and social development.

The United Nations Convention on the Rights of the Child

The UNCRC (1989) outlines the basic human rights which children everywhere are entitled to. Initially it was an extension of the 1924 Geneva Declaration on the Rights of the Child which was adopted into the General Assembly of the UN

Working with children, young people and families

as late as 1959. The UNCRC was first ratified on 20 November 1990 and has since been adopted by all but two countries (the United States of America and Somalia).

The UNCRC is clear that respect for the rights of others lies at its heart, and below are some of the articles that are most appropriate, and are being, or have been, fostered in education:

- We must not treat people in a degrading way (Article 3).
- Anyone charged with an offence is presumed innocent until proven guilty (Articles 5 and 6).
- Everyone is given a fair hearing (Article 6).
- Respect each other's privacy (Article 8).
- Respect someone's religious beliefs even if they are different to your own (Article 9).
- Listening to the views of others even if you disagree (Article 10).
- The value of peaceful protest (Article 11).
- There should be an effective remedy for people who feel their rights have been denied (Article 13).

(United Nations Conventions on the Rights of the Child, 1989)

As well as the above, Articles 12, 13, 14, 15 and 29 are also relevant to listening to children, and are included in more detail at the end of this chapter.

Activity

Some might argue that the UNCRC is not sufficiently embedded into training, education or practice in schools and other settings where adults work with children and young people. As you reflect on the rights articulated within the UNCRC, to what extent do you consider they underpin practice in settings with which you are familiar?

Citizenship in educational settings

The practice of listening to children and more importantly acting upon what they say, in terms of primary and secondary education is a fairly new concept (Erickson and Schultz, 1992). The main way by which schools attempt to listen to the opinions of children is through the development of a School Council, as identified and initially suggested in the Crick Report (1998). Citizenship is one strand of the non-statutory guidance for Personal, Social, Health and Economic education (PSHE) at Key Stage 1 and 2 and citizenship is now statutory at Key Stage 3.

Giving children and young people a say in decisions that affect them is at the core of many government initiatives regarding education such as Every Child Matters (DfES, 2004b) and Excellence and Enjoyment (DfES, 2003a). It is intended that such an approach will have a positive impact on standards, behaviour and inclusion. Recently schools have encouraged children and young people to

Listening to children's voices

participate more effectively in democratic procedures. For example, most secondary and primary schools now have a School Council. Whether or not these are effective is a separate issue and one that will be explored later in this chapter.

In the Crick Report (1998) the lack of engagement that young people feel with political issues is noted, as it states that 'there are worrying levels of apathy, ignorance and cynicism about public life' (Crick, 1998: 8). Following the recommendations of the Crick Report, citizenship education was made a statutory subject in 2002 for all secondary pupils, and was further categorised into three strands: social and moral responsibility; community involvement; and political literacy (Crick, 1998).

As well as researching knowledge and understanding within citizenship, each strand (in KS3) in accordance with the Crick Report 'should also cover practical skills that enable young people to participate effectively in public life and prepare them to be full citizens' (Crick, 1998: 19). The main strategy that was proposed in the Crick Report was the active promotion of listening to young people's views, the cultivation of School Councils and an appreciation that 'schools should make every effort to engage pupils in discussion and consultation about all aspect of school life' (Crick, 1998: 36).

Activity

Before we move on to the section on School Councils, reflect on ways in which settings you have worked in, or currently work in, consult with children. How are children's views sought? Issues of inclusion and power make genuine consultation a challenge in many contexts, but before some of these issues are considered, identify the selection processes, agenda setting, supervision, attendance (for example) and then analyse how these aspects may suggest who has the power to make decisions, and who does not.

School Councils

The Crick Report (1998) supports the promotion and implementation of School Councils as much of the report is concerned with promoting pupil activity. Guidance on how such forums could be organised are available from the Qualification Guidance and Curriculum Authority (QCA) and although these are specifically for School Councils, much of the suggestions are appropriate for any setting which includes children. According to the QCA 'Involvement in the running of the school through school or class councils and other decision making also promotes responsibility and learning about democracy' (QCA, 2000: 9). Effective School Councils should be discussion and decision-making bodies. The main aim of such forums should be to encourage children, young people and staff (or adults) to learn collaboratively about forms of political interaction. An effective School Council could include the following features:

- The establishment of a Council that is a natural progression from circle time (class discussion) and class Council
- A democratic election of class representatives (each class should have at least two representatives on the Council)
- Regular meetings (monthly or half-termly)
- An annually elected School Council
- An agreed constitution
- Council members respecting and listening to each other
- Defined boundaries for the Council
- Training for class representatives
- A supportive and effective link with teachers/adults
- Easy access to the headteacher and governors
- A bank account and a budget.

One must be cautious, however, as the above list should not be viewed as a 'tick list' to ensure effective dialogue between adults and children in all educational settings. Each setting is distinctive and as such one needs to be careful regarding advice that may not be entirely appropriate for that setting where you are either working or are on placement (Holdsworth, 2001; Lansdowe, 1994).

When developing School Councils or any forum by which youngsters are asked to generate their ideas, it is perhaps easier to encourage an adequate gender and ethnic balance amongst the School Council than it is to promote inclusion of those with Special Educational Needs (SEN). Children with SEN may include those whose experiences may mean they have the most to gain from being asked their opinions and who will particularly benefit from being given responsibilities. By ensuring that pupils with SEN are included on School Councils there could also be benefits to the whole school community. One example is that other children will experience working with youngsters of differing abilities and therefore be enabled to empathise with others. Below are a few practical suggestions in order to promote inclusion on School Councils:

- Have a specific SEN representative with an advocate
- Have a liaison representative on the School Council who meets with a SEN committee
- Be proactive in encouraging the participation of young people with SEN
- Provide Council members with diversity training to recognise and embrace people's differences, leading to a greater awareness of other people's needs
- The School Council should contribute to the accessibility plan and be included in curriculum design and support in terms of assistive technology, adapting seating arrangements, different formats for reporting and linking to the Special Educational Needs Disability Act (2001).

(Adapted from UK School Councils Network Newsletter, 2002)

How effective School Councils may be in promoting inclusion and participation is difficult to assess. It is important though to mote that inclusion necessitates practitioners, institutions or settings to critically evaluate their role as facilitator

Listening to children's voices

of all needs. One must not assume that mere representation of a specific need will ensure successful implementation or indeed an ideal philosophical approach to SEN. When considering the levels of participation that youngsters are engaged in when 'being' consulted, it is useful to consult the work of Hart (1992). Here one can observe how children's participation is compared with the steps on a ladder, with the lower steps (starting at 1) describing low-level participation but in a negative context. (Hart's ladder is also presented in Chapter 10 in the context of research with children.) The steps are:

1 **Manipulation**. Children are engaged or used for the benefit of their own interests, formulated by adults, while the children themselves do not understand the implications.
2 **Decoration**. Children are called in to embellish adult actions. Adults do not, however, pretend that this is in the interest of the children themselves.
3 **Tokenistic**. Children are apparently given a voice, but this is to serve the child-friendly image adults want to create, rather than the interest of the children themselves.
4 **Assigned but informed**. Adults take the initiative to call in children but inform them on how and why. Only after the children have come to understand the intentions of the project and the point of their involvement do the children decide whether or not to take part.
5 **Consulted and informed**. Children are intensively consulted on a project run by adults.
6 **Adult-initiated shared decisions with the children**. In the case of projects concerned with community development, initiators such as policy makers, community workers and local residents frequently involve interest groups and specific age groups.
7 **Child-initiated and directed**. Children conceive, organise and direct a project themselves without adult interference.
8 **Child-initiated shared decisions with adults**.
(Adapted from Hart, 1992)

Ideally all adults working with children would want the children to feel empowered on the highest three levels. A particularly powerful example of this is the type of democratic schooling as embodied by Summerhill School where both pupils and staff have equal voting rights and all aspects of the school's governance are open to debate within the school 'meeting' (Neill, 1998).

Activity

Consider a recent occasion when you were working with a group of children in a setting where consultation was taking place. Using Hart's ladder model, decide which step is the best fit when considering student voice and participation.

- What strategies could be used to ensure that the children move closer to step 8 (Child-initiated shared decisions with adults)?
- If the process was effective at step 8, what strategies were successful?
- How could you ensure that the young people you are working with are closer to step 8 rather than step 1?

Working with children, young people and families

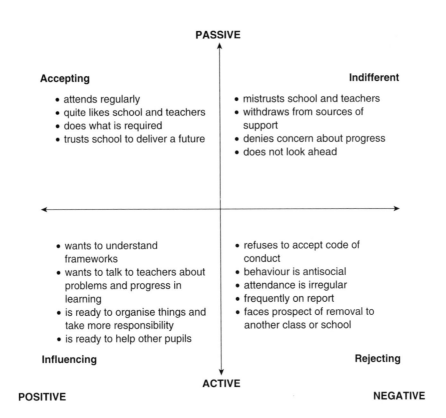

PASSIVE

Accepting

- attends regularly
- quite likes school and teachers
- does what is required
- trusts school to deliver a future

Indifferent

- mistrusts school and teachers
- withdraws from sources of support
- denies concern about progress
- does not look ahead

- wants to understand frameworks
- wants to talk to teachers about problems and progress in learning
- is ready to organise things and take more responsibility
- is ready to help other pupils

- refuses to accept code of conduct
- behaviour is antisocial
- attendance is irregular
- frequently on report
- faces prospect of removal to another class or school

Influencing

Rejecting

ACTIVE

POSITIVE

NEGATIVE

Figure 6.1 Indicators of engagement for school pupils (Adapted from Nixon et al., 1996: 113)

Another important issue to consider when discussing pupil voice is how to encourage students to be active rather than passive participants. After all 'well placed trust grows out of active enquiry rather than blind acceptance' (O'Neill, 2002: 76). The quadrant in Figure 6.1 illustrates that ideally, through effective citizenship education and by listening to children's and young people's voices, one would anticipate that the majority of young participants should be in the 'positive and influencing section'. However due to constraints placed on schools regarding raising achievement, performance issues and competitiveness it could be argued that to comply with such agendas, practitioners may prefer children to be in the top left quadrant (passive and accepting).

Activity

Again identify a recent occasion when you were working with a group of children (a different occasion to the last task). Using Nixon et al.'s quadrant (Figure 6.1), decide on which quadrant you could apply to the adult's expectations of the overall process when considering student voice and participation.

Listening to children's voices

- What strategies could be used to ensure that the children move to the bottom left quadrant (positive and influencing)?
- If you selected the bottom left quadrant (positive and influencing), what strategies were successful?
- Do you consider that all practitioners you work with have similar views about how to ensure that children and young people in the setting take a positive and influencing perspective? What are the implications of potential differences?
- Why is it important to consult children and young people when working with them?

Listening to children in educational settings

Davies and Yamashita (2007) highlight the various ways by which educational settings can capitalise by listening to young people's voices, such as being involved in staff appointments, school improvement policies, contributing to teaching and learning and improving academic achievement. Young people's voices, in educational settings, should occur in different forms. Whitty and Wisby (2007: 5) identify four reasons for schools to establish student voice processes: children's rights; active citizenship; transferable and social skills; and personalisation. If schools merely play nominal attention to the involvement of children without fully incorporating their objectives, than there could be a counterproductive effect upon the students. Potentially this could actually work against one of the aims of the National Curriculum which aims at developing 'responsible citizens who make a positive contribution to society' as well as 'participating actively in decision making and voting in order to influence public life' (DfEE, 1999). Furthermore Davies and Yamashita (2007) recommend that after systems have been put in place 'School Councils could usefully be made compulsory in schools' (p.3).

As citizenship and thus student voice are subjects that are in their infancy, the literature and research on such subjects is fairly limited, although the introduction of citizenship as part of the National Curriculum is not without its critics (Pykett, 2008). However, research has been undertaken by the National Federation for Educational Research (NFER) in the form of a longitudinal study (DCSF, 2008b) which aims to track the first cohort of pupils studying statutory citizenship education through the duration of its implementation. In this most recent review the DCSF (2008b: 7) has reported that students 'feel less empowered in their schools in Year 11 than they were in Year 7. Interestingly, this is in contrast to their head teachers, who believe that student empowerment and voice has increased in schools between 2002 and 2007'. There could be various reasons for this discrepancy in results but it is of concern that citizenship was introduced in 2002 as a strategy to address young people's apathy.

Working with children, young people and families

Consider the reasons for the provisional results in the National Federation for Educational Research longitudinal study. Why do you think the majority of Year 11 pupils feel less empowered about their role in education? Make a list of these reasons. Think of at least two strategies or methods that could empower young people and enable their voices to be heard which are appropriate to your work placement or employment.

Reservations regarding the effectiveness of School Councils

As School Councils become more common and popular in schools it is vital that schools do not 'concern themselves with the *process* of School Councils, rather than the *purpose* they would like the Council to fulfil. The frequency with which councils are set up only to fade away again may be linked to this issue' (Whitty and Wisby, 2007: 7). There must be a clear purpose of what the educational setting hopes to accomplish as well as why and how it should be included in the school agenda in order to achieve a successful school voice.

Students are often referred to as 'consumers of education' and although various government initiatives have attempted to listen and implement their ideas, this does not always seem feasible. Traditional methods of teaching may not always sit comfortably with the notion of acting upon students' suggestions. The overall demands now made on teachers and the constraints on their time have also been highlighted (Arthur et al., 2006; Ball, 2008; Thomas, 2007). It has been suggested that 'teacher concerns include workload, already busy timetables in relation to the formal curriculum and whether pupils will act responsibly. There may be a fear of the unknown, particularly in terms of changes in the balance of power in the classroom' (Whitty and Wisby, 2007: 7). Many practitioners would argue that the above concerns are reasonable and understandable as these could provide added pressure for overburdened members of staff. The shift in terms of 'power' and the changing role of practitioners is also of significance: 'adults making decisions on behalf of young people is entrenched within the social hierarchies of schools. The dominant social constructions of childhood affect the relative status of young people and the underlying assumptions about their competence to make decisions ...' (Thomas, 2007: 3). Traditionally schools have been based upon established hierarchies and there is unease that a merging of roles, be that of student as professional or teacher as facilitator, could lead to ambiguity or, at its most extreme, resentment.

Read the case study below and consider the bullet points after.

In a School Council meeting pupils raised concerns that the paper recycling bins purchased for each class by the Council were not being used effectively. Some students had observed the Building Sites Supervisor (BSS) removing all the contents of bins in each class together and not keeping the contents from the paper recycling bins separate. The Chairperson stated that she would pass on delegates' concerns to the school's Senior Management Team (SMT). The SMT indeed agreed and supported the School Council and the headteacher suggested a joint meeting with the BSS, SMT and School Council. When the matter was put to the BSS he simply said no he would not separate the paper and he was not going to be told what to do by some 'bossy kids'!

- How could the school ensure the whole staff are committed to pupil suggestions?
- Identify at least three action points to improve a whole school commitment to listening to youngsters.
- What needs to be done in order for the suggestions of the Council to be implemented?
- What strategies need to be implemented in order to prevent the above occurring again?
- How does the SMT ensure that after this meeting there is a satisfactory conclusion for the School Council and the BSS?

The school hierarchy may have a direct influence on children's willingness and commitment to engage as well as debate issues surrounding in-school policies (Thomas, 2007; Whitty and Wisby, 2007). One must also consider the effectiveness of School Councils and indeed whether:

> ... there are many reasons why schools should endeavour to include all pupils in school decision making. If a school's provision for pupil voice only involves a small number of pupils – for example, as an 'elite' group of council representatives not really connected to the school – this will be viewed by Ofsted as essentially an extra-curricular activity rather than activity that forms part of the school's citizenship. (Whitty and Wisby, 2007: 8)

Therefore it does seem unrealistic to agree that all students will want to be involved in any systematic portrayal of their voice. It may be viewed by some students as being complicit with school systems which may be perceived as not being 'street-wise' or 'cool'. Research states that, overall, practitioners in school, 'generally agreed with pupil's suggestions' (Mcintyre et al., 2005: 6). Considering this to be the case educational settings should invest in the student voice and be

Working with children, young people and families

active in implementing student views and requisitions in an attempt to motivate and engage youngsters regarding all aspects of their education.

Other strategies for listening to youngsters in educational settings

As well as utilising School Councils there are various strategies that educational settings adopt in order to actively listen to youngsters. In educational settings, student consolidation can assist with at least four elements of citizenship education: skills of participation; skills of responsible action; skills of enquiry; and skills of communication (Rudduck, 2003: 15).

This section outlines some strategies which are used in educational settings that do not necessarily rely on formal reports from the School Council in order to ensure youngsters are consulted regarding relevant issues. This may be relevant for children with SEN or disaffected youngsters who may feel that their voice is not really listened to but would indeed benefit the most from being consulted regarding education and wider issues – thus focusing on supporting individuals rather than a section of children who feel they may represent the majority of children. For example, in the SEN Code of Practice (DfES, 2001a) when an Individual Educational Plan (IEP) is constructed around the needs of pupils with SEN, the child's opinion should be sought. It is worth considering at this point the National Youth Agency's Hear By Right framework (2009) which has been developed to 'assess and improve practice and policy on the active involvement of children and young people.' Hear by Right is based around a model for organisational change which considers shared values, strategy, structure, systems, staff, skills and knowledge, and style of leadership as indicators which detail the degree to which young people's participation is actively encouraged. As such it is a very useful tool for encouraging positive change at an institutional level through the development of detailed action plans.

Throughout this chapter we have concentrated on how educational settings consult with groups of pupils via the School Council. The individual voice of a child, while it needs to be catered for, can be very difficult to obtain. MacBeath et al. (2003) suggest three basic modes when consulting young people:

- **Direct consultation**. Children are asked their views through questions posed in interview or group discussions. This takes the form of closed and open questions, a questionnaire or checklist.
- **Prompted consultation**. Children are prompted and supported into expressing an opinion which may be rather uncomfortable or contentious. Sharing previous comments from other pupils may be utilised as a starting point or asking the children to complete a sentence.
- **Mediated consultation**. Pupils' responses are communicated by various ways such as drawings, photographs or drama. Pupils are invited to talk about their mode of communication and answer relevant questions using their creations as support. This may be helpful if questions are abstract.

(Adapted from MacBeath et al., 2003)

very often	quite often	some-times	rarely or never		learn a lot	learn quite a lot	learn a little	learn nothing

Figure 6.2   Double checklist for children to evaluate school activities (Adapted from Rudduck, 2003: 20)

Rudduck (2003) offers a range of practical strategies which could be utilised to ensure individual voices are listened to, such as questionnaire-based approaches and surveys, writing-based approaches, talk-based approaches, and image-based approaches (Rudduck, 2003: 17). A particularly useful method for engaging with and analysing pupil responses for older students is the double checklist, an example of which is provided in Figure 6.2. The middle column has been left blank in order for the child to decide on the item to be debated. The left hand column indicates how often the activity occurs and the right hand column enables pupils to evaluate its appropriateness in relation to learning. Subjects that could be discussed include working in groups, problem solving, etc. ...

Activity

The next time you work with a group of children use the double checklist shown in Figure 6.2 to evaluate how well the children believed the activity went. The kind of themes the children could comment on could include:

- Working with a partner
- Role-play
- Working outside
- Working in the computer suite
- Giving a short talk to the rest of the class.

You could ask the children to decide on the subject to place in the middle of the box. When the children have completed the double checklist analyse their responses and construct an action plan on how you could improve your practice for future, similar activities.

Working with children, young people and families

Character Education

In secondary schools and many primary schools citizenship operates as a subject in its own right. When discussing citizenship education and provision one needs to consider the notions of 'Character Education'. To enter a discourse about character and Character Education is to enter a minefield of conflicting definitions and ideology. It is rare to find an educational topic about which there is so much fundamental disagreement. The only general agreement position seems to be acknowledgment of its importance, particularly when linked to listening to children.

One needs to consider the question of how to define character and whether such a thing can exist as a fixed set of habitual actions in a person that constitutes his or her character. For example, a Marxist might regard character as a fluid entity determined by the power structure of an existing society. There are of course many more views. The variety of approaches results in bewildering differences in educational schemes and curriculum. It has proved a difficult task for teachers and academics to arrive at a clear and workable definition of character and more particularly, Character Education. Why then enter this minefield? In short, because it is intrinsically linked to listening to children. The current government, with its heavy moralistic ethos, has taken up the baton. The establishment of citizenship education as a compulsory secondary school subject (DfES, 2002) was accompanied by the Green Paper, *Schools: Building on Success* (DfEE, 2001) and the White Paper, *Schools Achieving Success* (DfES, 2001b). The latter refers at length to 'education with character', the goal of which appears to be to instil certain virtues so that they become internal principles guiding young people's behaviour, decision making and voice for operation within a democracy. This is ultimately connected with the aims of citizenship education as outlined in the Crick Report (1998).

Ultimately, character is about who we are and who we become, and can be seen to result in 'good' or 'bad' character. Character Education is normally viewed as a specific approach to moral education. The argument is that Character Education is not simply about the acquisition of social skills; it is ultimately about what kind of person a child will grow up to be. The following list contains examples of concerns that have increased despite many attempts by the government, educational settings and welfare agencies to address these issues:

- Suicides – especially of young males
- Teenage pregnancy and abortion
- Crime rate – particularly theft by minors
- Alcohol and drug abuse
- Sexual activity and sexual abuse
- Teenage truancy and mental health problems.

Consider the list above in relation to your own setting, either on work placement or in employment. Add to the list any concerns that you feel are relevant to the children and young people that you are working with and begin to suggest or recommend solutions or strategies to support youngsters that you are working with relating to your list of concerns.

The lives of most British young people are often considered another significant factor in the perceived decline in moral standards. We do need to consider, however, whether there has ever been a 'Golden Age'.

Every Child Matters

In 2003 the government published a Green Paper called *Every Child Matters* (ECM). This coincided with the public inquiry into the death of Victoria Climbié resulting in the Laming Report (2003) which outlined huge failings in the systems in place to protect children as well as failings by agencies to listen to children (see Chapter 7). According to Reid, the ECM agenda 'proposes the most radical changes in services for children and their families since the Children Act 1989' (Reid, 2005: 12). This agenda and philosophy is a radical change which incorporates protection yet places more emphasis on prevention by listening and acting upon concerns regarding children.

One of the government's visions in implementing ECM is to support the principle of personalisation linked to individual needs and pupil voice as well as supporting the work schools are already doing in order to raise educational standards. The five outcomes (be healthy, stay safe, enjoy and achieve, make a positive contribution, achieve economic well-being), have been identified in consultation with young people, and are significant to the well-being of children from birth to 19 years of age. All practitioners working with children need to promote the five outcomes.

Central to supporting children and young people is the responsibility of practitioners to understand and apply any process in an educational context that seeks the views and opinions of the child.

The implementation of the Every Child Matters initiative recognises the importance of 'promoting children's interests and listening to their views' (DfES, 2004b: 19). One context in which this is essential is if for any reason a child you are working with is not progressing towards the five ECM outcomes. One outcome of this may be to consider using the initial checklist as part of the Common Assessment Framework (CAF). Central to this process are the views and opinions of the child which should not be underestimated or neglected from the start. The process that this may take will vary in each local authority (see Chapters 1 and 7).

Read over the following case study and consider the questions afterwards.

Before early intervention

Jada had been receiving help at school whilst in Year 6 from the Behaviour Support Service due to her aggressive behaviour. However, over the summer her behaviour worsened and her father was concerned that the transition to Key Stage 3 in a Year 7 class may mean that she would not get the same level of support. He contacted the secondary school, who agreed to liaise with other agencies. A check on the data held for Jada revealed incomplete records and Jada's Health Visitor confirmed concerns about her sleep routines and an outstanding referral for speech therapy, while the school revealed concerns about Jada and her father's difficulties.

After early intervention

The secondary school undertook a Common Assessment with Jada's father and with Jada and from that planned how services could come together to form a 'team around the child', including an Education Welfare Assistant, a Social Worker, a Health Visitor and a Learning Mentor. As a result, the Education Welfare Assistant worked with Jada at home and at school; a re-referral for speech therapy was made; and the Health Visitor continued to offer support to her father, suggesting strategies for dealing with her behaviour. Practitioners in schools may be the first point of contact for the family and information needs to be shared on request with the other specialists about Jada's behavioural difficulties. Due to the integrated approach to identifying and addressing the causes of Jada's behaviour, Jada's family now feels they are receiving co-ordinated support that meets her needs. Her re-referral for speech therapy was prioritised due to her needs being set within a broader context of her educational and social development and the team continues to work with Jada and her family to achieve more improvement.

- How do you think Jada's primary school might have been more proactive in easing transition to KS3 for Jada and her family?
- To what extent do you consider that Jada's perspectives and views have been taken into account in the scenario described above? Justify your response and consider the reasons why some people have had more 'say' than others.
- If you were working closely with Jada, and acting as the first point of contact, you would have to make time to talk to her and listen to her concerns. How could you ensure that you act appropriately and listen to her concerns?
- What skills might you need to develop in order to do your role effectively?

Child protection issues

Clearly one of the most pressing concerns when listening to children is the issue of child protection. Whilst we do not have space here to provide an exhaustive analysis of current guidelines and policy, there are some fundamental principles that need to be adhered to when practitioners have concerns about a child's welfare or when they make a disclosure. Individual institutions will have specific guidelines and policies for child protection and there will be a child protection officer who should be available to discuss issues with. If you should find yourself in a situation where a child directly or indirectly discloses information to you that leads you to become concerned about their welfare it is imperative that the following guidelines, as well as institutional policies, are followed:

- Listen carefully to the child, reassure them that they are not to blame.
- Do not try to investigate or ask leading questions – these can become prejudicial should any court proceedings arise.
- Explain what you are going to do and that this may mean having to tell someone who can help them.
- Report your concerns to the designated teacher or senior member of staff. Be specific. They will advise on the next steps.
- Maintain confidentiality.
- Record what the child has said (as far as possible in their own words) or what you observed. Include times and dates, child's name and age and any SEN or disability they may have.
- Remember that you have a statutory duty under the Education Act 2002 to pass on any child protection concerns.

Conclusion

One of the major aims of citizenship education is to encourage youngsters to be active within society as well as enabling youngsters to recognise their individual ability to affect and modify society.

The option for schools or educational settings to organise Schools Councils as affirmation of achieving government standards is appealing. However, if not implemented and maintained effectively there is a danger that the student voice merely becomes 'tokenistic' and is in fact only utilised as evidence to impress Ofsted, Advisers, Inspectors and other such external agencies.

> Genuine provision for pupil voice requires some power and influence to be passed, at which point pupil voice becomes unpredictable. In contrast, where this does not happen, there is the danger that pupil voice and school councils in particular, could produce a cohort of young people who are cynical about democratic processes. (Whitty and Wisby, 2007: 21)

In order to have any successes with youngsters' voices in educational settings then it is vital that all staff need to be committed to any initiatives or policies introduced to support this. Such policies need authentic endorsement rather than a compliant approach to implementation.

The citizenship that is currently apparent in educational settings is influenced by Crick's notions of social and moral responsibility, community involvement and political literacy. There is not and cannot be one clear definition of citizenship education and this debate is ongoing. Throughout this chapter we have highlighted that pupil participation and student voice are key to ensuring meaningful links between learning in educational settings and youngsters' lives beyond such environments (Holdsworth, 2001; Lansdowe, 1994; Rudduck, 2003).

Further reading

The following books are particularly useful because they provide carefully considered, research-based approaches to encouraging young people's participation.

Davie, R., Upton, G. and Varma, V. (1996) *The Voice of the Child: A Handbook For Professionals*. London: The Falmer Press.

Hallett, C. and Prout, A. (2003) *Hearing the Voices of Children: Social Policy for a New Century*. London: Routledge Falmer.

Hodgkinson, S. and Mercer, N. (2008) *Exploring Talk in School*. London: Sage.

Appendix: The UN Convention on the Rights of the Child – why it is vital to listen to children
(From United Nations Convention on the Rights of the Child, 1989)

Article 12

1 States Parties shall ensure to the child who is capable of forming his or her own views, the right to express those views freely in all matters affecting the child, the views of the child being given due weight in accordance with the age and maturity of the child.

2 For this purpose, the child shall in particular be provided the opportunity to be heard in any judicial and administrative proceeding affecting the child, either directly, or through a representative or an appropriate body, in a manner consistent with the procedural rules of natural law.

Article 13

1 The child shall have the right to freedom of expression; this right shall include freedom to seek, receive and impart information and ideas of all kinds, regardless of frontiers, either orally, in writing or in print, in the form of art, or through any other media of the child's choice.

2 The exercise of this right may be subject to certain restrictions, but these shall only be such as are provided by law and are necessary:

(Cont'd)

Listening to children's voices

(a) For respect of the rights or reputations of others; or

(b) For the protection of national security or of public order or of public health morals.

Article 14

1 States Parties shall respect the right of the child to freedom of thought, conscience and religion.

2 States Parties shall respect the rights and duties of the parents and, when applicable, legal guardians, to provide direction to the child in exercise of his or her right in the matter consistent with the evolving capacities of the child.

3 Freedom to manifest one's religion or beliefs may be subject only to such limitations as are prescribed by law and are necessary to protect public safety, order, health or morals or the fundamental rights or freedoms of others.

Article 15

1 States Parties recognise the rights of the child to freedom of association and to freedom of peaceful assembly.

2 No restrictions may be placed on the exercise of these rights other than those imposed in conformity with the law and which are necessary in a democratic society in the interests of national security or public safety, public order, the protection of public health or morals or the protection of the rights and freedoms of others.

Article 29

1 States Parties agree that the education of the child shall be directed to:
The development of the child's personality, talents and mental and physical abilities to their fullest potential;

- The development of respect for human rights and fundamental freedoms and for the principles enshrined in the Charter of the United Nations
- The development of respect for the child's parents, his or her own cultural identity, language and values, for the national values of the country in which the child is living, the country from which he or she may originate and for civilizations different from his or her own
- The preparation of the child for the responsible life in a free society, in the spirit of understanding, peace, tolerance, equality of sexes and friendship among all peoples, ethnic, national and religious groups and persons of indigenous origin
- The development of respect for the natural environment.

Working with children, young people and families

7

From safeguarding to Safeguarding

Mark Cronin and Claire Smith

The aims of this chapter are to:

- Examine the historical context around child protection and safeguarding children
- Explore how policy changes in child protection have been influenced
- Consider the government's moves from a reactive to proactive agenda in order to safeguard and improve the life chances of all children and young people.

The safeguarding agenda has undergone some significant changes in the past 20 years. Attempts have been made to move the focus of work with children and families away from the management of risk in order to make greater use of preventative strategies to support early intervention in circumstances where children may be vulnerable. This chapter will explore the historical context in which these changes have developed, from the Children Act 1989 to the more recent Every Child Matters initiative. It will examine the drivers behind the early intervention approach and consider the implications of some of the strategies employed in this new safeguarding policy landscape.

Historical context

Prior to the 1970s, social work practice was seen primarily as a private activity involving the client and the professionals who employed their skills and techniques in order to tackle or even solve social problems (Parton and Thomas, 1983). In fact the changes which led to the establishment of social services departments and the legitimatisation of social work in 1971 had received little public or even political attention (Hall, 1976). However, this was to dramatically change as this decade witnessed an increasing focus on child welfare practices in the form of both public inquiries and media scrutiny, the outcomes of which had a considerable impact on how the issues they raised were managed. One such significant example was the public inquiry into the death of Maria Colwell in 1973 at the age of 7 (Secretary of State for Social Services, 1974). This inquiry brought the issues of child abuse and associated professional practice to the centre of public, political and media attention.

Maria Colwell died on the 7 January 1973 in Hove, Brighton as a result of extreme violence at the hands of her stepfather William Kepple who was initially convicted of her murder (reduced to manslaughter after appeal) and sentenced to eight years imprisonment. Prior to this Maria spent over five years in local authority care being fostered by her aunt only to be returned to the care of her mother and stepfather at the age of 6 years and 8 months, despite Maria's opposition to the return. As Hendrick (2003: 163) noted, 'Maria herself opposed the return and on earlier visits had shown signs of trauma, so much so that in June 1971 she was diagnosed as depressed'. During her time living with her mother and stepfather she was visited by a number of social workers from both the local authority and the NSPCC and numerous concerns were reported to these organisations regarding her welfare, but this did not prevent her subsequent death.

In response to Maria's death Sir Keith Joseph, the Secretary of State at the time, decided to open a public inquiry the results of which were published in September 1974 (Secretary of State for Social Services, 1974). During the course of this public inquiry there was significant media coverage around what was described as a 'national scandal', and the level of public interest generated was to prove pivotal in terms of its impact on future policy and practice. Although the report was highly critical of the professionals involved, its main conclusion was that 'it was the system ... which had failed her' (Secretary of State for Social Services, 1974: 86) a theme which was reflected in the media coverage. The lack of a formalised inter-agency system for dealing with child abuse was highlighted and the fact that much of this work was left to individual initiative was seen as a significant weakness. As a direct consequence of this inquiry a new system of child abuse management was introduced (Department of Health and Social Services, 1974) which focused on both the ability of professionals to identify signs of abuse and the establishment of mechanisms for sharing information. The primary task for policy and practice was to identify signs and symptoms, share information, co-ordinate action and intervene to protect the child (Parton, 2006). As a consequence of this series of events, public inquiries became significant forces in the development of change in policy and practice around safeguarding in the UK.

In addition to the inquiry around the death of Maria Colwell, there were a number of subsequent inquiries that followed in the 1980s (Jasmine Beckford 1985, Tyra Henry 1987, Kimberley Carlile 1987, amongst many others) which mirrored the issues identified around the lack of co-ordination between agencies and inadequate professional practice in terms of protecting children and young people from harm. Many of the inquiries suggested that the childcare professionals had not made use of their legal mandate to protect children and young people. They were criticised for being too sentimental in respect of the parents' needs,

Working with children, young people and families

failing to focus on the children's and young people's interests and consequently their interventions were seen as doing too little, too late.

Activity

Consider (in groups or individually):

- Why you think that findings from case inquiries were always deemed to be similar?
- Why were lessons allegedly not being learned?

However, the Cleveland inquiry (Secretary of State for Social Services, 1988) provided a very different critique regarding appropriate interventions around the protection of children and young people. It was in the summer of 1987 that concerns began to be raised about the alarming increase in numbers of children who were being removed from their families as a consequence of the practice of two paediatricians and social workers in a hospital in Middlesbrough. Between February and July of 1987, 121 children were removed to a place of safety (the hospital) as a consequence of the diagnosis by health professionals of sexual abuse. The inquiry found that most of the allegations of sexual abuse were unfounded and all but 27 children were returned to their families. This was significant as it was not only the first public inquiry to raise questions regarding the medical diagnosis of child sexual abuse but more importantly for policy and practice it implied an overreaction in terms of professional intervention.

In this inquiry it was suggested that professionals had failed to recognise the rights of parents and had intervened prematurely. Despite the fact that there were parallels with previous inquiries in relation to the lack of co-ordination/communication between agencies and inadequate professional practice, the emphasis was very different. Questions were being raised about the appropriate balance between family autonomy and state intervention and the focus was on the damage caused by over-zealous professional interference. The sense of injustice felt for wrongly accused 'normal families' in combination with the emotive issues around sexual abuse resonated powerfully with the public and the Conservative Government of the time was not unaware of the power of this feeling and its potential for directing the safeguarding children agenda.

The political context in which these inquiries were taking place would be crucial in terms of the direction of travel for the safeguarding agenda at this time. That is, the election of the Conservative Government in 1979 resulted in a new approach to tackling social problems which emphasised the importance of individual responsibility, choice and freedom from state interference. The family was seen as an essentially private domain which should be encouraged to

From safeguarding to Safeguarding

take responsibility for the care of children and young people, with the state's role reduced to one of minimum intervention (see Chapter 1). Therefore, the social and political context in 1987/88 seemed to present a number of challenges in terms of redefining the relationship between the power of public authorities and the private family in the safeguarding of children.

Activity

Conservative Party ideology under Margaret Thatcher was very much about individuals and families, rather than societies and communities. The Conservative Party believed that the state should have minimal intervention within the family home and that responsibility for this should very much be left to the head of the household.
 In light of this:

- Why do you think the government's intervention following the Cleveland scandal was deemed to be unusual?
- Why do you think the government responded in this way?

The Children Act 1989

It was in this context that the Children Act 1989 (hereafter referred to as the Act) was developed, a document which would not only provide a framework for social care interventions but also redefine how public authorities would interact with the family in relation to child welfare. This legislation was heralded as a new approach to social care which both supported families and gave central importance to the child's welfare. The core principles of the Act encouraged an approach to child welfare which utilised consultation with both parents and children in agreed plans. The role of the state was defined in terms of the ways it could support parents to care for their children. The 'no order principle' in section 1 (s.1(5)) of the Act set the tone, stating that the court in considering an application 'shall not make the order or any of the orders unless it considers that doing so would be better for the child than making no order at all'. It was clear that the intention was to work in such a way that allowed the families to care for children if this was at all possible and that state intervention in this dynamic would be minimal.

Under section 17 of the Act, which became known as the 'Family Support' section, it talks of a 'duty to safeguard and promote the welfare of children in need', whilst where possible 'promoting the upbringing of such children by their families' and advocates 'providing a range and level of services appropriate to those children's needs' (s.17(1)). In principle this marked a significant shift in terms of preventative interventions which were not only about avoiding care

Working with children, young people and families

proceedings but supporting families in the care of their children. This concept was further supported by what appeared to be quite a broad definition of the concept of a 'child in need'. That is, a child or young person was taken to be in need if they 'were unlikely to achieve a reasonable standard of health or development without the provision of services by the local authority' (s.17(10a)). Therefore, the provisions outlined in this section of the Act were potentially wide ranging and the extensive support it advocated would have been applicable to a growing number of vulnerable children and young people in the UK (20 per cent living in child poverty between 1991 and 1994, according to HBAI, see Chapter 4). However, in reality, according to the Department of Health's Children in Need Survey (2000) a relatively small proportion of vulnerable children annually received support via section 17, approximately 317,000, representing just under 3 per cent of all children.

Activity

Do you think the state should intervene in how parents and carers run their family home? What do you think the advantages and disadvantages to state intervention might be for children, young people and parents/carers?

In addition to this, section 47 of the Act outlined new assessment processes and threshold criteria which had to be satisfied before state intervention into the family was considered necessary. This section placed a duty on the local authority where they

> have reasonable cause to suspect that a child … is suffering, or is likely to suffer, significant harm, the authority should make … such enquiries as they consider necessary to enable them to decide whether they should take any action to safeguard or promote the children's welfare. (s.47(1a))

The threshold for significant harm being defined as an impairment of health or development (physical, intellectual, emotional, social or behavioural) (s. 31(9)) compared to that which could be reasonably expected of a similar child (s. 31(10)). This section of the Act was important because not only did it provide the context in which child protection procedures should operate where significant harm could be evidenced but it also advocated intervention where there was reasonable cause to suspect significant harm is 'likely' to occur, therefore, providing the scope for professionals to hypothesise and act before this harm occurred. The duties outlined in both sections 17 and 47 seemed to support an element of prevention and broadened the responsibilities of the local authority in terms of its safeguarding role. However, the combined focus on assessing a child's welfare on the basis of their development in terms of expected outcomes or milestones, alongside greater accountability of professionals and local authorities, would have a significant impact on the delivery of services by social services professionals.

Furthermore, with particular relevance to the recommendations of previous child inquiries, the Act makes reference to the need for agencies to support the local authority in the exercise of these functions as well as others outlined in part three of the Act. Under section 27

> where it appears to a local authority that any authority ... could, by taking any specified action, help in the exercise of any of their functions under this part, they may request the help of that other authority or person, specifying the action in question. (s. 27(1))

The specified agencies being the local education authority, local housing authority, health authority or another local authority or person authorised by the Secretary of State (s. 27(3)). However it also states that 'An authority whose help is so requested shall comply with the request if it is compatible with their own statutory or other duties and obligations and does not unduly prejudice the discharge of any of their functions' (s. 27(2)). This caveat, alongside the fact that this function is not a duty, effectively allows other agencies to prioritise the delivery of their own services above the safeguarding functions in this Act and clearly fixes the lead responsibility for these services with social services.

The refocusing debate

In 1994 the Dartington Research Unit produced a series of reports which were collectively published under the title *Messages from Research* by the Department of Health (1995). These reports summarised the child protection services that were being offered at this time and amongst other conclusions they found that too many children and young people were receiving a service only as a consequence of being the subject of a child protection investigation. It also found that once the investigations were complete, many children did not receive any long-term services. These reports were illuminating a dynamic which was beginning to develop in the wake of the Children Act 1989 which saw interventions in the main only taking place where child protection or concerns around significant harm were being identified. The emphasis on developmental models advocated in the Children Act 1989 to measure child welfare alongside the limited resources allocated to deliver these services seemed to be resulting in an increased focus on significant harm as a threshold for social work intervention.

In addition to this, in 1994 the Audit Commission published a report entitled *Seen But Not Heard* which reviewed the ways in which services to children and families were delivered under the Children Act 1989. The report suggested that

Working with children, young people and families

a shift in the balance of social services work with children from child protection to family support might promote children's welfare more effectively and represent better value for money. It recommended that Children's Service Plans should be produced jointly by social services, health and education a requirement which was introduced in 1996 for all social services departments. These plans were intended to ensure that arrangements were put in place across all the services responsible for children and young people to recognise and act on warning signals that may be available, and to make all local services for children and young people coherent. These two documents started a national discussion led by the Department of Health which became known as the 'Refocusing Debate'. The focus of this debate was how services could be delivered or redefined so that more children and young people received services and ensured that statutory intervention was not the only route to services.

In 1999 the government launched Quality Protects (Department of Health and Department for Education and Employment, 1999) which was its programme for transforming the management and delivery of children's social services. This programme emphasised the importance of effective assessment which discriminated between different levels of need and the requirement for a timely service response to the identified need. Shortly after this the *Working Together to Safeguard Children* (Department of Health, Home Office, Department for Education and Employment, 1999) and the *Framework for Assessment* (Department of Health, Department for Education, 2000) documents were produced which were intended to stimulate more effective assessment processes as well as supporting the co-ordination of a multi-agency approach to safeguarding children and young people. However, it is significant that these documents still operated in an environment created by the Children Act 1989 which placed social services departments as the lead agency with the support of other agencies, provided this did not unduly prejudice the discharge of any of their functions.

At this time social service departments nationwide (and more acutely in the metropolitan boroughs) were experiencing increasing retention and recruitment problems as social workers were leaving the profession due to sickness or disillusionment. Increasing levels of regulation and paperwork were putting pressure on the time available to engage with children and families and as this balance shifted the problem worsened. The widespread use of initiatives such as the 'Golden Hello' and the 'Golden Handshake' which offered cash incentives to enter and remain in the profession reflected the desperation of some authorities to hold on to social workers. The increasing use of international recruitment drives further illustrated this point as did the growing percentage of social workers in area office teams recruited via employment agencies. These methods brought with them their own problems such as the lack of knowledge of UK social work practice for those recruited internationally and the transient nature of agency social workers whose employment terms were flexible. The former of these two points remains an issue today and was highlighted in the recently published *The Protection of Children in England: A Progress Report*

From safeguarding to Safeguarding

(Laming, 2009). All of these issues combined did not make for a sound foundation from which to launch new initiatives designed to bring greater consistency and co-ordination.

Illustrative material – social work experience 1999–2003

My desire to become a social worker revolved around a commitment to support families to provide a home environment for children which would see them thrive. During my training I became aware that although Area Office social work was stressful it would provide essential skills and the necessary experience to realise this aim. However, despite numerous attempts to secure some taste of this environment there was a serious shortage of available placements and as such until I qualified it remained largely an unknown quantity. Peers who had managed to obtain such a placement came back to college with stories which reinforced the image of these work environments as pressurised and stressful. On completion of the diploma I secured a job in an inner-city care management team and during my first few days was reassured that I would not be exposed to the 'heavy' and complex cases for some time. However, in my third month I was attending Care Proceedings in the Family Proceedings Court and had the responsibility of preparing care plans for two young boys. The countless procedures, quantities of paperwork and meetings required meant that the time available for working with children and families was limited. The minimum requirement to undertake a monthly visit to the numerous looked after children on my caseload became a target which I had to work hard to attain. During the course of my four years in this position I was not allocated a single family support case and my caseload included only families where either the children's names had been placed on the Child Protection Register or they were looked after by the local authority. It quickly became my aim to acquire the necessary professional knowledge and find an alternative position which would allow me to engage with families in support work. This was a feeling which was mirrored in the majority of my colleagues who were coming under increasing pressure to remain by way of 'golden handshakes' which were large cash incentives given in exchange for continued service (repayable if they left before this extended term of service was reached). Increasing levels of agency and internationally recruited social workers who were ill-prepared to manage the demands of their new posts resulted in a disjointed and disillusioned team. I recall the immense feelings of relief when I managed to leave this team.

Activity

The above is an account of one social worker's experience in a Social Services Area Office environment which illustrates some of the pressures which can lead to many leaving the profession. At present consideration is being given to the need to

Working with children, young people and families

remodel the social work role in order to tackle problems around recruitment and retention. In light of this consider the following questions:

- What is the current public perception of social workers and what impact might this have on those considering entering this profession?
- What changes could be made to encourage newly qualified social workers to stay in positions in Social Services Area Offices?
- How might the current trend of 'scapegoating' individual social workers impact on initiatives designed to attract people to the profession?

In 2001 a second series of reports was published by the Department of Health under the heading *The Children Act 1989 Now: Messages from Research* (Department of Health, 2001). The scope of these reports was widened and it provided a much broader reflection on the operation of the Children Act 1989 in the decade that had followed its introduction in 1991. In all, 24 studies were completed which were grouped into five areas; children and parents in courts; safeguarding children at risk; services for children in need; care of looked after children; and interagency co-operation. This report provided an ideal opportunity to reflect on the 'refocusing debate' and see at what point social work interventions were happening. The report looking into the operation of section 17 or the family support function concluded that 'resources were focused on "high risk" families at the expense of promoting the welfare of a broader group of children through the provision of family support services' (Aldgate and Tunstill, 1995: 154). This seemed to suggest that social work provision had continued to focus its resources on those families where significant risk was identified. This was reiterated by the report which looked into the provision of family support services and concluded that 'assessment was still based on risk rather than need and opportunities were thus missed to provide services that might have prevented more serious problems developing' (Thoburn et al., 2001: 232).

The report which looked at safeguarding and the use of the new significant harm threshold reinforced this point. It found that 'In 42% of cases the formal child protection assessment and monitoring system was judged necessary' but in '73% of cases it was used' (Brandon et al., 2001: 166). This suggested that the child protection system was being overused as a means of intervention into family life. It went further by concluding:

> earlier provision of services to children in need could have prevented some situations of stress deteriorating into cases of 'significant harm' and that 'more discriminating use of the formal child protection system could free up resources to support children at an earlier stage of need. (ibid., p. 166)

It seemed that despite the dialogue around the 'refocusing debate' little had been achieved in terms of changing the point at which social work intervention was taking place.

From safeguarding to Safeguarding

Victoria Climbié, Laming and Every Child Matters

In 1997, Tony Blair and the 'New' Labour Government proposed changes to extend the refocusing debate as mentioned previously to 'embrace wide-ranging concerns about parenting, the need for early intervention to tackle crime and anti-social behaviour, supporting the family and regenerating communities more generally' (Lonne et al., 2009: 44). The Children Act 1989 highlighted that the child's needs were of paramount importance and where possible the child should remain in the family home. This was taken further under 'New' Labour; it was acknowledged that the needs of children and young people could not be separated from the needs of parents or the family and therefore a more integrated and joined-up approach by services and professionals working with children, young people and families needed to be undertaken. This connected with New Labour's broader approach to social policy initiatives which was to consider how services could be managed more effectively without the requirement for significant investment. This would entail not only greater interventions in family life with a focus on maximising the potential influence of children's early years but also a significant emphasis on closely monitoring the delivery of services and a greater role for inspection agencies such as Ofsted. With its aim of tackling child poverty and social exclusion, the Labour Government placed children and young people at the heart of their policies in an attempt to improve outcomes for all children and young people.

Activity

'New' Labour's political ideology was very much about intervening in the family home in order to improve outcomes for all children and young people.

- Why do you think early intervention strategies in children's lives are deemed to improve their life chances?
- Is this a strategy for further state control over family life and if so with what consequences?

In 2000, child protection issues again hit the media headlines and stirred up another moral panic. On the 25 February 2000 aged 8 years and 3 months Victoria Climbié was pronounced dead after having endured a catalogue of abuse at the hands of her great-aunt Marie-Therese Kouao and Carl John Manning, the great-aunt's boyfriend. Similar to Maria Colwell in the seventies, Victoria was known to social services (albeit under the name of Anna Kouao), and concerns were raised about her welfare – as with Maria Colwell. Intervention on the part of services, however (social, health, housing and police departments) was lacking. In fact it was noted that:

> Victoria was known to no less than two further housing authorities, four social services departments, two child protection teams of the Metropolitan Police Service (MPS), a specialist centre managed by the NSPCC, and she was admitted to two different hospitals because of suspected deliberate harm. The dreadful reality was that these services knew little or nothing more about Victoria at the end of the process than they did when she was first referred to Ealing Social Services by the Homeless Persons' Unit in April 1999. (Laming, 2003: para 1.16)

However, during the 11 months that Victoria was living in England she sustained 128 injuries to her body caused by deliberate abuse and neglect. No one pieced together the various bits of information on Victoria in order to draw up the full picture of her circumstances. Alarmingly, it was not until her death that her true identity was revealed.

The subsequent inquiry by Lord Laming, published in 2003 into the circumstances surrounding her death and the failings of numerous agencies to protect her, has had a wide-ranging effect on the organisation of children's services. Lord Laming made 108 recommendations to improve the child welfare systems in place in the UK. The subsequent Green Paper *Every Child Matters* (DfES, 2003b) and the ratification of its legal framework, the Children Act 2004, 'marked a significant shift in thinking about children's services in England and heralded a major period of reform and change' (Lonne et al., 2009: 47).

Whilst it appears that the death of Victoria Climbié instigated these changes, as already acknowledged reforms were already taking place. Victoria's death, however, provided 'the immediate catalyst' (Barker, 2009: 8) for the government to push through its planned changes with greater urgency and little dispute from opposing political parties. As Parton states (2006: 139) the Green Paper *Every Child Matters* (DfES, 2003b) 'aimed to take forward many ideas about intervening at a much earlier stage in order to prevent a range of problems in later life'.

The government's sweeping reforms, however, have altered the systems from being ones of *reaction* – reacting only when a child protection concern was raised – to being *proactive* – working with children, young people and families early in order to *prevent* a case of protection being needed. Early intervention strategies were to be a key element in identifying families where children might be at risk of harm or neglect at some stage in their lives. Therefore, intervening earlier to work with parents would help to overcome issues before they became a problem. With this move to early intervention and being proactive, there was a shift from child *protection* as discussed in the former part of this chapter to *safeguarding* all children and young people, regardless of their social, cultural or economic background. As the name of the Green Paper suggested, the proposed reforms were designed for all children and young people and not just those deemed to be at risk and requiring protection from abuse or neglect.

But what does the term 'safeguarding' actually mean in this context? The term derives from a concern around the continual practice failings to protect those children and young people being subjected to risk and harm. Whilst safeguarding is a key responsibility managed by central government, the Department of Health defines safeguarding as:

- all agencies working with children, young people and their families take all reasonable measures to ensure that the risks of harm to children's welfare are minimised; and
- where there are concerns about children and young people's welfare, all agencies take all appropriate actions to address those concerns, working to agreed local policies and procedures in full partnership with other local agencies. (Department of Health, 2002: para. 1.5)

This highlights a clear move towards multi-agency working and joined-up approaches. Previously child protection and child welfare issues were very much left to social services departments to manage. More often than not, when a child died at the hands of their parents/carers a social worker would be scapegoated and castigated for seemingly failing to intervene. The role of the social worker became one of being 'damned if you do and damned if you don't'. These latest government moves, however, attempt to remove this traditional 'witch-hunt' of social workers and place the responsibility of children's and young people's welfare in the hands of all services working with children, young people and families; health, social services, education, police, voluntary organisations. Such was the emphasis on sharing this responsibility that the government announced plans to merge the children's social services department and education services into one department – Children's Services. The former roles of Director of Children's Social Services and Director of Education, therefore were merged into the single role of Director of Children's Services. These moves, however, created a rather heavily education-led department with social workers being outnumbered by education professionals. Three-quarters of the new Director of Children's Services roles were filled by those with an education background rather than social services experience.

This concept of social services and education providing a more joined-up approach, however, is not new. In the 1990s, Staudt and Kemp Powell (1996: 433) noted that 'the school has come to be seen as a logical base from which to provide a range of social and support services to children and families'. There are, however, concerns regarding this. American research (Abrahams et al., 1992; Burns and Lake, 1983; Kenny, 2001; Tite, 1993) states that teachers are best placed to identify changes within children's and young people's behaviour and therefore to identify possible cases of abuse. Teachers, however, face many concerns in light of this. Many do not feel that the training they have received is adequate enough to help them identify signs of abuse, especially sexual abuse (Beck et al., 1994). Many report that they do not know how to make a report (Kenny, 2001) and they fear the consequences for the child if a report is made (Kenny, 2001). Furthermore, they also fear legal consequences for themselves if they make a false allegation against a parent or carer or other adult (Abrahams et al., 1992).

Following the publication of the Green Paper *Every Child Matters* (DfES, 2003b) and the Children Act 2004, those working with children, young people and families were hit by a tidal wave of new guidance, frameworks and publications to inform them how best to work with all children everywhere. There were moves to improve multi-agency and inter-professional working. The aforementioned document *Working Together to Safeguard Children* (Department of Health, Home Office, Department for Education and Employment, 1999) was updated in 2006 to include more detailed guidance on the roles of all agencies working with children, young people and families. This included information on how organisations should be working across boundaries and joining-up practices.

Further changes were afoot in 2007 upon Tony Blair's resignation as Prime Minister and leader of the Labour Party. In his first few days as Prime Minister, Gordon Brown announced plans to separate the Department for Education and Skills (DfES) into two departments, one arm of which is now the Department for Children, Schools and Families (DCSF). Under the leadership of Ed Balls, Gordon Brown charged this new department with responsibility for the welfare, protection and care of all children and young people. The DCSF also includes the management of children's social services and the Respect Agenda, previously under Home Office control. Gordon Brown also highlighted that this Department, in conjunction with the Ministry of Justice, would also lead the way in preventing youth offending – another government priority.

However, whilst ECM was deemed to be a national framework and an approach led very much by central government, Barker (2009: 9) notes that 'a key premise is that local needs should be met via "what works best" locally', acknowledging that the previous acclaimed 'one-size-fits-all' type of approach would not be appropriate. Instead, services delivered through a 'mixed-economy of welfare' structure were to be tailored to meet individual needs, yet monitored and evaluated through government inspections systems (namely Ofsted) as part of its closer surveillance measures. This has led to services being set up at different paces in different geographical areas (with the more affluent areas being slower to adopt the ECM agenda than more deprived and urban areas). Also there has been confusion in particular areas regarding how to establish initiatives. This has been exacerbated by differences in budget, staffing and other allocated resources.

Early intervention initiatives

One of the government's pre-ECM initiatives aimed at early intervention was Sure Start, established in 1998. Based on the American programme 'Head Start', Sure Start Local Programmes (SSLP) were initially aimed at pre-school children and their families living in deprived areas in England, as it was deemed that services were not reaching those most in need. With a view to alleviating social exclusion in adult life, the programme's aim was 'to work with disadvantaged parents and children to promote the physical, intellectual, social and emotional development of children, in order that they could thrive when they went to school' (Parton, 2006: 96), and thus hopefully break the cycle of deprivation and poverty that they may have been born into. Five hundred and twenty-four SSLPs were set up between 1999 and 2004 (see www.everychildmatters.gov.uk).

Find out where your nearest Sure Start Children's Centre is. What services do they offer – for children? For parents/carers? Can you identify from the government ideology and policies discussed elsewhere in this book how their services have been influenced?

Since the implementation of Every Child Matters, Sure Start has become a cornerstone in the government's agenda to tackle child poverty and social exclusion. Under the ECM agenda, all of the SSLPs will become Sure Start Children's Centres, and it is anticipated that every community in England will have a Sure Start Children's Centre by 2010, resulting eventually in a nationwide network of 3,500 centres.

To date evaluations attempting to measure the success of the Sure Start programme have been varied. It has been suggested by Ofsted (2008) that children who attended a Children's Centre were well prepared when entering school and that where services had been used by the most vulnerable parents, their lives had been transformed and there were also positive benefits for the children. However, the programme has also been criticised for not doing well enough in terms of meeting the needs of its primary target, the socially excluded. Ofsted (2008) also reported that settings were not doing enough to reach out to particularly vulnerable individuals or families and the National Evaluation of Sure Start (2007) stated that more needed to be done in terms of outreach work to engage with excluded communities. In one report examining good practice in terms of engaging with these excluded communities (Capacity and Esmee Fairbairn Foundation, 2007), the issue of limited resources is identified as pivotal and it suggests that 'with tapering levels of funding, the pressure to attract and retain a more middle class clientele, who can afford to pay for services, will almost certainly increase' (Capacity and Esmee Fairbairn Foundation, 2007: 2). The issue of funding alongside the demands of monitoring the uptake of services have undoubtedly influenced the delivery of services in Children's Centres. The removal of the protection offered by government ring-fencing of the Sure Start funding in 2010 will add extra pressure as Children's Centres face the challenge of securing their medium and long-term survival.

The government's new child and family-focused initiatives centred heavily around education, which was a move away from plans under the Children Act 1989 which, as noted above, placed social services as the lead agency. The Children's Plan (DCSF, 2007a), whilst concerned with addressing the needs of deprived and vulnerable children and families, also addresses multi-agency working with an aim of building a partnership between government, children, families and professionals. Similar to Sure Start Children's Centres, the Full Service Extended Schools (FSES) model introduced under the Children Act 2004 encourages schools to develop partnership with other agencies across other public service and voluntary sectors, not just education. Any child within the school requiring additional, non-educational support should be able to gain access to this support through his or her school, thus dismantling any barriers and maximising the chances for the child to attain his or her full potential, improve their life chances and achieve the designated five outcomes. FSES, however, offer more than 'other' services and support. Schools' hours have been increased with the intention that working parents have reliable childcare for their children before and after school to fit in with their working day. Former Education Secretary, Ruth Kelly, allocated an extra £680 million to enable schools to open between 8am and 6pm both in term time and during school holidays. An evaluation of extended schools (Cummings et al., 2007) has evidenced that this initiative has, on the whole, been welcomed by schools and that it has already had a positive impact on children's attainment. FSES, therefore, along with Sure Start Children's Centres were deemed to be at the heart of all services (see Figure 7.1). These are seen as a one-stop-shop for parents to be able to access a variety of services, including outreach services, that they might need, for example health, education, wraparound care, and employment and benefits information. It was deemed to

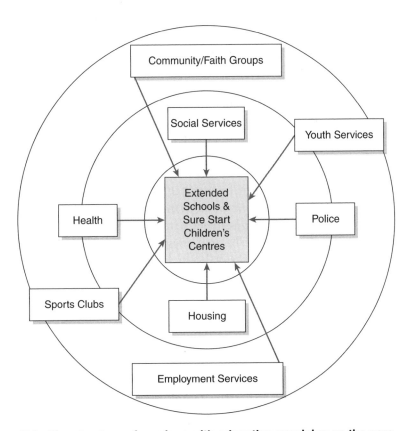

Figure 7.1   The structure of services with education provision as the core

From safeguarding to Safeguarding

be easier for the services to operate from one hub rather than parents/carers struggling to find services that might help them. This could also be viewed as a strategic move in order to enable services and practitioners to join up more effectively by breaking down physical/geographic barriers, while also enabling them to make more efficient use of resources including staff and budgets.

Whilst, therefore, the notion of education and social services collaborating to safeguard children is not new, the development under the Children Act 2004, is that in some cases a social worker is co-located within a school. On the one hand the advantage is that there is a social worker for school staff to liaise with if any signs of abuse are noticed. On the other, however, the social worker may feel isolated from their own colleagues and may not have contact with other social services staff with whom they can discuss cases or issues (Moran et al., 2007).

Other tools for early intervention delivered through FSES and Sure Start Children's Centres include the CAF, Lead Professional and Contact Point. In view of the vast range of services that some children, young people and families come into contact with (as highlighted in Figure 7.1), and therefore the amount of information that is generated for each child, young person or family, ECM introduced the Common Assessment Framework. The aim was not only to avoid service users having to repeat themselves to each professional they met, but also an attempt to enable communication and information sharing between agencies. The CAF can be used by practitioners who have received the relevant training to assess the needs of children and families, thus intervening early in a situation before the child or family gets into severe difficulty. As Jones and Leverett (2008: 136) state 'the CAF is seen as a preventative measure as well as a tool to provide compensatory intervention before things reach crisis point'. It is designed to be used with children and families with 'additional' needs (in terms of not meeting the five ECM outcomes) and not for those children requiring child protection plans or with disabilities or special needs. The desire for early intervention strategies has gradually evolved as a consequence of the limited interventions which resulted from the Children Act 1989. However, the effectiveness of this assessment tool will be measured not in its ability to identify these additional needs but in its capacity to connect with the services which can support families and improve their lives. This will require significant investment in support services which have historically been designed to support a minimum intervention ideology.

In line with the aims of the CAF, the Lead Professional role was introduced to operate in circumstances where families required the support of numerous agencies. This is a single practitioner known to the child and family who liaises between the family and all of the agencies identified through the CAF. The aim is to reduce the number of practitioners dealing with the child but also to eliminate the confusion of services and agencies involved with a child or family. Where it is identified that the family requires a Lead Professional it is their responsibility to ensure the family receives the services necessary to address the 'additional' needs identified by co-ordinating agencies' responses.

Working with children, young people and families

The Lead Professional role is key to the success of the CAF in circumstances where families have the most complex needs and has been the source of much debate. In particular the availability of the time and training required to undertake this responsibility as well as issues associated with differences in professional power have resulted in significant tensions for practitioners considering taking on this role.

Connected to the development of the CAF was the introduction of a computer database which would provide a means to indicate to professionals instances where the family have been the subject of previous assessments. This database became known as the Contact Point and would be the first database to include the basic details of every child in the country as well as the contact details of professionals who had been involved in previous assessments. However, the introduction of this database has not been without its problems. The launch of this database had been postponed twice, at the time of writing, and suspended once due to a compromise in its security systems designed to keep individual data secure. The value of such a database in ensuring professionals are aware of previous assessment in terms of aiding the information sharing agenda has yet to be proved. The on-going debate regarding the use of electronic systems to record sensitive data alongside the regular loss of such data will undoubtedly influence the long-term success of this initiative.

Early intervention versus child protection

But how well is the government's early intervention strategy working? The Every Child Matters Agenda was hailed as a major reformation of the children's and young people's workforce (DfES, 2005b) and it has helped many children, young people and families to improve their circumstances. Yet four years on and another child death hits the headlines creating a media frenzy (not forgetting the child deaths that the media does not scandalise across its headlines). Baby Peter was killed in August 2007 by his mother, mother's boyfriend and their lodger in the same London suburb where Victoria Climbié was killed (it might be argued that this is the very reason why this case was brought to national attention). Unlike the inquiry into the death of Victoria Climbié which laid the blame immediately on the social worker, the inquiry into Baby Peter's death highlighted several failings on the part of health practitioners involved in the case, including his GP who failed to notice that he had a broken back.

The government restructured services placing education services at the heart of all others on the premise that most children and young people at some stage in their lives will have a school-experience. It was argued, therefore, that a holistic approach needed to focus on the school if the well-being of all children is to be protected. It is also deemed to be the most logical place to deliver universal services for children and families. As Munro states (2007: 46) 'to some degree, parents' willingness to accept help depends on how it is made available. It can be argued that there would be greater take up of services on a voluntary basis if they were offered in a more accessible and user-friendly way'.

Victoria Climbié, however was not registered at a school in London. The Laming report (2003: para. 3.19) notes that 'No effort was made, either by Kouao or by Ealing Social Services, to enrol her [Victoria] in any form of educational or day care activity, and there is no evidence to indicate she had any friends or playmates'. Baby Peter was 17 months old when he was killed in August 2007. It has not been highlighted that he was attending any day care provision, although Lister (2009) noted that the mother was attending parenting classes but nearly half of these she attended without Baby Peter (Lister, 2009). Looking back to July 1984 when Jasmine Beckford was killed by her stepfather, Munro (1998) noted that Jasmine Beckford's attendance at nursery was marred by long absences which were never queried by the social worker. Furthermore, the social worker did not inform the nursery school of Jasmine's violent home-life, thus the teachers did not assume child abuse when they saw injuries on the odd occasion that Jasmine was brought to nursery. Laming (2009: 24) cites figures from the DCSF biennial overview report of Serious Case Reviews between 2003 and 2005 stating '68 per cent of children aged 4 and over who subsequently died or experienced significant harm had been showing signs of poor school attendance'.

Whilst the government promotes the idea of preventing another tragedy like that of Victoria Climbié, it might be argued that such changes would not actually have prevented such a tragedy, as these policy changes 'were only tangentially concerned with child abuse' (Parton, 2006: 139). In relation to Climbié and Baby P and other cases like these, has ECM therefore only really masked the real problem? According to Munro (2005), the new changes and systems could hinder professionals in safeguarding children and young people as 'tools do not always have the intended effect' (Munro, 2005: 376). Munro likens safeguarding children's systems to that of a nuclear disaster that occurred in 1979. An inquiry into the disaster initially pinpointed human error as the cause of the disaster – that of the engineering operatives. A further independent inquiry, however, discovered that engineers had been so thorough in implementing safety devices that when such a major disaster broke out operatives could not read and interpret the signals. Munro states:

> Yes, they had misread the signals, but, when such a major accident ocurred so many red lights started flashing that the human brain would have difficulty in accurately interpreting their significance. Efforts to improve safety had inadvertently introduced new dangers. (ibid., p. 382)

With all of the legislation being implemented surrounding safeguarding children and the move from a protective state to a preventive one, are we facing the same danger concerning safeguarding children and young people?

In terms of the government's response to the emerging debate in respect of the value of early intervention, it seems that there are some fundamental flaws in the initiatives which are designed to implement this strategy. In fact, apart from a major investment in the building of 3,500 Children's Centres, these initiatives almost exclusively focus on processes which will better connect the existing services. Whilst the arguments supporting the need to improve joined-up working are convincing, they only address part of the agenda for early intervention. In order to significantly improve the outcomes for families who are 'socially excluded' not only do we need to be able to identify any additional needs much earlier but we also need to reform the support services who are expected to address these needs. At present, the resources available to support families with 'additional needs' are based on a welfare system which was only designed to respond to safeguarding issues on a minimum intervention basis. Therefore, in the absence of significant investment in support services in order to meet the identified additional needs, the early intervention initiatives are effectively toothless.

Conclusion

State intervention into child welfare generally has become more apparent over the last 20 or so years, teaching to what some might refer to as a 'nanny state' (Ashley, 2004; Pratt, 2006). Regardless of what one's own view might be on this issue, when we explore the political reasons behind such intervention in our children's lives maybe the government has a plausible reason for telling certain parents how to raise their children. The move from child protection to safeguarding placed an emphasis on the safety and well-being of all children and young people highlighting that Every Child Matters. The shift from services only working with children in need of protection to being able to work with any child who may have additional needs can surely only be a positive notion. However, in order for this change in strategy to be effective major investment is needed in the support services. The absence of a commitment to supporting families once these additional needs have been identified represents an empty promise and merely paying lip-service to the idea of effective early intervention. This would represent a missed opportunity to significantly improve the lives of the most vulnerable families.

The government's ECM agenda focuses heavily on education, moving it to the core of all agencies. This is an attempt to establish early intervention strategies with easier access for children, young people and parents, and also to improve multi-agency working. It will, however, only benefit those children, young people and families having frequent access to such education services. As noted, though, the changes do not yet seem to go far enough in protecting those children and young people still subject to deliberate harm and abuse. It is too early to tell whether or not the recommendations made by Lord Laming (2009) following the death of Baby Peter will be successful.

Further reading

Corby, B. (2006) *Child Abuse*. Maidenhead: Open University Press.

Lonne, B., Parton, N., Thomson, J. and Harries, M. (2009) *Reforming Child Protection*. Abingdon: Routledge.

Parton, N. (2006) *Safeguarding Childhood: Early Intervention and Surveillance in a Late Modern Society*. Basingstoke: Palgrave MacMillan.

Appendix: A summary chronology of this chapter

Labour Party elected	**1966**	
Seebohm Report	**1968**	
Local Authority Social Services Act	**May 1970**	
Conservative Party elected	**June 1970**	
Establishment of social services depts	**1971**	
	1973	Death of Maria Colwell
Public inquiry into the death of Maria Colwell	**1974**	
Labour Party elected	**June 1974**	
Children Act	**1975**	
Conservative Party elected	**1979**	
Conservative Party elected	**1983**	
	1985	Death of Jasmine Beckford
Conservative Party elected	**1987**	Deaths of Tyra Henry and Kimberley Carlile
Cleveland Inquiry	**1988**	
Children Act	**1989**	
Working Together to Safeguard Children (1)	**1991**	
Conservative Party elected	**1992**	
Audit Commission Report *Seen But Not Heard*	**1994**	
Introduction of Children's Services Plan	**1996**	
'New' Labour elected	**1997**	
Establishment of Sure Start	**1998**	

Working with children, young people and families

1. Quality Protects Programme launched	**1999**	
2. Working Together to Safeguard Children (2)		
Framework for Assessment	**2000**	Death of Victoria Climbié
'New' Labour elected	**2001**	
Safeguarding Children: A Joint Chief Inspectors' *Report on Arrangements to Safeguard Children*	**2002**	
1. Laming Report into the death of Victoria Climbié	**2003**	
2. Green Paper, *Every Child Matters*		
1. Every Child Matters, Next Steps	**2004**	
2. Children Act		
'New' Labour elected	**2005**	
Working Together to Safeguard Children (3)	**2006**	
The Children's Plan: Building Brighter Futures	**2007**	Death of Baby P
1. *The Protection of Children in England: A Progress Report by Lord Laming*	**2009**	
2. The Protection of Children in England: Action Plan (the government's response to Lord Laming)		

From safeguarding to Safeguarding

8

Interpreting risk: factors, fears and judgement

Stan Tucker and Dave Trotman

The aims of this chapter are to:

- Understand how risk impacts on our day-to-day lives and the different forms that it can take
- Explore the implications of risk for children, young people and their families and those who work with them
- Use a range of explanatory frameworks to consider the relationship between risk and judgement
- Consider and analyse the reasons why different forms of risk differentially impact on particular groups and individuals within society
- Use the 'typology of risk' provided to examine the different levels of risk that children, young people and families encounter and their implications for developing responsive practice and services
- Offer an understanding of the range of interrelated factors that impact on judgement forming processes.

In this chapter we explore the idea of *risk* and how we can understand this in relation to work with children, young people and their families. At the heart of the chapter lies the key aim of increasing understanding of the complex worlds that the young live in and how risk increasingly shapes their day-to-day experience. We use the discussion to introduce you to a range of explanatory frameworks that it is hoped will prove useful in encouraging you to think proactively about the nature of risk. Crucially, we set out to create an important link for any work with children, young people and families. The notions of risk and judgement are connected to increase your understanding of how effective decisions can be made in the development of more responsive practice and services.

In our day-to-day lives we all encounter some form of risk. Crossing the road, using the internet, making a career decision all involve risk. In some instances we may be conscious of the risks that certain activities involve, for example the danger of physical harm from a fast moving vehicle, in others we may be more blasé, such as the financial and psychological risks of identity theft on the internet.

The sorts of risk and the degrees of risk we encounter can be subject to any combination of physical, emotional, financial, socio-cultural, environmental, psychological and moral or ethical factors. And these factors can change depending upon the nature of the activity, for example commuting to work by bicycle, taking recreational drugs, being unfaithful to a partner or selling our home. Crucially, our understanding of risk is contingent upon our *situation, perception* and *disposition.* For example, the risks associated with the lifestyles routines of a 'developed' western society may be radically different for those in less privileged circumstances: a routine trip to the supermarket in England involves considerably less physical and psychological risk to shoppers than for people shopping at their local market in war-torn Iraq. The physical risks associated with making a cup of tea in England are minor compared with those faced by communities whose only available drinking water is either infested with parasites or polluted with effluence from their local factory. We can call this *situated risk.*

Our 'situatedness' to risk can be dependent upon any number of factors: our geographical location, our race and culture, our homeland, our genetic heritage, our socio-economic circumstances, happenstance or as a consequence of deliberate choice. Consider the following, for example:

- The range of situated risks for young Afghan women whose ambition it is to attend their local school. Compare these to the risks facing disaffected girls truanting from an inner-city high school in the UK.
- The risks associated with a high-altitude trekking holiday in the Himalayas. Compare these to those faced by Tibetan refugees attempting to evade an armed Chinese border patrol in the same region.
- According to epidemiological research there is a greater risk of dying from heart disease in Glasgow or Belfast than anywhere else in the UK.
- Particular activities or occupations may carry different and higher levels of situated risk: putting out fires, playing the stock market, or diffusing landmines.

Activity

Look at the images in Figure 8.1 (a–g) and place them in the order of high to low situated risk and think about your reasons for doing so. Think about whether the risks are physical, emotional, financial, environmental, socio-cultural, psychological and moral and ethical.

Interpreting risk

(a) Young men in Glasgow, photograph taken on 5 April 2006 by User: Dave souza at Wikipedia. Category:Charles Rennie Mackintosh

(b) A boy from an East Cipinang trash dump slum shows his find, Jakarta Indonesia. (Jonathan McIntosh, 2004: Wikipedia)

(c) Unknown paddler using a playboat at Paddle for the People, July 2007, Manchester New Hampshire, Crackpipe playwave on Merrimack River. (Original uploader was Mikespenard at en. wikipedia, 2008-03-01)

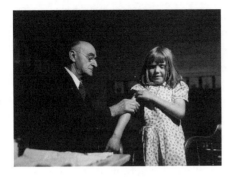

(d) Dr Schreiber of San Augustine giving a typhoid innoculation at a rural school, San Augustine County, Texas.Transfer from U.S. Office of War Information, 1944

(e) Turret lathe operator machining parts for transport planes at the Consolidated Aircraft Corporation plant, Fort Worth, Texas, USA. (This image is available from the United States Library of Congress's Prints and Photographs Division under the digital ID fsac.1a34951)

(f) Industrial landscape (attributed to Danang government website Vietnam www.danang.gov.vn/photo/ pictures/050720-O-nhiem. jpg&imgrefurl=http://www.danang. gov.vn/home/view.asp)

(g) Unknown source

Figure 8.1   Images of potential risk

This is an important activity to reflect on. The intention was to get you thinking about the nature of risk and the various forms it can take that is high or low risk. We wanted you to start categorising different forms of risk and in doing so decide on the factors that might influence the extent and impact of the risk on those involved. Did you struggle to decide on the actual nature of the risk? Perhaps you thought that a range of factors came in to play in deciding whether a risk was high or low. This is a fascinating activity to do with a group of people, particularly if you are required to defend your ranking order.

Risk can often be thought about in terms of 'calculated risks' where our *perception* of risk is shaped by our previous experience of similar actions or situations, or the social forces that govern our behaviour, our sense of intuition, or our moral imperative, for example risking the late arrival to work by taking a short-cut to avoid a traffic jam, risking the long-term detrimental effects of smoking cigarettes, concealing the 'whole truth' from a friend for fear of causing offence or rejection. The actions we take as a consequence of our perceptions involve us in making *judgements*. Judgement then becomes a critical agent in our ability to calculate risks, our understanding of the potential consequences and our decisions about what action, or not, needs to be taken. Critical judgement is necessary in ensuring our perceptions of risk do not become subject to distortion through the vagaries of particular 'moral panics', for example, the risks portrayed in the popular press around 'hoodies', 'yobs' and 'chavs' and the 'so-called' phenomenon of 'black-on-black' shootings.

Activity

Consider the following and decide what factors will have a bearing upon how we determine risk.

- 'Chat rooming'
- Holidaying in a different country to your own
- Buying goods on the internet
- Walking underneath a ladder
- Having unprotected sex
- Playing video games
- Buying a lottery ticket
- Going to the gym
- Deciding who to marry.

So far we have framed risk as a largely *problematic* social phenomenon. However, research tells us that certain forms of risk are important to the well-being of the individual and society. For example, risk-taking appears as a consistent feature of creativity; without risk-taking the pursuit of innovation would cease, as would invention and exploration.

Consider the following. In any number of contexts the positive aspects of risk have to be balanced against the potential negative outcomes of risk activity, for example risk is an essential attribute of entrepreneurialism, but an uncritical approach may negatively impact upon the locations and people situated within and around that risk. For example, a decision to build a new plant to create the next generation of G4 mobile phones in India may have considerable financial risks for the company directors; it may result in significant liberating technological benefits for particular phone-using communities; it may yield considerable financial returns for the shareholders; it may also result in the forced relocation of a small farming community with no possibility of local employment; it may result in catastrophic levels of environmental damage as the plant diverts water from a site of natural heritage. All these factors involve moral and ethical judgements about risk that extend beyond the material and the financial.

When we consider risk we also have to account for personal and collective *dispositions* to risk. What may appear as 'risky' to one person may be regarded as nothing more than a challenge to someone else. Our disposition to risk is likely to be based upon such things as our prior experience, our ability to adapt to new experiences, our calculation of the odds of success or failure. So far we have considered risk as something that involves 'doing', however, risk can also be connected to inactivity, inertia, or 'risk avoidance'. Indeed, we often have to weigh-up the risks of choosing to do nothing, in 'sitting-tight' or 'hoping it will go away'.

Communities of risk

An important question to ask is whether some people live in communities that may be considered to be more 'risky' than others? And if that is the case what factors are likely to define the nature of such communities? Now, you might want to argue that such a question is relatively easy to answer. Communities of risk are likely to be those that experience high levels of poverty and it is important to remember that despite government efforts, significantly large numbers of children are still living in poverty in the United Kingdom (Harker, 2006b). You might define a community of risk in terms of, say, the high levels of unemployment experienced by its members (Nickell, 2004), reported incidents of anti-social behaviour (Brown, 2004), the incidence of chronic illnesses such as heart disease or the prevalence of obesity (Lobstein et al., 2004), or the quality of social housing available (Harker, 2006a). All of these indicators might seem to the impartial observer to be entirely appropriate. However, we want to argue that the debate can't be seen solely in such terms and other factors and outcomes need to be carefully considered.

Interpreting risk

Let's reflect on what we might usefully call the *internal life* of a community by considering the educational and social facilities available to its children and their families. The internal life of a community can be most usefully described as consisting of a set of common experiences that serve to shape future life chances and aspirations, day-to-day interactions, the availability and use of resources and the way a set of shared problems are defined and responded to. In approaching the discussion in this way a more complex debate is revealed for consideration concerning the idea of communities at risk. You might find it helpful to complete the activity below in order to assist your thinking around this notion.

Activity

Think about a community you know that you would define as a 'community of risk'. Then reflect on how you think poor quality experiences of primary or secondary education, or, say, the availability of appropriate play or youth facilities might increase exposure to risk. Note down some of the factors that are likely to be highly influential in shaping the *internal life* of the community.

We hope that the activity helped you to begin to reflect in a little more depth on the nature of communities of risk. If we take the educational experiences of children and young people, for example, we would want to argue that such experiences have a profound impact on the *internal life* of any community. Let's take just one group of young people, white working-class boys. The one thing we know from research is that this group of young people experience the lowest level of educational achievement when compared with that of any other group of young people (Evans, 2006). Now if that is the situation, and you don't accept the view that white working-class boys are in some biological sense 'less able' than their peers, we need to gain a clearer understanding of factors that place this group at higher levels of risk than other potentially disadvantaged groups. As you might expect the explanation is far from simple in that a range of factors combine to foster what has become an enduring outcome for many white working-class males. These factors include the influence of peer culture, the value placed on education within the home environment, the response of schools and individual teachers to individual and collective learning needs and the perceived relevance of the curriculum in terms of creating higher levels of career expectations.

Similarly, when we consider how a lack of social facilities might impact on the *internal life* of a community, the argument can be made that elements of individual and collective risk are again increased. Impoverished backgrounds are as likely to be generated out of physical and social environments that offer little opportunity for developing creativity, where, for example, play is seen as an unimportant learning tool, as they are from social exclusion and poverty-induced alienation. Indeed recent government policies in this area, through, for example, the development of Children's Centres, recognise the importance of holistic responses to meeting need through the integration of education, social welfare and health education programmes (Payne, 2008).

However, there is one more important idea we want to consider here when it comes to thinking about communities of risk. On first consideration the concept can be a little difficult to comprehend, not least because the terminology used to describe it appears complex in itself. However, we want to argue that specific individuals and groups of young people are consistently 'problematised' (Griffin, 1993) in terms of their lifestyles, the way they present themselves in public, the way they speak and describe their worlds and the ways in which they are presented through the media. And it is the action of 'problematisation' that effectively separates them out as a community of risk. Griffin (1993), in her seminal text, argues that a range of dominant discourses (the way we think, speak and act towards the young) impact on our perceptions of them. Such discourses are used to declare individuals and groups of young people as 'mad', 'bad', 'diseased', 'perverted', etc. As you can no doubt see, in speaking of young people in such a way essentially we stereotype and categorise areas of their day-to-day existence. Moreover, Griffin maintains that these forms of discourse are so dominant that they are highly influential in shaping the way services for young people actually respond to them. Reflect for a moment on the question that if young people are essentially seen as a problem within society then how are those charged with working with them likely to see them? This is more than just a debate about media representations of the life of the young or the way as a society we 'panic' (Cohen, 2002) from time to time when we find the lives of young people difficult to understand. The power of such dominant discourses, Griffin argues, actually goes a long way towards shaping the nature of the treatment that young people are given, their life chances and their aspirations.

Activity

Having read through this section you should now be in a better position to understand what constitutes different kinds of communities of risk. Make notes on the various factors that can increase the level of risk that children and young people face. Reflect on whether you think some children and young people might be more at risk than others.

The last part of the activity, in particular, moves us into an area for debate that certainly generates a whole range of views and ideas. You might have argued that risk increases according to the social class you are born into, or the ethnic group

Interpreting risk

you are part of, or because of your gender. You might have noted that those young people who spend most of their time in public spaces are exposed to increased levels of risk. You might be convinced by Griffin's argument that risk is a by-product of the dominant representations. Whatever your position, perhaps you now feel that risks come in all kinds of shapes and forms and some are potentially more serious than others. This is an issue we explore in the next section.

Typology of risk

In this section we present the idea that one way of understanding the idea of risk is to start from the position that different kinds of risk will have a range of very different outcomes attached to them. We want to argue that there is a whole range of risk that people routinely encounter in their everyday lives and that such risks can only be really understood when we delve beneath their surface manifestations. To help with this task we offer for consideration what we term as a *typology of risk*. As the name suggests it attempts to draw together different types of risk by looking at what specific forms of risk have in common and their potential outcomes for some children and young people.

In Table 8.1 you will find below our typology of risk. Have a look through it and then undertake the following activity.

Activity

Look carefully over the typology of risk presented in Table 8.1 and write notes on how you think each category is likely to impact on the future aspirations, ambitions and life chances of individual and groups of young people.

Hopefully you picked up on the fact that not only does the typology offer us a useful way of looking at risk but it also brings into sharp focus the fact that risk does not fall equally on all groups of children and young people in society. There is ample evidence to suggest that children who live in poverty, for example, are likely to be exposed to increased levels of risk in terms of experiencing negative outcomes in the areas of health, education and social care (Beckett, 2007). At the same time it is also important to remind ourselves that different forms of risk are often connected. For illustrative purposes the typology separates out different forms of risk but clearly the chances of becoming involved in 'high personal risk' are likely to be increased, for example if 'environmental risk' is significant.

Did you find yourself reflecting on the nature of 'pathological risk'? This idea is highly contentious in the sense that it is used to 'blame the victim' for many

Working with children, young people and families

factors that shape their lives and yet are out of their immediate control. The 'historical risk' category provides examples of the way this can happen – educational failure, for example, has clear and enduring social class and ethnic foundations. Yet, the power of pathology is undeniable and it is frequently presented in the media as the 'explanation' for those 'solutions' that are concerned to punish, regulate and control the activities of the young – particularly in public places (Cohen, 2002). There is also a neat simplicity involved in that cause and outcome are directly connected. The young are effectively 'blamed' for the situations they find themselves in.

Table 8.1 Typology of risk

Type of Risk	Common Characteristics	Examples and Outcomes
Positive-intentional risk	• Risks that are intended to build skills, widen horizons, promote imagination • Risk arises out of exposure to new ways of thinking, working, or challenging perceptions and stereotypes • High level of creativity, ingenuity, tenacity and self-motivation required to achieve desired outcomes	• Taking part in a play for the first time where a high degree of public presentation of self is required • Learning to speak a new language with a group of peers • Travelling to a new area of the country as part of a youth exchange programme
Environmental risk	• Living in an impoverished community • Having limited access to social facilities and support networks • High levels of family and community poverty • Inadequate housing, high levels of chronic illness and exposure to crime	• Experiencing significantly high levels of illness throughout childhood • Lack of public parks and spaces to encourage creative play • Exposure to and possible participation in low-level crime
Historic risk	• Enduring and endemic failure of children and young people to achieve positive educational outcomes • 'Cycle of deprivation' preventing social mobility and reinforcing economic insecurity • Weak community infrastructure produced by consistent and significant lack of investment	• Ongoing individual and collective underachievement by young people in public examinations • High levels of youth unemployment produced by long-term economic decline of an area • 'Failing' schools that suffer from low levels of inward investment, long-term staff shortages and poorly designed and furnished buildings
Pathological risk	• Based on perceived and stereotypically informed representations of children and young people	• High level of public supervision of behaviour, particularly in public places, e.g. extensive use of ASBOs

(Cont'd)

Table 8.1   (Cont'd)

Type of Risk	Common Characteristics	Examples and Outcomes
	• The young perceived as 'mad', 'bad', 'diseased' 'perverted', sexually promiscuous • Characteristics used to justify early and high levels of service intervention • Lives of specific individuals and groups of young people are consistently 'problematised'	• Premature labelling of individual and groups of young people to justify early intervention into their lives • Some young people begin to conform to dominant discourses and stereotypes
Personal risk	• Involvement in substance abuse and excessive use of alcohol • Involvement in situations where there is the possibility of abuse and/or neglect occurring • Weak peer/family/community ties • Low sense of self worth and esteem	• Drug dependency and alcoholism • Depression, possibly leading to suicide and attempted suicide • Physical and mental trauma born out of the experience of an abusive relationship

Yet, despite the many negative outcomes of risk presented above it is important to consider another important question 'why do some children and young people seem to be resilient, and continue to grow and thrive, despite the negative risks and outcomes facing them in their daily lives?' One way of understanding such a situation is by considering the concept of 'resilience' (Daniel and Wassell, 2002) in more depth. The idea of resilience is a fascinating one. Here the child is seen as anything but 'the victim' of the circumstances they find themselves in. Resilience is generated through the development of a sense of inner purpose that enables them to cope with crises, set-backs and challenges (see Chapter 2). Crucially then it is important to consider how such a sense of resilience might be fostered and generated. Here, we would argue that the availability of 'creative risk' has an important role to play in any work with children and young people (see Nickerson, 1999: 413–14). As we indicate in the typology such risk is concerned with developing skills, widening horizons, promoting imagination, etc. The issue of understanding and exploring choice and opportunity comes into play here especially when a choice to act in one way or another has clear negative and positive connotations attached to it.

Hopefully you are beginning to understand the complex nature of risk in work with children, young people and their families. The fact is that those working with the young encounter risk in a variety of different ways throughout their professional careers. Some forms of risk may require a level of immediate reaction whereas others offer more time and space for critical reflection. However, those working with children and young people are required to make judgements – a matter explored in more detail in the next section.

Working with children, young people and families

The idea of judgement

We move into yet another fascinating area for consideration. To begin with it is important to make a vital connection – increasingly debates about judgement are connected to debates about accountability. Pressure for the public and professional accountability of those working with children and young people has significantly increased in recent years. For example, poor professional judgement has been seen as a central factor in contributing to the death of a number of children at the hands of their parents and carers. Those investigating such cases, like Lord Laming (2003), have gone out of their way to connect matters of judgement with issues of public accountability.

Public debate of this kind has made it all the more important to understand on what basis judgements are made in work with children and young people. We have moved a long way from being able to explain our actions in terms of a 'gut response' or seeing them as 'the right thing to do' – many judgements will require a level of analysis and ultimately justification if called into question. Use the next activity to help you to start thinking about this matter.

Activity

Read the three scenarios presented below and reflect on the factors that you might consider in forming a judgement about the circumstances and needs of the child concerned. How would you respond to each of the scenarios?

- Halima, a 5-year-old, has become very isolated in the classroom, sitting alone for long periods of time. The risk is that her communication skills will deteriorate further as she has always been a very shy and withdrawn child.
- Rex is 15 years old and a very good guitarist. He has been invited to perform at a youth music festival but his mother can't afford to let him go as it means staying in a hotel overnight. The risk is that this will severely damage his self esteem. He was heard to say, 'Kids like me never get any real breaks and chances because of where we come from'.
- Mandy is 12 years old. She has turned up dirty and tired to school on four separate occasions during the last fortnight. One of her best friends has told you that her mum is really ill and she has to look after her. The risk is that in looking after her mother Mandy is suffering an unacceptable level of neglect.

These kinds of scenarios are relatively common and as such are ones that those working with the young are likely to encounter on a reasonably regular basis. Yet to make effective judgements in such situations it is argued here that a range of linked factors have to be carefully considered. The factors concerned are

Interpreting risk

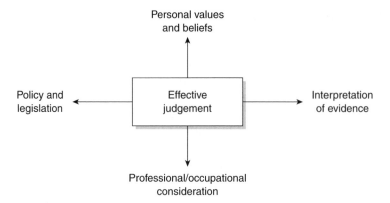

Personal values
and beliefs

Policy and
legislation

Effective
judgement

Interpretation
of evidence

Professional/occupational
consideration

Figure 8.2   Effective judgement

represented in Figure 8.2 and explained in more detailed below. What is demonstrated through Figure 8.2 is that the development of judgement has to be related
to a number of interrelated factors.

Personal values and beliefs

It is impossible to come to an informed judgement without acknowledging
the influence of the personal values and beliefs you hold. This is not just a
debate about levels of objectivity or subjectivity. Personal values and beliefs
often drive people in making a choice about the kind of work they want to do
and the way they use that work to influence change. However, it is also important to acknowledge that personal values and beliefs can have both a positive
and negative impact on judgement-making processes. An important aspect of
this is our ability to know something of our own dispositions and predilections;
for the Greek philosopher Socrates this was the province of 'knowledge of the
self'. Although Socrates was arguing his case over 2,000 years ago, developing
an understanding of our personal values, feelings, vulnerabilities and convictions is an important judgemental skill. A useful development of this can be
found in the work of American 'care theorist' Nell Noddings who invites us to
consider whether the unexamined life is worth living (Noddings, 1995: 191)?
This is particularly important if we are then able to recognise and set to one
side those features in our own biographies that may cloud or colour our judgements – this is known in some fields of philosophy as 'bracketing'.

Policy and legislation

Current policy and legislation can be highly influential when it comes to inform-
ing judgement-making processes. Those working with children and young people

have to fulfil their legal obligations to, for example, meet the demands of the national curriculum, enforce child protection procedures and respect human rights and choice. Policy is also highly influential in shaping the way work is prioritised and responses to national and local policies can shape the outcomes of internal review and national inspection activities. We should not assume, however, that all policy and legislation is chronologically designed to be in concert with one another. Hence, it can often be the case that collective judgement is required to mediate and interpret competing policy interests, for example ministerial ambitions for enabling creativity in the school curriculum do not sit well with a parallel preoccupation with national tests in literacy and numeracy (see Chapter 5). On this point connection and collaboration with the wider community is imperative.

Professional/occupational considerations

At the heart of any professional training programme it is usually possible to identify key values, ideas, methods and approaches, views on evaluation and assessment and theoretical frameworks that are likely to be highly influential in shaping the judgements of practitioners (Coles, 2002). At the same time notions of multi-professional practice now require individuals and groups from very different professional backgrounds to work more closely together, and communicate effectively, when it comes to developing informed judgements (Glenny and Roaf, 2008). Professional judgement can no longer be regarded as an independent or solitary activity. In addition to this, new professions are emerging that appear to be challenging the traditional 'authority' of more established ones. For example, within a classroom setting teaching assistants and learning mentors may well see their views as being as valuable as those of the teacher when it comes to matters of judgement formation (Cajkler et al., 2007). The important point to make here is that the right to judge is no longer seen as the sole province of the 'established' professions.

Interpretation of evidence

This represents a very important element of any judgement-making process. The way that evidence is interpreted and who is actually involved in the process of interpretation is central to the making of sound decisions. Clearly evidence that is opened up for scrutiny and questioning is more likely to emerge as sound evidence than that which is reviewed and evaluated by a single individual or group. Increasingly, emphasis is being placed on the need for all stakeholders to be involved in the review of evidence including children, young people and their families whenever possible. Once again, this emphasises collective rather than isolated individual judgement making. It also has considerable ramifications for the contexts in which judgements are situated.

Interpreting risk

Regional and local contexts

Myriad decisions will be made in our day-to-day encounters governed by those features described above. However, these decisions will not take place in isolation; a recurrent theme throughout this discussion has been the need for collaboration. Moreover, for collaboration to be in any way meaningful it also has to be transformative, through empowering and maximising those 'voices' that are situated in particular, and often unique, cultural contexts.

The argument constructed in this section has been used to demonstrate the complex processes and factors involved in producing informed judgements. One of the main themes to emerge is that the generation of judgement is seen to lie beyond traditional professional boundaries, that is with teachers, doctors, social workers, police officers, etc. All those involved with children and young people in whatever capacity have important information and perceptions to offer that should help in producing better quality evidence. In addition, the views of the young should also be treated with respect and dignity when it comes to making informed decisions.

Some concluding thoughts

You will no doubt remember that the key aim of this chapter was to encourage you to reflect on the complex world that children, young people and their families live in and how various kinds of risk shape day-to-day experience. We have used the discussion to highlight not only the nature of the kind of risk that the young face but also how that risk is intricately linked to matters of judgement. Our purpose in pursuing this line of argument was to emphasise how a range of different factors mediate perceptions of risk. We also provided you with a framework to help you reflect on how it is possible to come to what might best be described as informed judgements when working with children, young people and families.

Yet we also raised some important ethical issues through the discussion on communities of risk. The fact of the matter appears to be that for some individuals and groups, levels of risk are significantly influenced by matters of poverty, educational underachievement, poor housing and health, lack of play facilities, etc. However, were you also left pondering why it is the case that certain people appear to be more resilient when it comes to surviving personal and collective risk and seem to have both the internal resources and external networks to grow and thrive despite the adversity they face? You need to give this matter more consideration when it comes to developing effective forms of work with the young. Through the typology of risk we introduced the notion of 'positive-intentional risk'. Perhaps one of the key matters we need to consider in working with children, young people and families is how work strategies can be developed that foster exposure to risk without fatally injuring confidence, future aspirations, skill and knowledge development as well as the courage to take risks. We also want you to reflect again on the ideas of both 'pathology' and 'problematisation' and the ethical underpinnings of both of these ideas. Essentially, the argument has been made that these concepts are so powerful that they determine the nature, philosophy and priorities of the services provided for children, young people and families.

Our purpose in raising these issues at one level is very simple: services for the young will only ever really change if and when such ideas are positively challenged and countered. We would want to argue at a very fundamental level that the transformation of services has to be predicated on a rights promoting agenda that advocates the importance of seeing children, young people and families as crucial contributors to decision-making activities and any processes that are used to evaluate service effectiveness. Here of course new risks are introduced onto the agenda in that service users might advocate approaches and strategies that are at odds with professional views and expectations. Thus, any judgement that is made to change policies and practices will require a level of resilience to see things through even when other approaches appear easier and therefore more attractive in the short term.

Further reading

Robb, M. (2007) *Youth in Context: Frameworks, Settings and Encounters.* London: Sage and Open University Press.
Wilkinson, I. (2010) *Risk, Vulnerability and Everyday Life.* Abingdon: Routledge.

Interpreting risk

9

Situating child development

Roger Willoughby

The aims of this chapter are to:

- Assist students in approaching and critically reflecting on the substantial literature on child development
- Discuss the paradoxical nature of development as a concept
- Detail illustrative key areas of and theoretical perspectives on child development
- Outline some social and interpersonal origins of the self
- Emphasise the key role of language in development
- Illustrate concepts with a case example and provide brief activities to assist students in deepening their engagement with core issues.

The study of child and adolescent development represents a core area of concern not only within psychology, health and the social sciences, but also more generally within all disciplines that take human beings as their focus. Thus, conceptualisations of the subject may, for instance, be equally found in the humanities, English, drama, and the various creative arts. Beyond this, each and every one of us will have implicit, if not explicit, ideas (constituting a 'folk psychology') on what makes us, and those around us, the way we are. The present chapter, rooted in both psychological and interdisciplinary perspectives, provides a critical overview of the above noted key topics and themes within the literature on child development and points readers to further sources of information.

Conceptualising development

When initially considering development as a concept, it is common to begin with a discussion and definition of the term. Before moving on to consider specimen views on this from the literature, complete the activity opposite.

Think back about the course of your own life. List some of the ways you have changed over time. Try to cluster items on your list into meaningful categories. Draw a timeline (or series of timelines) marking key points within these changes. Note factors that appear to have either prompted or inhibited such changes. Discuss your results with others and note the areas of similarity and difference between your individual findings.

Unsurprisingly, the literature offers a wide range of ideas on the essence of development. Rutter and Rutter (1992: 64), for example, define human development as 'systematic, organized, intra-individual change that is clearly associated with generally expectable age-related progressions and which is carried forward in some way that has implications for a person's pattern or level of functioning at some later time'. While Harris (2008: 1) argues that 'change in a positive direction, that is towards greater accuracy and better organisation, is regarded as being "development"' and that 'developmental change' is 'change that can be seen as part of the process by which, over time, children move from a less mature to a more mature way of thinking and behaving where greater maturity is seen as being more adult-like'. Such definitions can be seen to incorporate individually focused normative conceptions of development, involving relatively linear notions of what constitutes progress.

Challenges to such modernist normativity have been widespread in academic and wider socio-cultural domains, particularly since the Second World War. Widespread disenchantment with previously hegemonic discourses, such as the benignity of western civilisation, social stratification, and scientific progress, was fostered by the industrial-scale slaughter and horrific genocide of World War Two, a war fought between some of the most supposedly civilised nations in the world. Such catalytic experiences contributed to the growing influence of post-modernism and more general scepticism towards mainstream scientific, socio-political and cultural claims (Giddens, 2009). In such a context, concepts of development and progress need to be themselves critically questioned. When the horizons of developmental psychology expanded from a concentration on child and adolescent development to consider adulthood and life-span perspectives (e.g. Erikson, 1950) some of the challenges became more evident. Here, issues of symbolic as well as tangible losses within adult life (such as the failure to achieve personal ambitions, the death of parents or friends, and the prospect of one's own death) can appear somewhat paradoxical when situated within the concept of development. Yet, the incorporation of such features arguably considerably enriches the concept of development.

This may be approached through considering Schaffer's (2006: 6) description of life-span development as 'the process of change associated with age which characterizes all human beings from conception to death'. Here, the deceptively simple notion of change over time avoids overt value judgements and at the same time allows for variegated patterns of change and scope for consideration of *decline* within the life course. Such conceptualisations encourage consideration of non-uniform and domain specific change within individuals, such that the rate and processes of change within one area may occur relatively independently of change in other areas. Similarly, as considerable diversity is possible within the phenomena that constitute a life course, this type of definition opens up the way to situate experiences of adversity, decline, loss, and death centrally within the discipline. Thus, experiences such as illness, disability, physical aging, the loss of vigour and beauty, career set-backs, the loss of family members and friends through death or other causes, and the prospect of one's own death may be situated with the fabric of development. Such events clearly may alter the direction of a life course, as it is both objectively and subjectively experienced and unfolds. The essential issue here is that the fallout of such events on a life course is often complex and multi-directional.

To illustrate this further, apparent setbacks, for example, may often entail various levels of suffering and can constrain psychosocial functioning. However, when viewed from a longer-term perspective, such experiences can also contribute to the creation of other life opportunities, while their cognitive and emotional processing can enrich mental life, for instance through the fostering of insight and empathy. This is not to sentimentalise, romanticise or otherwise recommend suffering or the experience of adversity in itself. Rather, it is to highlight the complexity of development. This area has been briefly reviewed by Schaffer (2006), building on Baltes' (Baltes, 1987; Smith and Baltes, 1999) concepts of multidimensionality and multidirectionality, as well as his delineation of age-graded, history-graded, and non-normative influences on the life course (Baltes et al., 1998). These concepts highlight some of the ways in which humans *typically* develop along a range of dimensions within particular social domains (e.g. the changes in cognitive, social and emotional functioning when a child commences in primary school in England). Such contextualised views of development can contribute importantly to an understanding of developmental statistical norms: what developmentally might be averagely expectable within a certain timeframe and context. Normative profiles are useful benchmarks against which individuals may be gauged and their development judged. It is important, however, to recall that such normative views are statistical compilations of developmental data derived from a sample of individuals, that there is often significant variation within such samples, and that the individuals and phenomena considered are historically and culturally situated. Thus, for example, history-graded (e.g. the experience of the Second World War or the introduction of computers or the internet) and non-normative influences (e.g. the use of reproductive technologies, divorce, family breakdown or emigration) should alert us to some situating factors that are likely to modify development for particular cohorts, groups or individuals.

It is useful at this point to highlight that within this formative flux of life events, developmental change has typically multi-factorial origins and its processes and outcomes are usually complex, essentially involving simultaneous gains *and* losses. Consider, for example, a child learning to walk, taking her/his first steps. This might be regarded as a clear-cut achievement, giving satisfaction to the child as well as her/his caregivers, and measurable against normative developmental milestones (e.g. Illingworth, 1987). All this would be entirely appropriate. At the same time, however, there is the loss of the child-in-arms, of that intimacy of body contact and greater dependency of the former developmental stage for both infant and caregiver. Such losses can be emotionally painful and entail having to face a degree of mourning for the states that are relinquished. This represents one of the essential costs of developmental change, the experience of which can itself promote further (typically social and emotional) growth.

Theoretical perspectives

Developmental psychology is a 'site of contest' and as such its data exist within competing theoretical frameworks (e.g. psychoanalytic, behavioural, cognitive, constructivist, maturational, and so on). These differing perspectives offer alternative ways of ordering and synthesising observations, each in accord with the fundamental tenets of the framework employed. Such approaches should permit predictions about the future course of development and at the same time contribute to the testing of the models themselves (see also Feyerabend, 1975; Kuhn, 1962; Popper, 1963). Three prominent models: psychoanalysis, behaviourism and cognitivism will be briefly noted here in order to highlight examples of these features. In approaching developmental change from the perspective of a particular psychological model, students should deepen their understanding of that model, assessing its history, strengths and limitations (see Miller (2002) for a good critical review).

We shall begin with psychoanalysis, which in the contemporary context is fragmented and covers a diverse series of competing schools, such as ego-psychologists, Kleinians, object-relations theorists, Self-psychologists, Lacanians, and Intersubjectivists. Psychoanalytically influenced models (e.g. Erikson, 1950; Freud, 1965; Klein, 1993; Rayner et al., 2005; Vaillant, 2003) are likely to emphasise the roles of emotion, subjectivity, symbolisation, and unconscious conflicts, among other elements. Developmental change within one or other of these schools may be variously tracked through a series of psycho-sexual stages and interpersonal relations, prompted variously by drives rooted in instincts (particularly love and aggression) or desire, all mixed in with the constant ebb and flow of the individual's fantasy life. This dynamic day-to-day narrative flux for example, contributes incrementally to the formation and structuring of the personality, influences social encounters, and fosters or inhibits curiosity, creativity and intentional action.

Among the classical psychoanalytic efforts to chart developmental change, Anna Freud's (Freud, 1965; Neubauer, 1984) concept of developmental lines, Mahler et al.'s (2000) views on symbiosis and individuation, and Erikson's (1959, 1963; Eagle, 1997) concept of ego identity (being shaped by socio-cultural

Situating child development

forces), as well as his extension of developmental stages across the life-span, may be taken as illustrative of significant work in this area. Probably the most notable contribution to conceptualising development from a psychoanalytically informed perspective over the last 50 years, however, has been Bowlby's (1951, 1969, 1973, 1980, 1988; Holmes, 1993) attachment theory. Given both its importance and social dominance, this will be discussed separately below.

From a very different perspective, behaviourism (e.g. Pavlov, 1928; Skinner, 1948, 1953, 1971, 1974; Watson, 1930) typically stresses externally observable patterns of behaviour, with an understanding of the association (or adjustment) between each element of behaviour in the pattern being sought in environmental stimuli rather than in internal (subjective) mental states. Behaviourism thus sought to deconstruct behavioural sequences and experimentally discover the functional links that determined or 'conditioned' these, with the partial aim of being able to predict and regulate actions through various types of encouragement ('positive and negative reinforcement') or inhibition ('punishment'). The central element of study thus is the 'stimulus-response' (or S-R).

The initial work of Pavlov (1928) introduced what came to be known as *classical conditioning*, in which he famously showed how a dog's (unconditioned) salivation to food, when paired several times with a previously neutral stimulus (e.g. a certain noise, such as a ringing bell), resulted in the salivation appearing when the hitherto neutral stimulus was presented alone. The response was thus said to have been *conditioned*. Following Pavlov's lead, Thorndike (1911) attempted to state laws of behaviour, the best known of which is the *law of effect* which can be summarised as, 'the greater the satisfaction or discomfort, the greater the strengthening or weakening of the bond' (Thorndike, 1911: 244).

Thorndike's ideas in turn influenced Skinner's (1938) development of *operant conditioning*. In this, Skinner argued that initially random elements of behaviour (what he at times termed 'operants') may be increasingly *shaped* into intentional or goal-directed behaviour by the subsequent pattern of reinforcement. Classical and operant conditioning thus differed from each other in their temporal focus: the former emphasising the antecedents to the particular behaviour being examined, while the latter considers the subsequent patterns of reinforcement. Some of these principles are applied today in behaviour management regimes in schools. Initially based on experiments using animals, behaviourism claimed the same principles applied equally to humans and that development occurred through the shaping of behaviour by reinforcement (e.g. Beck et al., 2009; Harris, 1979; Watson, 1928; Watson and Rayner, 1920).

The third theoretical perspective, cognitivism, arose in part out of dissatisfaction with the severe restrictions of behaviourism, particularly its lack of engagement with higher mental mechanisms and processes. The roots of cognitivism may be discerned in several related areas such as Gestalt psychology. The development of computers during and after the Second World War began to be seen to offer an interesting alternative model of human thought, with Turing's (1950) ideas on artificial intelligence being influential. Relatedly, Broadbent's (1958) information

Working with children, young people and families

processing model offered a means of conceptualising the mental steps involved in cognitive tasks. The final significant spur to the cognitive revolution came from linguistics, particularly the work of Noam Chomsky. Chomsky's (1959) critique of the behavioural account of language development argued that innate mechanisms, such as 'universal grammar', are essential for language acquisition.

Selectively building on such foundations, cognitively oriented psychologists (e.g. Flavell et al., 2002; Piaget, 1970, 1985; Siegler, 1998) have sought to outline the nature and development of a wide range of mental phenomena. The most prominent exponent of this group is Jean Piaget and his core theories, though criticised, should be familiar to students. Piaget (1970) proposed a stage theory of cognitive development, with the developing child and young person progressing through each successive stage in a set order, this movement entailing qualitative changes in the individual's cognitive structures and hence in the individual's knowledge of their experiential world ('genetic epistemology'). The four stages or periods: Sensorimotor (roughly birth to 2 years), Preoperational (2 to 7 years), Concrete operational (7 to 11 years), and Formal operational (11 to 15 years) are marked by distinct structural changes. The attainment of each of these successive stages allows the individual to revise previous cognitive *schemes* (or schema) so that they more closely represent reality. However, in his later work Piaget (1985) de-emphasised this step-like stage model, smoothing out the radical shifts between stages, and placing more emphasis on mechanisms of cognitive change (Miller, 2002). Development, for Piaget, was promoted by interaction between four principal innate and experiential factors: (1) physical maturation; (2) experience with the physical environment; (3) social experience; and (4) equilibration. The last was seen as the central catalysing process of development. Essentially, equilibration involves the resolution of the cognitive uncertainty or disequilibrium that arises when perceived reality fails to fit neatly with existing preconceptions, ideas or schemas, through modification and development of the schema. Such adaptations to perceived reality underscore the emphasis Piaget placed on rationality and on the child and young person actively problem-solving, constructing and reconstructing their cognitive architecture (see also Harris and Butterworth, 2002; Parke and Gauvin, 2009; Schaffer, 2006).

Clearly, some of these perspectives attempt to offer overarching models of child and adult development that comment on multiple areas of development, while others are more modest in their scope. The above sketches provide only outlines of elements within these specimen perspectives and they are here intended to emphasise the differing conceptual lenses developmental commentators *actively re-construct* their data through. Students should thus note the theoretical stance and its underlying assumptions, strengths and shortcomings, when studying developmental literature. Similarly, when considering questions relating to development that may arise in your own fieldwork or other settings, consider what theoretical position you are closest to adhering to. While it may be implicit or only tentatively explicit, you will have one!

Situating child development

Activity

Considering either your own results from the first activity above or the case study of Jane D (see p. 147), how might these different models frame some of these life-events? What aspects would be either stressed or minimised? Does one model appear to provide a 'better' account of the reported developmental data?

Historical and cultural contexts

Just as understandings of development exist within various psychological frameworks, both of these occur in turn within wider historical, philosophical, political and socio-cultural contexts. Traditionally, few developmental theorists paid much attention to these, despite sometimes suggesting that their theories could be applied universally. One notable exception to this trend was the Russian psychologist Vygotsky (1978), whose socio-cultural approach emphasised the essential interconnectedness of the individual with their social context, history and culture: the minimum meaningful unit of analysis from this perspective for developmental study is 'an individual participating in some cultural practice' (Miller, 2002: 373). Winnicott expressed a somewhat similar idea within the domestic British context when he declared that 'there is no such thing as a baby' (1952: 99), emphasising that *infants* only exist as part of an environment-individual context. Vygotsky, however, went further in arguing that individuals of all ages are thus embedded and that the mind is itself given shape though ongoing social (interpersonal or 'intermental') interactions which are then appropriated or internalised by the developing child or young person to form part of their own ('intramental') mental architecture, their own ways of thinking, feeling, and problem-solving. Mind, from this perspective, thus partly reflects and recapitulates the individual's culture and social experience, with the developing mastery of tools being a key way in which such development of mind is fostered. Physical tools, for example a penknife, a watch, a doll, or a computer, require the development of skills in their use and in the exploitation of their function, with different tools having differing cultural and historical resonances. Similarly, psychological tools (with *language* being the most significant of these) have similar profound cultural heritages and are used to transform *elementary* into *higher* mental functions. A developing capacity to use language, Vygotsky argued, frees the child from being dependently reactive to the environment, allowing intramental representation of absent objects (e.g. from history, future worlds, or the imagination). Thinking itself is thus transformed with the child's accession to language (see also Daniels et al., 2007; Miller, 2002; Smidt, 2008).

Working with children, young people and families

Activity

Reflect back on the first activity. Indentify key physical tools that you were taught to use and/or were given. What significance did this object have for you, your family, and the wider society? How did you learn about the object and master its use? What figures in your family or wider community assisted you in this process? In what ways has this object contributed to your development and identity? Share the history of the item you have chosen with those in your work group.

The socio-cultural approach offers one way in which lives can be situated within a wider matrix of influences that each contribute to a richer understanding of developmental change. Another approach to such important contextualising is ecological systems theory (Bronfenbrenner, 1979, 2005). Intellectually influenced in his development of this theory by Vygotsky's ideas, Bronfenbrenner depicts people as living within multiple circles of influence: he thus systematises the inter-relations of multiple aspects of development within a dynamic series of domains. These domains constitute a series of systems and sub-systems, organised as a nesting structure, one inside the other (rather like a series of Russian dolls), each exerting an influence on each other and on the individual. Most immediately, an individual actively exists on a day-to-day basis within a series of *microsystems*, such as their own biology, the family, school, childminders, and so on. Each of these microsystems itself incorporates differing subsystems (such as the family, including sibling, marital couple, and extended family subsystems). Beyond the microsystem is the *mesosystem*, which consists of *points of connection* between various microsystems within each of which the child or young person exists (e.g. the family and the school). Beyond this is the *exosystem*, which incorporates linked settings, one or more of which does not typically include the child or young person in question (e.g. a parent's workplace and the family). Surrounding this is the *macrosystem*, or wider politico-cultural context, which itself is constructed out of a matrix of the preceding three systems. This offers a 'blueprint' or structure for cultural reproduction, shaping lower level events. Finally, *time* as a central dimension within development is represented by the *chronosystem*, which highlights the specific historical factors that impact on an individual's life course.

This approach to contextualising development is useful in highlighting both proximal and more remote factors that contribute to shaping the trajectory of an individual's life or that of a larger group. While Bronfenbrenner emphasises sociological influences in his model, the general conceptual framework can be readily extended to incorporate biological and psychological factors. These could, for example, be represented as sub-systems nesting within the microsystem and would thus yield a bio-psychosocial developmental context.

Alongside such contextualising efforts coexists the related need for critique, deconstruction and reflective practice. Feminist approaches (e.g. Gilligan, 1982) offer a vital perspective in this context and provide a useful antidote to the sometimes essentialising binary discourses of traditional psychology, which at times concentrated on white male experience as though that was representative of the norm. Similarly, issues of ethnicity and diversity within developmental studies have been increasingly highlighted, though much work remains to be done in these areas (see also Baraitser, 2009; Burman, 2008; Jagger, 2008; Miller, 2002).

Observing development

Gathering information on children and young people's development takes many forms and students should familiarise themselves with the principal modalities (see Parke and Gauvin, 2009; Slater and Bremner, 2003; Sugarman, 2001). Common to all methods will be some element of observation. Systematic observation of infants and young children has a long history (Dixon and Lerner, 1992). In popular culture Wordsworth's observations would lead him to declare that 'The child is the father of the man' (Wordsworth, 1802; Kavka, 1984), while more scientifically Darwin's (1877) 'Biographical sketch of an infant' influenced many and is a notable early example of an observational study.

Let us consider an observation classic, the case of one 18-month-old boy as reported in the literature:

> This good little boy, however, had an occasional disturbing habit of taking any small objects he could get hold of and throwing them away from him into a corner, under the bed, and so on, so that hunting for his toys and picking them up was often quite a business. As he did this he gave vent to a loud, long-drawn-out 'o-o-o-o,' accompanied by an expression of interest and satisfaction. (Freud, 1920/1955: 14–15)

What is going on here? Is there a pattern or purpose within this infant's behaviour? If so, what does this relate to? Does it suggest anything about this infant's particular developmental struggles and what role does the environment play in these?

This particular case was actually observed by Freud and discussed in his *Beyond the Pleasure Principle* (1920/1955). Freud hypothesised that infant behaviour (e.g. play and vocalisations) can be seen as a mental developmental process spurred on by separation and loss. Considering this particular infant, who was in fact Freud's grandson, he wrote that:

> I eventually realized that it was a game and that the only use he made of any of his toys was to play 'gone' with them. One day I made an observation which confirmed my view. The child had a wooden reel with a piece of string tied around it. It never occurred to him to pull it along the floor behind him, for instance, and play at its being a carriage. What he did was to hold the reel by the string and very skilfully throw it over the edge of his curtained cot, so that it disappeared into it, at the same time uttering his expressive 'o-o-o-o.' He then pulled the reel again

Working with children, young people and families

by the string and hailed its reappearance with a joyful 'da' [there]. This, then, was the complete game: disappearance and return. As a rule one only witnessed its first act, which was repeated untiringly as a game in itself, though there is no doubt that the greater pleasure was attached to the second act. The interpretation of the game then became obvious. It was related to the child's great cultural achievement – the instinctual renunciation (that is, the renunciation of instinctual satisfaction) which he had made in allowing his mother to go away without protesting. (Freud, 1920/1955: 14–15)

Activity

What do you think of Freud's hypothesis, his interpretation of the sequence of observed behaviour and the strength of his evidence? Discuss the observation with your group and identify any methodological weaknesses. How might these be addressed?

Freud's observation of the 'fort-da' game and his willingness to explore its potential meaning, particularly in the light of patterns of continuity and discontinuity, offers a useful approach to this framing behaviour. His argument is that his grandson's play and accompanying vocalisations constituted a form of symbolic activity. This was not only related to language development (as itself a means of representing that which is not present), but also was a form of psychological mastery of loss and the recreation in play of a particularly valued and missed relationship, namely that with his mother whose everyday comings and goings inevitably gave rise to powerful feelings. Similar developmental processes may be discerned in other infant and childhood activities, with perhaps the 'peek-a-boo' game being one of the most familiar examples. Here, the game occupies a more explicitly social context. The manipulation of absence and presence, as well as the delight in the reappearance phase, of what is a stylised activity involving reciprocal roles, repeats the essentials of Freud's 'fort-da' game. Hide-and-seek might be regarded as a variant of the same exploratory dynamic for older children.

Unsurprisingly, modern observational methods have developed considerably since 1920 and are varied and often sophisticated. Systematic observation, recording, and theoretical interpretation of the results are central. In considering both pre-existing case material and in attempting to conduct your own observations, students should give careful consideration to the methods used, including their theoretical alignment with the specific orientation of the piece of work.

Communication and symbolisation

Most developmental texts discuss language development, quite correctly, at length. It is a central theme, linking diverse areas of development together.

Situating child development

Building on the earlier discussion of the socio-cultural approach, I shall here simply underline the psychosocial matrix of language development, drawing theoretically also on structuralism and psychoanalytic ideas (Lacan, 2007), in order to situate development within a broader context.

Communication is a base that permits one person to relate to another (Newson, 1982), a base on which the human infant can acquire the language and modes of thought of their speech community (Vygotsky, 1978). As an active process, the infant over time absorbs the surrounding language through a continuing process of dynamic interaction, of reciprocity and progression, between the infant and her interlocutors. The pre-existing speech community and culture here represent the symbolic order (Lacan, 2007), through which meaning is conveyed using not only spoken and written language, but also other forms of sign systems, gesture, mime, and non-verbal means of communication. The child enters into the symbolic order at various points in time. Prior to birth and indeed prior to conception, the child may be thought about, discussed and debated, often in emotionally charged terms. This 'possible child' is here constituted of the desires, wishes, fears and fantasies of an indeterminate number of people, in one or more speech communities, and who are individually involved in possibly numerous discourses. These people will include not only the potential biological parents, a particular woman and man, but also their friends, relatives, colleagues, and health and social care staff, among others. Such discourses are further complicated with the advent of assisted reproductive technologies (e.g. IVF, egg or embryo donation, surrogacy, and donor insemination). Nevertheless, within such discourses a gap is created into which the actual child will enter as it (sexual and gender identity having yet to be instantiated) assumes a role within the world. Where the child thus begins and ends is in this context a somewhat arbitrary issue.

Meaning and its ownership within such contexts are essentially distributed and paternity rights are closely related to the response of the audience or particular speech community via the symbolic order. The construction of discourse and its meaning can thus be regarded as a shared responsibility, emerging out of reciprocal relations. Part of the infant's task is to appropriate language from the discourses and various communicative modes that exist as a surrounding sea of shared social meanings. This is development, though the western-centric individualist bias should be noted. How might language development, which as Vygotsky (1978) emphasised goes hand-in-hand with acculturation, be manifest in other cultures, say in China or India, where there is less emphasis on the monadic individual and more on the family or group identity (Miller, 2002)?

Attachment theory

This has become perhaps the dominant theoretical framework for considering an individual's development of a sense of self, emotional security, esteem, and the foundations for these in interpersonal relationships. Beginning with the pioneering

Working with children, young people and families

work of John Bowlby (1951, 1969, 1973, 1980, 1988; Holmes, 1993), who linked key ideas from psychoanalysis and ethnology, as well as Darwinian evolutionary theory, in constructing this model, attachment theory has become a dominant model within many child and social care settings.

Essentially, the theory is a scientific way of considering the importance of love, or what Bowlby would refer to as 'affectional bonds', in human development. Love relations promote the seeking of proximity; you want to be close to the person you love. From an evolutionary perspective, being close to another held survival value. Concentrating initially on early development (up to about age 3), Bowlby suggested that infant 'attachment behaviour', such as crying or smiling, encouraged care-giving behaviour by key adults, stereotypically the mother. A limited hierarchy of such attachment figures – people with whom the infant felt safe, secure, confident, and loved – could also contribute to their care, on a temporary or adjunctive basis. Through proximity, regularity, confidence and love, the infant could begin to develop internal working models of such interactions (analogous to Vygotsky and Piaget's varying emphases on processes of internalisation). These models contributed to the infant's developing capacity for prediction of others responsiveness (self-confidence) and to their own analogous capacity to self-regulate their emotional states and behaviour. Burgeoning research using the attachment paradigm has modified and extended its utility to cover, for instance, relationships throughout the life cycle, cross-cultural applications and social policy implications, while at the same time offering robust critiques of the theory (see also Burman, 2008; Parke and Gauvin, 2009; Miller, 2002; Rutter, 2008).

Conclusions

Conceptualising development is challenging. For students, some difficulties emanate from the 'usual suspects': definitions, competing explanatory models, fragmentation of the topic, and a vast literature. Further problems come from the at times non-linear and paradoxical nature of developmental change within which losses are as central an experience as are gains. Indeed, the very activity of studying the subject is itself a form of developmental activity, which almost unavoidably breeds a degree of resistance. As a student, one is inevitably reflecting on one's own life course and that of others close to us. Such challenges however also enrich the topic, imbuing it with *personal* significance as well as future *utility* as an aid to on-going relational development at work and in the home.

Contextualising development within an overarching cultural, historical and socio-political matrix allows richer complex perspectives to emerge. Combinations of inter and intra-personal influences contribute to shaping development in multiple ways, which – in combination with the open nature of the system – gives the discipline a real vitality.

It is important to emphasise the need for a critical approach to the subject, particularly given its applied nature within child, educational, health and social care, and other human settings. Normative developmental benchmarks can be helpful at times, though their utility is dependent on students and practitioners being able to not lose sight of the individual or the wider context. Development in this sense is not a checklist. Rather, it is a dynamic process involving – among many other things – love and the search for meaning. Students are encouraged to follow up these ideas through the recommended reading list below.

Further reading

Burman, E. (2008) *Deconstructing Developmental Psychology*. Hove: Routledge.
Miller, P. H. (2002) *Theories of Developmental Psychology*. New York: Worth.
Parke, R. D. and Gauvin, M. (2009) *Child Psychology: A Contemporary Viewpoint*. Boston: McGraw Hill.
Schaffer, H. R. (2006) *Key Concepts in Developmental Psychology*. London: Sage.
Slater, A. and Bremner, G. (eds) (2003) *An Introduction to Developmental Psychology*. Oxford: Blackwell.

Appendix

Case study: Jane D

Jane was aged 7 when her parents divorced. They had been married for 10 years. Her mother was white British, worked in a canteen, and had mild learning difficulties, while her father was a Turkish immigrant who worked in a moderately paid technical role. When they had initially met they had formed a caring relationship, seldom argued, and any problems that arose were attributed as coming from outside sources. As time went on, some disillusionment and frustration crept into the relationship, though they both avoided talking about this as neither wanted to cause distress or upset.

Following Jane's birth, Mrs D took Jane to sleep in the parents' bed and Mr D went to sleep in the spare room, a situation that soon became the norm. The divide between the parents increased from this point onwards such that Mrs D and Jane returned to live with her family and Mrs D subsequently sought a divorce. Maintaining she and Jane were afraid of Mr D, alleging that he was now stalking them and treating Jane cruelly, Mrs D opposed access by Mr D to Jane. A court granted an order for access at a Contact Centre and directed that an independent social work report be prepared.

An assessment suggested that Jane was a bright, lively and neatly turned out girl. Her most recent school report suggested her general educational and social development was satisfactory, though it did note she lacked self-confidence in working independently. The family doctor noted Jane had been brought to the surgery nine

---

Working with children, young people and families

times over the previous year with sore throats or colds. On one such visit Jane's mother claimed Mr D had stamped on Jane's hand in an attempt to get her to say where she was then living, although no injury was evident to the GP.

At the Contact Centre, Jane greeted her father warmly and they engaged together in both quiet table-top activities and more strenuous play. Jane clearly enjoyed such contact and appeared appreciative of the efforts her father had gone to in bringing some toys and food. Jane appeared to find being observed by a previously unknown independent social worker disconcerting and at times responded by hiding her face in her father's clothes and crawling under furniture while her sometimes strenuous play perhaps also offered her some sense of security. By the end of the two hours contact her wariness and anxiety had diminished somewhat. Separating from Mr D and returning to her mother was difficult for Jane. She sought to extend the contact and then, Centre staff having intervened to escort Jane back to her mother, she ran back to her father. It took some 20 minutes before the separation was accomplished. Both parents, and particularly Mrs D, seemed to find it difficult to establish effective boundaries with Jane in this situation.

One week later Jane was observed on two consecutive days with her mother in her home by the same social worker. Jane and her mother worked together baking a tray of jam tarts, Jane taking the lead and accepting direction from Mrs D. Jane showed marked anxiety again about seeing the social worker on the first day. Asked by her to draw a picture of her family, Jane began by drawing herself, then her maternal grandparents and finally two small figures representing her mother and father. She also suggested that her father should not be included in the picture as he 'doesn't live with us'. Jane said she felt closest to her maternal grandmother, as she was 'kind' and a 'nurse'. She said the same about her mother, whom she said she felt next closest to. When asked about her father, Jane ran away to Mrs D. Mrs D seemed unable to encourage her to speak further to the social worker, particularly when Jane would cry and protest. Jane appeared very concerned about the observer speaking not only with her, but also with her mother. She thus told her mother not to say anything and attempted to push the social worker out of the room. Mrs D feebly reproved Jane, though without any visible effect. On the second day Jane was protesting loudly and crying that she did not want to see the social worker even prior to her arrival home, this continuing once inside the house. She ran into her own bedroom and cried and shouted there in continuing protest for about 20 minutes, at the end of which time she fell asleep.

Activity

Imagine you had been asked to independently comment on Jane's development. Using the information available here what hypotheses might you make about her cognitive, personality, social and emotional development? What other types of

(Cont'd)

Situating child development

evidence would you want to obtain to clarify your ideas further? How might you describe Jane's attachment status with her mother and also with her father? Discuss alternative theoretical formulations of this case. Consider the social: micro-, meso- and macro-systems within which Jane exists. What impact do these have on Jane and does Jane have on them? What predictions might you make about Jane's future development? What recommendations would you make regarding Jane's future custody, care and other possible professional involvement? Present your conclusions to your group or class, who might adopt the roles within a multi-disciplinary team meeting. Be prepared to defend your decisions.

10

Research with children, young people and families

Claire Smith

It is 'an old saying that a child, a fool and a drunken man will ever show ... the truth'. [1537 in Letters & Papers of Reign of Henry VIII (1929) Addenda I. i. 437]

(Speake, 2004)

The aims of this chapter are to:

- Consider the notion of child-centred research
- Examine the issues surrounding ethics in child-centred research
- Explore some of the methodological issues to be considered when conducting research with children, young people and families.

Never a week passes by these days without some news report about latest research findings or new research discoveries highlighting a new health, social, scientific or economic revelation. Quite often, the term 'research' conjures up images of people in white lab coats involved in scientific experiments. Research, whilst being scientific, does not necessarily involve laboratory work. So then, what exactly is research? And in particular what is social research? According to the *Concise Oxford Dictionary* (Thompson, 1995: 1169) research is 'an endeavour to discover new or collate old facts etc, by the scientific study of a subject or by a course of critical investigation'. Social research, with which this chapter will mainly be concerned, is the scientific study, measurement or forecasting of social and economic factors or attitudes.

Historically social research was concerned with generating data from adults. Research about children's perspectives was derived from those living or working with children, for example gathering the parents'/carers' or teachers' perspectives on children, as children were seen as unreliable informants. More recently, however, with the growth of theories around the sociology of childhood, and with particular reference to the late 1980s and the United Nations Convention on the Rights of the Child (UNCRC; see Chapter 6), children and young people are being viewed as individuals in their own right, as opposed to possessions of their parents or carers. More recently, the Every Child Matters (ECM) Agenda (DfES, 2003b) specifies five outcomes for children and young people, one of which is to 'make a positive contribution' (DfES, 2003b: 14), therefore acknowledging the question, who better to give perspectives on children's lives other than the children and young people themselves?

Despite this, debate continues around the age that a child is competent to fully understand the concept of participating in a research project, and therefore give informed consent (which will be discussed in greater depth under the subsection on ethics). Theories around child development and developmental psychology focus on the cognitive ability of the child and developmental levels, building on the work of Piaget (1896–1980). Piaget identified several stages in a child's life when they would begin to develop new skills. He categorised these stages by age groups.

The American Academy of Pediatrics Committee on Drugs (Cuskelly, 2005), for example, notes that children aged 7 years or younger, or who have a cognitive ability of 7 or younger are not competent enough to assent to participate in research. MacNaughton and Smith (2005), following their research with pre-school age children however, argue that 4-year-old children are capable of assenting or withdrawing participation from a research project. Margaret Donaldson criticised the work established by Piaget (Fraser, 2004: 23). She proved that younger children were cogent thinkers, as MacNaughton and Smith (2005) in the aforementioned research also found. The sociology of childhood theory, therefore counter-argues the notion of children reaching a particular age before being able to participate in research. Whether or not a child feels able to participate in research is dependent upon their self confidence and experience coupled with appropriate research tools being employed. Therefore, in relation to the work carried out by Donaldson, Woodhead and Faulkner (2000: 24) state that she 'helped developmental psychologists recognise that children's true competencies are revealed only in situations which make sense to them'.

Advocates of the sociology of childhood theory argue that children should be seen as competent, capable and autonomous in deciding whether to participate in the research (Danby and Farrell, 2005). In other words, by virtue of being a child and being active participants in the social world they are competent in participating in research about their social worlds, if they feel confident to do so, regardless of age.

This chapter will explore some of the factors that need to be considered prior to conducting any research involving children. It will examine the ethical considerations, including some of the debates around gaining informed consent. It will also focus on methodological issues that researchers face, with particular reference to research carried out by Newman University College between 2005 and 2007, and funded by the Birmingham and Black Country Strategic Health Authority on black and minority ethnic children as advocates of their own healthcare (Simon, 2007).

Working with children, young people and families

Child-centred research

Further to the escalating acceptance that children and young people have rights and the growing acknowledgement that children and young people can be participants in research exploring their own social worlds, increasingly we hear the term 'child-centred research'. But what is meant by this term? Research, historically, has generally been a process which has been *done* to people. You may choose to complete a questionnaire, telephone interview or in-depth interview, and possibly you may never hear from the researcher again after they have acquired the information or data that they need for their research project. However, there is a move to incorporate participants more into the research process by involving them in the design of research or regularly feeding back on progress, or asking the participant to verify details which they gave during an interview. Where the participants are children there is a greater move to try to involve them more throughout the whole process, from research design to dissemination.

Child-centred research refers to the level of involvement of children in any research process. Christensen and James (2003: 3) identify that children and young people should be viewed more as subjects of research rather than objects. In addition, the level of authority and power of the adult in the research also has an impact on the level of child-centredness of a research project. Research is a principle from an adultist society in which adults have power/authority over children and young people. The less power the researcher has over the child participants and the more involved the children and young people are in the design and organisation of the research project, the more child-centred the research. Fraser (2004: 23) simplifies this notion slightly by suggesting that '"child-centred" could mean that research attempts to negotiate an understanding of research aims in a situation and in terms that "make sense" to the children and young people concerned'.

Roger Hart (cited by Nieuwenhuys, 2004) compared children and young people's participation with the rungs on a ladder, with those children and young people with least 'power' or participation being situated on the bottom rung (see Chapter 6 for an alternative context in which Hart's ladder can be applied). Alderson describes the first three rungs, listed by Hart as Manipulation, Decoration and Tokenism, as 'the pretence of shared work' (Alderson, 2000, cited by Robinson and Kellet, 2004: 86). This might be where children and young people are asked for their opinion in order to tick a box that children had been consulted on a particular matter but they were not involved in any other way.

Of the eight rungs on Hart's ladder, Nieuwenhuys (2004: 217) notes that only rungs four to seven are concerned with children's and young people's actual participation. The top rung ('Youth-initiated, shared decisions with adults'), according to Nieuwenhuys, is the only level where children and young people's voices are actually included and acted upon in government decision making and this is because the children and young people themselves initiate the discussion. This, therefore, rarely occurs as it is more difficult for children and young people to

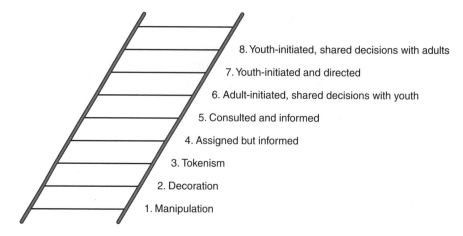

Figure 10.1   Hart's ladder of participation (adopted from, Hart, 1992)

make happen on their own. Hart (1992: 14) blames this on the fact there is an 'absence of caring adults attuned to the particular interests of young people'. In answer to the problem, however, Nieuwenhuys (2004: 218) reasons that 'it requires caring adults who are attuned to the interests of children and have themselves the means to help them voice their needs and desires'.

Ethics and children

Research ethics processes were established following the Second World War and the revelation worldwide of inhumane Nazi wartime experiments that had been carried out on prisoners in concentration camps. The Nuremberg Military Tribunal in 1949 drew up ethical, as well as legal and moral requirements (The Nuremberg Code) to be considered, enabling participants to volunteer (or withdraw) from research 'without force, deceit or coercion' (Farrell, 2005: 1). The Nuremberg Code stated, however, that children and those with mental illness do not have the ability to consent to participate in research (Alderson, 2004; Annas and Grodin, 1992). In 1954 the World Medical Association published its code of ethics which was then adopted in 1964 as the 'Declaration of Helsinki' (Farrell, 2005). This provided guidance to those conducting medical research that involved human participants.

The emphasis on research ethics has grown since this time, and is now embedded in social science research. The term ethics refers to one's moral principles and rules of human conduct. In relation to social research, ethical issues may arise from the issue needing to be investigated, the methods required to investigate said issue and the rights of the participants to be protected from physical or psychological harm.

Many of the social science research ethics committees, however, were born out of medical ethics guidelines and principles which in some respects do not fit the needs of social research, as they relate to medical testing and experiments. With the increase in child participants, social research exploring children and childhood is more open to ethical critique than other social research, to ensure that no harm or distress is caused to any child involved. But do current ethical guidelines, adapted from medical ethics procedures, adequately fit this purpose? In a society opening up to globalisation, and being more aware of safeguarding children and protecting children from harm, research ethics is being subjected to stricter guidelines and accountability to ensure that those conducting the research and the research process itself pose no risk to children and young people, either physically or to their mental and psychological well-being. Completing a research ethics procedure further protects the sample group from research-overload and being inundated with invitations to participate in research. It also protects the researcher from criticism or legal action being taken against them (Alderson, 2005). However, having had to complete the health service ethical process for the research cited earlier (Simon, 2007) in order to gain permission to interview black and minority ethnic young people in hospital, for what was essentially a social sciences subject area (citizenship and advocacy), we can categorically state that the ethics form was irrelevant in part to our needs or the requirements of the health service in this case as the research was not medically based. There is a need for a review of ethics procedures in the social sciences to make them more relevant socially rather than just medically.

Activity

What do you think are the main issues that you would need to consider in order to ensure that research with children, young people and families is ethical?

In relation to involving more children and young people in research, ethics procedures need to be more child centred. Skelton (2008: 23) acknowledges that ethics guidelines within non-medical institutions (e.g higher education institutions and research councils) do not have a child focus and have not been developed from the social sciences framework. She (Skelton, 2008: 23) goes further to highlight that 'ethical research practice can actually *close down* participation for children and young people and also fails to accord them the same rights as adults in terms of what consent means'. This indicates that institutional ethical guidelines can deny children's and young people's competence and ability to make decisions about their own lives.

Two children's charities (the National Children's Bureau (NCB) and Barnardos) have, however, included children and young people very clearly within their research and ethics guidelines. The guidelines from the NCB (which, at the time of writing in Autumn 2008, the writer was informed, were under revision by the

Research

research department) state 'this demonstrates, above all, that children are the primary focus of NCB's interest, rather than adults as parents, policy-makers or service providers' (NCB, 2003: 1). The values and principles section notes a commitment to listen to and include the views of children and young people. The guidelines also highlight a need to carefully consider requirements of very young children, and those with communication or learning difficulties when obtaining informed consent to participate in research. The Barnardo's ethical practice guidelines (Scott and Hayden, 2005) include two separate sections, firstly on conducting 'research involving children and young people' (Scott and Hayden, 2005: 6), and secondly on research with 'at risk and particularly vulnerable children and young people' (Scott and Hayden, 2005: 7), thus highlighting the centrality of the child, regardless of age or ability, when conducting research ethically.

Regardless of the aforementioned difficulties or issues, any research with children and young people will be subject to ethical clearance. This can take anything from a few weeks to a few months to be granted depending on the Research Ethics Committee to which the researcher needs to apply (and also depending on whether or not clearance is granted upon first submission or if it needs to be amended and re-submitted). This needs to be considered carefully when drawing up a timeframe for any piece of research.

Activity

Either on your own or in small groups, imagine that you are on an ethics committee and you have been charged with the responsibility of re-writing the ethics protocol to make it more child centred.

- What issues would you include to make research processes child friendly?
- What do you think children and young people would want to see in your protocol and why?

If possible, try to ask some children and young people what they might want included in this protocol.

Informed consent

Before commencing any qualitative research with adults or children, the researcher must obtain written informed consent. Informed consent is where the participant understands what the research is exploring and what is required of the participant to be involved in that research. On this understanding the participant can make an informed decision on whether or not s/he would like to participate in the research, and they should understand that they can withdraw at any stage throughout the research process.

Working with children, young people and families

For children 18 years or under consent must be sought from the parent/guardian first, before approaching the child (Skelton, 2008). So the debate here is the question who *actually* consents to participate in the research? Who should consent? Given the growth in awareness around children's rights, and the right of the child to make a positive contribution, should it not therefore be the child's or young person's right to consent regardless of their parent's decision? This has become a contentious issue because here there is an argument over children's right to be heard versus parental/adult control. Children over the age of 16 are able to make their own decisions regarding any medical treatment they may need, yet to participate in research, they still need consent from a parent or carer. Skelton (2008: 27) comments that 'within ethical research practices, the notion of children as competent actors is watered down somewhat when it comes to the rules around consent'. In spite of the efforts to make research relating to children and childhood more child centred, research practices are still situated in an adultist perspective.

Many argue (e.g., Connors and Stalker, 2003; Danby and Farrell, 2005) that children and young people do not consent to participate in research but rather they *assent* following parental consent. This raises questions around whether or not children and young people actually agree to participate because their parents/carers have said that they will, or whether they agree because they want to participate and have their opinions heard. Danby and Farrell state that:

> the activity of children signing consent forms typically has not been part of the research agenda with young children. Conventionally, once parents have given their permission, children are then invited to engage in the research process without additional discussions about their consent and involvement. (2005: 53)

Prior to commencing our research exploring BME young people as advocates of their own healthcare, leaflets were designed to be distributed to the young people with a separate one for their parents. The leaflets were colourful to attract attention. They outlined who was undertaking the research and for what purpose, the requirement of the young person wishing to participate, what the research would be used for, and a consent form to be signed and returned to the researcher. It was deemed that by giving the young people their own leaflet and their own consent form to return gave them some ownership over the decision to participate. Danby and Farrell (2005) suggested that asking children and young people for informed consent, made them feel like they had a choice, it gave them responsibility and, furthermore, made them more interested in what they were doing. The language on the leaflet was kept simple as some of our target group may not have had English as a first language. A draft leaflet was reviewed by the youth steering group, which was established to design the project with the researcher, to ensure that the language used was clear and that the leaflet would appeal to our target age group.

During this research, often the researcher would find that the young person was interested in participating in the research, but the parent would decline consent. In these cases the researcher and young person had to (by law) respect the final word of the parent and could not go ahead with the interview. Clearly this goes against the principles behind the UNCRC (which does not request parental permission before a child has freedom of expression) (Skelton, 2008). Possible reasons for this refusal by the parent during our research could have been due to language barriers. Within the BME groups, sometimes the children speak English but the parents may not. The child in some cases would have to interpret for the parent, the parent may therefore have been reluctant if the child had not interpreted all of the information, or if the parent could not communicate directly with the researcher him/herself. When language was not an issue, refusal to participate may have been because the parent was worried that participation in the research might jeopardise their child's access to medical treatment.

One argument that has been raised is that research is dominated by an adultist society. Therefore, in addition to adult researchers controlling the research process, parents and carers can control children's rights as to whether or not to participate in research. Whilst it is argued (Cloke, cited by Hill, 2006) that children and young people, particularly those from vulnerable groups, are not used to being asked for their opinions on matters, children and young people need to be empowered in today's society. In the current context, as Hill (2006: 63) highlights, 'adults are ascribed authority over children, who often find it difficult to dissent, disagree or say things which they fear may be unacceptable'. Children and young people will want to please the adult and may therefore give the answers which they feel the researcher or their parent/carer may want to hear.

Despite these issues, how can we make it easier for children and young people to have control over their research participation? It is important to emphasise to the child or young person that they can withdraw at any time. If the research takes place over several phases, remember to ask the child or young person at each meeting if they consent/assent to continuing with the research. Research (Hughes and Grieve, as cited by Dockrell et al., 2000; Waterman et al., as cited by Greene and Hill, 2005) has highlighted that very young children will try to give a response to nonsensical questions because they feel they have to give an answer and to please the adult researcher – again we see the adult power situation. It is imperative that the child or young person feels that they are allowed to respond with 'I don't know', and the researcher needs to make this clear from the outset of the research.

Methodological considerations

Finding the most suitable and appropriate method to use with children and young people is no mean feat. There is no simple formula into which you can type a child's age and ability and the method is revealed. As Greene and Hill (2005: 8) note 'the simple equation of age with a particular level of ability or knowledge or set of attitudes should be avoided. It is easy for adults to underestimate children's abilities and to patronize them'.

There are, therefore, several methodological factors to consider when conducting research with children and young people. Besides the usual questions to think about (e.g. How will I find a representative sample? Which methodology will generate the most useful and appropriate data to answer the question within the given cost and time constraints?), you also need to consider issues relating to the age and ability of the child or young person, language and communication issues (e.g. language ability – is English an additional language, do they have special needs which need to be taken into account when generating data), when and where you are going to obtain the data (e.g. in a school just after lunchtime may not be the most appropriate time, or in the room used for sick children, or children who may have been excluded for poor behaviour, or in the family home with other family members passing by where children may be overheard or easily distracted). You also need to consider how you record your data. For example, some young people may not wish to be video recorded and may prefer voice recording, while some younger children may deliberately 'act-up' if a video camera is in an obviously focal position, and others may turn very shy, when conducting observations.

Activity

Imagine that you are conducting some research with pre-school children, but few of the children seem willing to participate. Consider:

- What could be the issues behind this lack of participation?
- What might you do to overcome this problem?

Involving children and young people in the design phases of the research can give them more ownership of the research, and puts them in control, making the research less adult-centric. During the research we carried out on BME young people as advocates of their own healthcare, the researcher established a youth steering group to drive forward the research. The steering group consisted of BME young people in Year 10 in a local secondary school. They met regularly with the researcher in their school – a setting familiar to them where they felt in control. Over several weeks of discussions and meetings, the youth steering group designed the topic guide that the researcher used when visiting BME young people in hospital to interview them. This ensured that the language used was understandable to young people and the issues addressed were seen to be relevant by young BME people themselves. The youth steering group contributed to the dissemination event and also joined the adult steering group. Upon completion of the research, the members of the youth steering group were given a certificate which could go in their Record of Achievement at school and evidenced the

Research

commitment and effort they had shown in driving forward what could so easily have been an adult-led research project.

Quantitative research

Quantitative research, as its name suggests, is data which can be quantified and subjected to rigorous statistical analysis. It is seen to be more scientifically robust; as Denscombe (2003: 236) notes 'because it uses numbers and can present findings in the form of graphs and tables, it conveys a sense of solid, objective research'. Quantitative research, therefore, often takes the form of surveys and questionnaires, carried out by telephone, by post, face-to-face (e.g., on the street, usually used for market research purposes) and nowadays, online.

Children and young people are largely excluded from quantitative surveys, which are often directed at adults. Where children's and young people's views are required in quantitative surveys, this data is often generated by those adults with responsibility for children and young people. As Scott (2000: 98) states, 'in surveys of the general population, children have been usually regarded as out of scope and samples are usually drawn from the adult population, with a minimum age of 16 or 18'.

When conducting surveys with children and young people, care must be taken over several aspects. Firstly, it would be naïve of a researcher to hand children, especially very young children, a questionnaire and expect them to complete it on their own. Children and young people may not comprehend the questions and therefore may tick any response (or may lose focus and concentration and not complete anything if it does not make sense to them). Some may have poor literacy skills making them feel inadequate and excluded from participating at all. Thus the researcher would only generate data from the more able children and young people, which would not be representative of the whole group.

Online surveys conducted with children and young people present a further and yet different set of complications. In addition to the aforementioned reasons, it may be more problematic conducting online research surveys with children and young people due to safety software and parental blocks which may be installed on computers to protect children from harmful images and material, thus blocking 'spam' or access from unfamiliar websites and email addresses.

In relation to the point noted previously that children will respond to a question even if they do not understand it or if it is nonsense, Waterman et al. (cited by Greene and Hill, 2005: 9) note that caution needs to be taken when posing closed questions with young children, and that it is better to use open questions in order to probe answers more fully to ensure responses are reliable. Scott (2000) discusses using children and young people in quantitative surveys, but her findings tend to lean more towards being able to involve older children in quantitative surveys as opposed to younger children. That is not to say that younger children are incapable of participating in quantitative surveys, but the researcher needs to take extra measures to ensure that the questions elicit reliable data.

Measures could include questioning the children face-to-face with an adult noting down responses, or ensuring that the questions are very clear and unambiguous. Using pictures where possible may also assist the child in understanding and responding to a question.

Qualitative research

Qualitative research is less concerned with generating numbers and focuses more on generating in-depth data which explores the attitudes, beliefs and experiences of individuals. Most research conducted with children and young people is predominantly qualitative, generated through interviews, focus groups, observations and diaries, for example.

Whereas literacy skills may have been an obstacle in quantitative methods, qualitative methods can overcome these issues because the researcher is not relying on the child or young person being able to read questions for themselves. Due to the researcher interaction with children and young people in using these methods, any misconceptions by the child or young person can be explained prior to or during the research. Kelly (2007: 22) states 'the flexible nature of qualitative research means that researchers are not bound to standardized, rigid methods. This allows room for creative and responsive methodological approaches for consulting children'. In the case of observations, the researcher is simply relying on the target sample group being themselves within a given scenario, thus literacy issues or misconceptions of what may be required are not factors complicating the research.

It is good practice, where possible, to become acquainted with the children and young people whom you wish to participate in your research, although this is not always appropriate or feasible, perhaps due to time constraints or location. During our research with BME young people, the researcher did not have time to get to know the potential participant as in some cases they were admitted to and discharged from hospital within a very short space of time. The advantages of getting to know participants are that they may get to know you as a researcher and therefore feel that they can be more open and honest in their responses, thus increasing the depth of the data. This is more crucial when discussing subjects of a sensitive nature. Cree et al. (2002: 52) during their study on children and young people with a parent/carer with HIV noted that spending time with a child or young person participant before an interview 'serves as a good "ice-breaker"'. In addition they noted that the young people who participated in their research stated that they appreciated adults, moreover professionals, getting to know them as individuals. Mayall (2001: 123), on writing about her research of child healthcare which was carried out in a primary school, stated that 'in the first days, part of my aim was to become a familiar figure, for whom the children did not behave in special ways during their classwork and with whom children might talk confidently'. She found that this did not take as long as expected as many children are used to having other adults assisting the teacher in classroom activities.

Research

Obviously, any researcher wishing to undertake research with children and young people will need Criminal Records Bureau (CRB) clearance. As with the ethical clearance, timescales for applying to the CRB must be factored into any plan drawn up for the research project as sometimes it can take a few weeks to be processed and for the CRB certificate to be posted.

Triangulation, reliability and validity

These are terms which every researcher needs to be aware of and ensure throughout any research project. Whilst it is possible to conduct research using only one method, it is advisable to use several methods to avoid bias and increase the validity of your research findings. Whilst the term triangulation may be interpreted as meaning three methods, this is not a strict rule of thumb, and simply refers to the use of two or more methods. This can also mean mixing quantitative and qualitiative methods, which is termed as the 'multi-method approach' (Denscombe, 2003: 133; Ritchie, 2003: 37). Ritchie (2003: 43) points out that 'Triangulation involves the use of different methods and sources to check the integrity of, or extend, inferences drawn from the data'. Each method can explore the research aim using its own strengths or qualities and the data generated from those methods can not only be compared and contrasted to increase the quality and depth of the data but will also corroborate the validity of the collated data.

Validity, therefore, does not necessarily mean that what the research found from the sample group can be inferred across a whole population or particular group of people. It means that the data collated by the researcher for that specific sample group is trustworthy in view of all the methods employed for that particular research project; as Cohen et al. (2007: 133) state, validity in its most raw definition 'essentially demonstrates that a particular instrument in fact measures what it purports to measure'. The term can be defined in further detail to specifically discuss wholly quantitative or qualitative methodology (see e.g., Cohen et al., 2007).

Reliability, however, differs slightly in meaning depending on whether quantitative or qualitative research is used. In relation to quantitative data, reliability refers to the 'dependability, consistency and replicability over time, over instruments and over groups of respondents' (Cohen et al., 2007: 146). When the data is reliable, it ensures that if the research were to be replicated on a similar sample group, the research methods would generate almost identical data. With qualitative research, however, the researcher is a key part of the research tools, for example how the questions are explained, or in what order they are asked, or the researcher's relationship with a participant. The issue of reliability therefore must explore whether someone else conducting the same or similar research would deduce similar conclusions (Denscombe, 2003). Lincoln and Guba (cited by Cohen et al., 2007: 148) believe that other words such as credibility, neutrality, trustworthiness or even applicability instead of reliability may be used when referring to qualitative data.

Children and young people's role in the analysis and dissemination

As one might surmise, the analysis of quantitative data, whilst not entirely straightforward, is more subject to rules and guidelines. Although one of the later stages of the whole research process, it is important to identify how the data will be analysed prior to writing the research tools. How the analysis is carried out will inform the researcher as to how to structure their research tools and how to manage or organise the data into a meaningful and manageable format, regardless of the methods used. Statistical analysis packages for analysing quantitative data have been in existence for many years (e.g., SPSS), easing the data manipulation process. There are now some computer-assisted methods available to enable qualitative data to be manipulated and analysed (e.g., Nudist, Atlas/ti or NVivo), thus enabling the researcher to gain a lot more cross tabulations from the data without trawling through piles of papers or tapes, as was previously the case.

It is possible to include children and young people in the analysis stages of the research. As Morrow (2005: 154) states; 'one way to address the power imbalance in interpretation of data is to return to research respondents and ask for their input into the analysis of the data'. It can, however, be quite a challenging task involving children and young people in analysing either quantitative or qualitative research, but as Jones (2004: 125) highlights, children and young people are often omitted from this stage of the research process, thus losing the child-centredness of the research. Researchers may be put off involving children and young people in this stage because this would require time to teach the required skills to children and young people, and time may not be something that the researcher has if a deadline is impending.

There are, however, other ways to involve children and young people without them taking on the responsibility of the full analysis. Rather than the children and young people conducting the actual data manipulation, they could review the analysis and key findings that have been drawn out of the data, prior to a final report being written. Kelly (2007: 31) suggests that asking the child and young participants in the research to review the initial findings can reduce or avoid adult bias which may occur during the analysis phase, thus losing the child and young person's voice.

The dissemination phase is the stage where, according to Roberts (2004: 239), the listening to children and child-centredness of the research is giving an even bigger push to make those voices heard by those with the power to change and therefore respond. In order to involve children and young people in the dissemination process it is important to maintain contact with them throughout the research project. This may be done by circulating newsletters, for example, to keep participants up to date with how the research is progressing. Kelly (2007) also suggests sending pictorial bookmarks recording a chronology of the research progress, or photographs of the researcher at work (obviously this opens up a range of consent issues and child protection issues if using children and young people as researchers). Maintaining contact with the participants will hopefully maintain their interest in the research findings (Kelly, 2007).

There are several ways that children and young people could be involved in the dissemination process. Jones (2004: 128) suggests that asking children and young people to read through a draft report can highlight terminology or jargon that may be unclear or unnecessary. Children and young people may even be co-authors of a research report, or may co-present at a dissemination event. The youth steering group for our research exploring BME young people as advocates of their own healthcare were present at the dissemination event. Whilst none of them felt that they had the confidence to present at the event (and none of them were coerced into doing so), they were networking with stakeholders and attendees at the dissemination event who were very interested to speak with the young people present. It is important, however, to remember that research findings can be sensationalised in the media who may distort research findings to suit their needs, regardless of who may be offended. It is therefore important to reflect carefully upon how the findings relating to children and young people are portrayed, again another very good reason for involving the young participants in the analysis and dissemination phases. Morrow (2005: 154) states 'researchers must bear the responsibility for how children are represented in reports of research in the media'.

Conclusion

In summary, there is growing acceptance that children and young people are reliable informants, and they should be judged competent to participate in research based on their own experience and levels of self esteem rather than cognitive ability. Truly child-centred research will be a project that is devised by and driven forward by children and young people themselves. This is rarely initiated by the children and young people themselves but needs some encouragement from adults. The children and young people should inform the research design. It has also been proven that it is possible to teach children and young people research techniques so that they can conduct the research, collate the data, carry out analysis and become involved in the dissemination process, whether that is contributing to writing a written report or participating in the dissemination event. This, however, can be time consuming and therefore needs to be factored into the project timescale.

In order to generate the most useful data from a particular group of children and young people, care must be taken to ensure that the most appropriate research methods are employed. Gaining assistance from a relevant group of children and young people can overcome several barriers in relation to this factor. The children and young people themselves are best placed to tell you whether or not the instructions are clear and whether the wording or phrasing will be understood.

Despite this, there are still some research matters which reduce the child-centred element of a research project and impacts on the child's or young

Working with children, young people and families

person's right to have their voices heard; namely the ethics procedure and informed consent. The first hurdle to be overcome is gaining ethical clearance from a relevant research ethics committee, who may reduce the child-centred element if the project is not deemed feasible, or manageable. A more concerning barrier though is the willingness of the 'gatekeeper' (e.g. headteacher or manager of a setting or children's service, parent or carer) to participate. This may be due to other factors, for example Ofsted inspections, current workloads, staff shortages, exam periods, and not the fact that they do not want the research to be conducted, but this still affects the children's and young people's ability to participate and have their voices heard. If the 'gatekeeper' declines participation in the research, the researcher cannot proceed any further with asking a child or young person under the 'gatekeeper's' care to participate. The inverse of this, however, also applies in that the gatekeeper may agree to participation, thus possibly rendering a child or young person powerless to decline from participating. In these instances, the researcher's rapport with the child or young person is essential in order to make the child/young person feel secure enough to say that they do not wish to continue with the research. Where possible it is good practice for a researcher to get to know their participants before the research (especially if the research covers a sensitive subject). This also makes the participants feel more valued.

With the growing acknowledgement both by society and within political legislation of children's and young people's rights, it is important that as researchers we involve children and young people within the research process; from design to dissemination. The hurdles to conducting research with children and young people must be outweighed by the advantages of including children and young people as active participants and making their opinions count.

Further reading

Christensen, P. and James, A. (eds) (2000) *Research with Children: Perspectives and Practices*. London: Routledge Falmer.

Farrell, A. (ed.) *Ethical Research with Children*. Maidenhead: Open University Press.

Fraser, S., Lewis, V., Ding, S., Kellett, M. and Robinson, C. (eds) *Doing Research with Children and Young People*. London: Sage Publications.

Lewis, A. and Lindsay, G. (eds) *Researching Children's Perspectives*. Buckingham: Open University Press.

Research

11

Developing yourself as a practitioner

Gill McGillivray and Helen Davies

The aims of this chapter are to:

- Explore the notion of reflective practice in the context of working with children, young people and families and how practitioners can use a reflective approach to make the most of the work-based learning elements of their course
- Examine trajectories, aspirations and personal narratives that contribute to the construction of identity, as well as what is imposed by policy at national and local levels
- Use case studies to promote analysis, reflection and critique to support the reader to be strategic in further choices in their professional development.

The two case studies of Peter and Saira have been placed at the end of the chapter as a stimulus for reflection and discussion of what has been presented, but you may want to familiarise yourself with them before you proceed. The content of the chapter draws on conversations, outcomes, reflections and interactions with our students undertaking primarily work-focused modules on the Working with Children, Young People and Families programme. We have used the term 'client' in this chapter to refer inclusively to the children, young people, families, parents and carers you may come into contact with. Similarly, the term 'practitioner' includes full- and part-time students.

The skills, knowledge, understanding, education and qualifications required to become an effective practitioner are contested and unstable. Changes in national policy in relation to working with children, young people and families, specifically the Children Act 2004 and Every Child Matters (DfES, 2004c), with the subsequent re-configuration of children's services and workforce reform create change and uncertainty. Practitioners from all sectors are being expected to take on board the practice, beliefs and language of new policies and legislation (Hoyle, 2008). The introduction of the 2020 Children and Young People's Workforce Strategy (DCSF, 2009b) will undoubtedly bring further change and uncertainty. Dominant discourses of inter-agency working, safeguarding children, integrated services and Every Child Matters have underpinned the plethora of policies and initiatives (over 400 in the UK) that relate to children and young people during the last 21 years (Action for Children, 2008). Professionalisation (debatable as a term in itself) in the form of becoming a graduate profession, is being imposed on those working in early years and youth work. This chapter will explore the challenges to practitioners as they develop themselves in the shifting political and professional context. It will be argued that the personal dimension of who we are is inextricably linked to our professional identities and thus has a significant influence on how we undertake our professional roles and responsibilities. The chapter draws on multi-disciplinary research, specifically psychology, social policy, sociology, philosophy and education.

Reflective practice

Reflective practice is a term frequently used in relation to developing professional practice (see Schön (1983) and Boud et al. (1985) for further discussion). In this section, we examine some definitions and models of reflective practice, and encourage you to construct your own interpretation and application to work practice. Dewey (1933: 9) suggested that reflection is 'An active, persistent and careful consideration of any belief or supposed form of knowledge in the light of the grounds that support it and the further conclusion to which it tends'. Dewey's definition suggests the interrogation of internal or external constructs, and the basis on which they have been constructed, but may not convey the sense of new learning emerging as other definitions do. Boud et al. (1985) proposed that reflection is 'A generic term for those intellectual and effective activities in which individuals engage to explore their experiences in order to lead to a new understanding and appreciation' (Boud et al., 1985: 19). Alternatively, Reid suggested that 'Reflection is a process of reviewing an experience of practice in order to describe, analyse, evaluate and so inform learning about practice' (Reid, 1993: 305). Reflection may therefore be considered as an activity that requires review and examination of experiences, knowledge and learning in order for new understandings and interpretations to be constructed. Bolton (2001: 22) proposes that 'effective reflective practice can enable the practitioner to provide care or education which is not a working out of their own needs and wants but is alert and alive to the client's or student's needs and wants, whether professed or not'. The lens through which the practitioner examines their work therefore needs to be multi-faceted. The following two models provide a further basis for consideration of what is meant by reflective practice.

Developing yourself as a practitioner

Models of reflective practice

Ghaye and Ghaye's model (1998)
Descriptive stage (giving an account of something/an event)
Perceptive stage (linking the account and our own feelings)
Receptive stage (being open to different accounts of the event)
Interactive (linking learning from the event and future action)
Critical stage (questioning practice constructively, suggesting new ideas and ways of working)

Isles-Buck and Newstead 's model (2003)
Intention: what was intended
Experience: what actually happened
Actions: what were our actions
Outcome: what was the outcome for others
Development: what needs to happen now

These models have similarities: elements of analysis of our own perspective, but also the perspective of others, in terms of an event, incident or experience. They also propose that looking forward to the future and applying learning from the experience to change and improve practice (and it is assumed that this can be applied to individual or collective practice) is an outcome of applying such models. How intentional or aware practitioners are when applying such models is a key question; whether and how the lens is directed towards ourself and others may not always be in our control or intentions. Claxton (2000) might argue that some practitioners are intuitive in their ability to be reflective, and are able to apply mental processes that create strategic outcomes, as both models suggest. Others may need to apply such a model in a methodical way, and rehearse it in order to achieve a sense of 'being reflective'. One could also argue that two essential features of effective reflective practice are the ability to be self critical in a constructive manner, and to be able to understand the impact on others of our actions, and it is this point that has an impact on outcomes for children, young people and families.

Activity

Select an incident, event or experience from your work placement or employment that has caused you to take time to think it over. It could be an event that caused feelings of achievement, purpose and positive development or alternatively concern, obstruction or similar negative feelings. The event could be an exchange with a

Working with children, young people and families

client or a colleague, a conversation, meeting or an incident in the setting. Using either or both models in the box above, analyse the event by working through each stage. Be specific about outcomes (for you, for others) and any future action then answer the following questions. How useful was this process? Is this a way in which you usually reflect on your practice anyway? If not, will you adopt such a way of working in future? What learning has taken place for you as a result of the application of such models? What may create difficulties in applying such models? What was the impact on clients?

How confident or predisposed we are to be reflective could be influenced by our characteristics and dispositions, and it is these we consider in the next section.

Individual differences and dispositions

To what extent individual differences influence the way we work through such processes as described in the models above, or how individual differences may influence our responses to day-to-day work experiences, is worthy of consideration. Inevitably, there are common requirements that set out certain expectations in professional practice (National Occupational Standards; Qualifying to Teach standards; Early Years Professional Status standards; the Common Core, for example), but one can argue that it is not desirable to have clones of the 'perfect' practitioner or armies of technicians in each profession (Moss and Petrie, 2002). The need for autonomy and professional integrity is contentious, however, and regulation and inspection could be considered as measures to limit and control levels of agency (Osgood, 2006). Practitioners who are able to share values and apply principles in practice that promote positive outcomes for clients are desirable, so what elements within each practitioner create a predisposition to be reflective, analytical, altruistic and empathetic? Case study 2, Saira, illustrates how one practitioner acquired skills and confidence in reflection, and was able to apply these to communicate a rationale for her practice to colleagues. She recognised the shared values and commitment articulated by the team as being essential to extending debate about practice and provision. What the case study does not convey are the explicit personal qualities and dispositions that may have contributed to Saira's decision to respond to change as she did.

Since ancient Greek times there have been attempts to categorise people according to their traits, characteristics and dispositions, particularly in relation to their suitability to do specific roles or job (the Myers-Briggs Type Indicator, MBTI, for example). Although reality is far more complex, learning to become an effective practitioner could be seen as developing a professional personality alongside a 'personal' personality. Working with children, young people and families can be argued as being primarily concerned with verbal and non-verbal

Developing yourself as a practitioner

interactions between the practitioner, clients and colleagues. Using Holland's (cited in Chamorro-Premuzic, 2007) Realistic, Investigative, Artistic, Social, Enterprising, Conventional (RIASEC) typology for identifying vocational interests, those working in the children's workforce fit into the social category. Traits such as agreeable, friendly, understanding, sociable, persuasive and extravert are all associated with those dealing with people on a daily basis, alongside an aptitude towards interpersonal skills (Chamorro-Premuzic, 2007). The debate emerges in terms of what is innate or inherent in individuals, and what is potentially acquired through education, experience and training. Of pertinence here as well is to consider what influences career choices we make: do we reflect on our personality traits and use these to select careers that suit our traits (as careers guidance software prescribes)?

Activity

Take a few minutes to identify your characteristics, traits and dispositions. How have these intentionally influenced your career choices, or have other factors intervened? What characteristics predispose you to be an effective practitioner working with children, young people and families? Talk to other students about this. We often find it difficult to talk about ourselves; in professional practice, supervision meetings will tackle difficult issues, so rehearsing conversations with others should promote confidence and reflection.

Clients, whatever their age, need to have confidence in practitioners who are predisposed and competent in their ability to do their job well (Bolton, 2001). Practitioners who are secure and happy in themselves are more likely to be approachable, empathetic and relate well to others. Goleman (1995) introduced the notion of emotional intelligence that is 'the ability to understand oneself, to empathise with others and to understand human relationships and their influences on life' (Moylett, 2003: 23). A study by Petrides, Frederickson and Furnham (cited in Chamorro-Premuzic, 2007) found that students, whatever their intelligence quotient (IQ), did much better in their studies if they had high emotional intelligence traits. We can argue therefore that students should consider ways to develop their emotional intelligence traits, not only to enhance achievement in their academic studies, but also for the benefit of the clients they work with. In addition, research that investigated the impact of emotional intelligence traits in the workplace found that they were related to job performance and satisfaction (see Wong and Law in Chamorro-Premuzic, 2007). Therefore, the capacity a practitioner has to handle their feelings will have an influence upon their professional practice. The case studies at the end of the chapter both illustrate practitioners coping with situations that created feelings

Working with children, young people and families

of uncertainty and frustration, more as a result of interactions with colleagues than with clients.

The consequences of working with vulnerable people on a daily basis can result in conflict and heightened emotions. Decisions may have to be made 'on the hoof' and could be critical for clients in their consequences. Conflict often arises where competing demands on our time, clients' urgent needs for intervention, and regulatory, statutory and legislative requirements pull in different directions, leaving practitioners feeling stuck in the middle. Practitioners need to be able to apply a range of strategies, knowledge and understanding in such circumstances, and learn from them. The case studies of Peter and Saira show how they were trying to understand the demands and expectations of colleagues, but at the same time, keep focused on improving outcomes for the children they work with. Therefore, 'understanding each other's emotional messages as well as the ones we are sending out becomes even more important if we are to operate together through a shared understanding' (Griffiths, 2004: 23). Mortiboys (2005) suggests that practitioners who understand themselves are more likely to improve their day-to-day practice. For this reason combining our cognitive selves with our emotional selves will enable practitioners to become more reflective and in turn more effective practitioners (Stroobants et al., 2008). Petrie et al.'s (2006) research with children's care workers in Denmark, Germany and England found that ways in which emotional support was provided for clients varied across the three countries, but that all deployed empathic, discursive, procedural and organisational approaches. Empathic approaches include listening, cuddling, naming emotions and being a companion; discursive approaches include talking, discussing, suggesting strategies and reflecting. These approaches are commonly deployed by practitioners who have had education and training as a pedagogue, but social pedagogy training and education is not easily available, nor is the notion of a pedagogue (or social pedagogue) familiar to those working in the field of care and support for children, young people and families in the UK (Lepper, 2009; Petrie et al., 2006, 2008). As we end this section on individual differences and dispositions, the tensions that become apparent are those arising from regulation and anxiety in some work contexts of being too close to clients for fear of reprisal, or even litigation, set against one's instincts to be altruistic, empathic and caring. Policy, culture and related matters are critical issues for consideration in this context, but also developing certain skills can promote effective working to support ourselves as well as the clients we work with.

Skills in the workplace

Work-based placement provides the opportunity for students and practitioners to develop relevant skills and knowledge that will benefit clients, students and the organisation. It is therefore important to identify what skills and knowledge are essential to succeed in your work placement. In preparation for the following activity, you may want to examine job descriptions for those working with

Developing yourself as a practitioner

children, young people and families to see what skills are essential and desirable for the area of work you are in or wish to go into in the future.

Activity

Select a role in the children's and young people's workforce that you know well (this can be a role you have undertaken through placement or your current work role). Make a list of key skills and knowledge that you consider are essential to do this job effectively. The list may now be useful as a starting point for you to audit your own skills and knowledge. You could then extend this activity to consider which skills are generic or transferable and can be applied to another role that you may consider in the future. This list can be shared with other students and/or practitioners in a workplace for them to contribute to.

The skills that you have identified will probably be a combination of specific skills for a particular role, or generic and transferable skills needed by any effective practitioner working with children, young people and families. Work placement gives rise to opportunities to acquire and develop generic and specific skills and this requires a willingness to reflect and examine your experiences and practice. 'Workplaces do not permit skills to be acquired in a linear or structured manner. Instead, employees have to deal with challenges as and when they arise, and reflect on the holistic learning and development opportunities they present' (McGillivray and Davies, forthcoming). Reflection may be through a diary or personal learning journal, a discussion with a workplace mentor or tutor, or by using one of the models of reflective practice identified earlier (Ghaye and Ghaye, 1998; Isles-Buck and Newstead, 2003).

Activity

Consider how you would like to be seen by clients and colleagues and use the list you have created in the previous activity to note areas you would like to develop. In other words, are there specific aspects of your work that you think could be changed in order to enhance your practice?
   Consider the following prompts to help you with your reflection:

- What are your strengths and how do you know?
- What do you need to do to develop your strengths further (such as training course, journal to record your reflective practice, further reading, modify your behaviour)?

If you have a workplace mentor or tutor you may wish to discuss your thoughts with them to gain their insights.

Working with children, young people and families

Central to the Every Child Matters agenda was the introduction of a Common Core of Skills and Knowledge for the Children's Workforce (DfES, 2005a). It sets out six areas of skills and knowledge, and whilst it is not the intention of this chapter to discuss all of them in detail, some of the overarching skills, knowledge and understanding that encourage reflective practice are pertinent. Particular skills, such as the ability to empathise, listen and communicate well, in addition to the ability to work as part of a team, are key skills that are essential to develop in the workplace situation. Goleman (1998: 27) defines empathy as an 'awareness of others' feelings, needs and concerns' and it can be argued that this is the key to our understanding of relationships both in the workplace context and in our social lives. Situations in the workplace context can arise where it is difficult to be objective or emotions may be evoked that are sometimes difficult to handle. They can create conflict with our personal attitudes and prejudices. Bolton (2001) suggests that to be empathetic we need to be reflective and reflexive in our thinking. Being reflexive means having the ability to interpret situations through the eyes of others not just our own. This may lead to 'a form of learning where there is a fairly sudden and (to the individual at least) noticeable shift in personal outlook' (Moon, 2008). Change in our belief or opinion may be reflected in our behaviour, and Moon (2008) calls this 'emotional insight'. The Ghaye and Ghaye model of reflective practice outlined above encourages a receptive stage, which is being open to different accounts of the event. Reflexive thinking can not only bring insight into situations but can also help build trust and respect between different parties.

Activity

Revisit the incident, event or experience that you analysed earlier using either or both Ghaye and Ghaye's and Isles-Buck and Newstead's models of reflective practice. Examine the event again from the viewpoint of the others involved or an observer. Now consider the following questions. Does your perception of the event change? If your perception of the event has changed how will this change affect your practice in the future?

Alongside developing skills of empathy or reflexive thinking, the key skills of active listening and effective communication are essential skills to develop in the workplace. Prior experience and learning will inevitably make a difference to how capable and competent you are or feel you are in the work placement environment (McGillivray and Davies, forthcoming). The models of reflective practice have given you the chance to consider your skills of listening and communication; time to examine these in your working practice is essential to become an effective practitioner. Keeping a diary or personal learning journal is one way of developing your personal learning. It enables you to identify successes

Developing yourself as a practitioner

as well as what you need to consider for improvement. Developing such skills does not necessarily happen automatically. Bolton (2001) suggests that developing reflective practice can be compared to the grit in an oyster. It takes time to become beautiful.

The next section considers other aspects of learning in the workplace, and the role of others in supporting our continuing professional development.

Learning in the workplace

Research across a variety of employment sectors has found that expansive, more than restrictive, approaches to workforce development promote greater opportunities for learning and development (Unwin and Fuller, 2003). Features of an expansive approach typically include: access to learning beyond the immediate workplace; career progression as opposed to being static; support for employees as learners as opposed to producers; and the skills of *all* employees being valued as opposed to selective groups. The imposition of regulations will inevitably impact on how employers in any sector will be able to support their employees in accessing professional development and workforce reform. As youth work, early years, social work and care practitioners respond to workforce reform (DCSF, 2009b, 2009c), then employers are required to adapt to change, through funding, organising cover for study release, providing mentoring and information (such as policies and data) and support for assignments, for example.

Activity

Look at both case studies at the end of the chapter and consider how employer support for Peter and Saira has influenced their learning and outcomes so far in their studies and professional development. How is each being supported in terms of time (to attend university, to meet with mentors/supervisors, to reflect on learning and change)? What might be the longer-term implications for Peter and Saira as a result of their professional development, in terms of support and their relationships with their colleagues?

When we are new to a career, circumstances are critical in supporting the transition from being a novice to an expert practitioner. Michael Eraut (1994) sets out the Dreyfus brothers' (1986) levels of skill acquisition along a dimension of novice through to expert, with advanced beginner, competent and proficient as the intermediate levels. The features of the expert level can be summarised as: no longer relying on rules; being intuitive; drawing on tacit understanding; resorting to analysis only in novel circumstances or when problems require solving; and

Working with children, young people and families

having a vision. If this is a dimension that helps us crystallise practice aspirations, then what steps should we take to lead us there? And, significantly, who will help us on the journey? Also, individuals ideally will be provided with an appropriate level of challenge that provides opportunities to test out skills and knowledge, but to do so in a 'safe' context. It is important that we feel supported and able to learn from mistakes.

Activity

Who has taken on the role of supervisor or mentor to you in your career to date? How effectively has the relationship supported you in your professional development?

Identify at least three examples of how you have benefited from supervision or mentor meetings, with a specific focus on what changes you have made to what you do in the workplace as outcomes. Talking to others about this activity will strengthen your reflection. Use any medium available to you to share outcomes.

The role of mentor or supervisor is critical in allowing the novice to explore and reflect on successes and challenges in the workplace. Eraut et al. (2004) propose that as individuals develop in the workplace, the structures that determine work roles and tasks should allow for the observation of others with more or different expertise and for forming collaborative working relationships with them. Wenger (1998) chooses the term trajectory to suggest 'not a path that can be foreseen or charted but a continuous motion – one that has a momentum of its own in addition to a field of influences' (Wenger, 1998: 154). In Eraut et al.'s research, trajectories were found to be disrupted and discontinuous, determined by an increase in the difficulty and complexity of problems and tasks, widening competences and acquiring greater responsibility. The notion of multiple trajectories is useful as these can create 'learning pathways' that map out how we are progressing (and sometimes regressing) along various dimensions. It is important to understand that trajectories are not linear in terms of time or direction, and that we can all feel that career progression may enter times of dynamic change or become static. There will be periods as an employee or a student on placement when we feel we are moving forward or not, and when undertaking an applied degree programme such as Working with Children, Young People and Families, placements are designed to provide all students with opportunities to extend their professional development in a meaningful and purposeful direction.

When full-time students undertake a placement module, they may be entering a work setting for the first time. Their roles and responsibilities are likely to be different compared to those of a part-time student who undertakes placement in their place of employment. Collin and Tynjala (2003) suggested that the optimum model for work-based learning is to alternate theory and practice, underpinned by

Developing yourself as a practitioner

tasks that connect them together. They suggest that this promotes a personal narrative, whereby experiences are embedded into learning, connected by implicit and explicit knowledge being applied to day-to-day work experiences. This resonates with Wenger's model of knowledge creation in communities of practice. He proposes that the two complementary processes of participation (an active, social, mutual, interactive and dynamic process) and reification ('the process of giving form to our experiences by producing objects' (Wenger, 1998: 58) allow knowledge creation. Reification can result in objects such as journals, diaries, performance management and supervision notes or assignment tasks in the context of this chapter, for example. The way in which assessment tasks are presented to students undertaking placement modules attempts to take account of this point, as these tasks require students to engage in periodic discussions with each other about placement as well as requiring written reflective accounts as summative and formative assignments.

Activity

Reflect on the relationship between workplace learning and academic learning. What has worked well for you in terms of academic learning being applied to workplace experiences? You may want to choose a specific assignment task that has required you to draw on work-based experiences for analysis. How effectively were you enabled to make connections between 'theory' and 'practice' and what personal and professional learning emerged from the assignment tasks?

Construction of professional identities and their influence on professional practice

Consideration of the construction of professional identities is relevant to be included in a chapter on developing yourself as a practitioner as it opens debate in terms of collective and individual identities, drawing on socially constructed influences. If we agree with Stone and Rixon's (2008: 110) suggestion that professional identity is 'how professionals understand themselves and their role including the more informal and implicit aspects of professional cultures', then scrutiny of how we see ourselves as part of a profession may provide security and a sense of belonging, as well as strengthening aspirations. Literature that examines the professional identities of teachers, nurses, youth workers and early years practitioners (Fealey, 2004; Gillis, 1981; Griffin, 1993; McGillivray, 2008; Tucker, 2004; Urban, 2008; Weber and Mitchell, 1995) suggests that the interaction of numerous factors contributes to the construction of professional identities. These include, as Stone and Rixon (2008) suggest, professional cultures, roles, relationships, expectations (of self and others), socio-economic factors (such as discourse,

Working with children, young people and families

status, gender, macro and meso levels of influence), day-to-day working lives, ideological influences and personal histories. The dominance and interaction of these factors will create an ever-changing sense of professional identity, but it is a useful notion to take time to reflect on if we choose to be strategic in career development and to enhance our work role.

Activity

Take time to collate influences on the way in which you see yourself as a professional. You may want to use reflections from the previous activity to begin to consider how the reactions of others to you as a professional influence your construction of your 'work' identity. What and who have been most influential, and why? What has been the outcome of those influences, and how do you see your identity developing in the future?

Many groups of professional practitioners who work with children, young people and families experience tensions and conflict arising from the interplay between influences on their professional identities. Working in multi-disciplinary teams to support the needs of children, young people and families can exacerbate a blurring or confusion of professional identity as boundaries overlap and status and hierarchies interfere: 'professional identity can be challenged as roles and responsibilities change. Such changes can generate discomfort, anxiety and anger in team members as they struggle to cope with the disintegration of one identity before a new version can be built' (Frost et al., 2005: 188).

How practitioners manage their professional trajectory and career development will in part depend on the community, teams, environment and sector in which they work, and the notion of communities of practice is helpful in this context. Wenger (1998) outlines key components of a social theory of learning that underpins communities of practice. These include meaning, practice, community and identity. As a student on a programme such as Working with Children, Young People and Families, you will be a member of multiple communities: communities of students, communities of workers and other communities beyond your studies. To develop yourself professionally, it is helpful to locate workplace communities, and to identify who is central to a group or community, who may be peripheral, and why. Which communities exist, and why? Are communities determined by professional role, a management hierarchy, geographical location or are there other features that determine membership? Anning et al. (2006) cite research that uses a metaphor of tribes when considering multi-professional teams, and suggests that professional cultures, status and behaviours should be cast aside in order to promote effective working. This may be challenging for some. Whether we feel an 'affinity' to a particular workforce, and how a

Developing yourself as a practitioner

sense of belonging influences our practice and identity raises further questions, particularly in the context of multi-agency working.

Groups within society (children, elderly, young people) have certain constructions associated with them, and people who work with them attract similar 'labels'. We would argue that the client group we work with contributes to socially constructed identities of the workforce we consider ourselves as belonging to. There are other texts that explore dominant discourses of child, childhood and children's services (James et al., 1998; Jenks, 2005; Prout, 2005; Wyness, 2006) and how such regimes of power (Foucault, 1982) inevitably impact on those who work with them. The concept of atomisation (Moss and Petrie, 2002: 64) as 'the efficient production of particular outcomes achieved through breaking down the production process into component parts' illustrates one challenge for practitioners to grapple with if they are to take a critical perspective on dominant discourses. Practitioners are expected to accept the demands of government policy and initiatives, and react to meet the needs (often critical) of children, young people and families and adapt to changes imposed on them. Rodd (2006) identified certain aspects of change: it is highly emotional and can cause stress; it is resisted by many people; it can be adjusted to by individuals and groups with the support of a leader; it entails development growth in attitudes and skills; and it is best facilitated on the basis of diagnostic needs. Rodd (2006) suggests that effective change is facilitated by leaders who communicate reasons for change effectively to their team, encourage participation and provide feedback. As a student practitioner, you may have experienced change in guises such as becoming a member of a new team, entering a workplace for the first time (voluntarily or as a paid employee), working with a new team-leader or changing teams.

Activity

You may want to reflect on changes you have experienced in a work setting, and how effectively leaders have facilitated change to promote well-being and maintain quality provision. If an opportunity arises, share the outcomes with people you work with on placement or at work.

Change, policy initiatives, socially constructed views and the influence at micro, meso and macro level on professional identity is where we started to outline what contributes to professional identity. We would suggest that Peter's and Saira's professional identities are influenced by their gender, their place of work and their work role. Before we conclude the chapter, reflect on who they are in their place of work, who they interact with, and what other factors might contribute to their professional identities.

Working with children, young people and families

Case study 1: Peter

Peter works as a mentor in a secondary school. He has been able to secure release from his work to attend university for one afternoon and evening during term-time in order to study for his degree in Working with Children, Young People and Families. He had to be assertive in his approach to his line manager, the deputy head of the school, as initially he was informed that he had to study in his own time.

Peter has been working as a mentor for three years. The school where he works is an inner-city secondary school, located in a community where there is deprivation and high unemployment. Many children who attend the school come from ethnic minority families.

Peter had previously worked in the manufacturing industry, but when he was made redundant, he made a deliberate choice to change career rather than seeking a new post in manufacturing. He was offered voluntary work at first at the school, but found mentoring rewarding and the school offered him paid employment and training at the end of his first year there.

Recently, Peter has been concerned about several issues, and two in particular have been troubling him. Firstly, as Peter is developing his mentoring skills and expanding his academic knowledge and understanding of research, theory, and political and philosophical approaches to work with young people, he senses a widening gap between his professional philosophy and that of two teachers he works with in the school. Peter is increasing in his confidence to adopt an inclusive approach to the pupils he mentors, and to adopt pedagogical strategies that meet the mentees' individual needs. However, the learning and teaching strategies favoured by the teachers tend to be target as opposed to individual-orientated. This is creating internal conflict for Peter, as the pupils he supports in lessons taught by the teachers concerned are showing some disaffection and lowered motivation recently.

Secondly, Peter suspects that as his knowledge and understanding expands, he is being 'side-lined' by mentoring colleagues. The invitations to social events and the informal conversations between lessons are not as forthcoming as they used to be, and both these dilemmas are now causing Peter concern.

Peter does not have a mentor himself or supervision meetings. The support he and other mentors receive is provided by termly meetings with the deputy headteacher who is also the school SENCO (special educational needs co-ordinator). He meets with the class teachers of pupils he supports half-termly for updates and planning.

Activity

How can applying the following perspectives help Peter address his concerns?

- models of reflective practice
- aspects of multi-professional working

Developing yourself as a practitioner

- power differentials
- Wenger's notions of communities of practice and communities of learning
- taking a critical view of policy initiatives.

What are the competing priorities for Peter in terms of relationships and outcomes? Consider all parties involved in your response. What are Peter's needs currently as a professional practitioner? What actions could Peter (and others) take in order to begin to address either concern?

Case study 2: Saira

Saira is in the first year of her part-time degree programme. She works in a children's centre (previously a nursery school) and has worked there for eight years. She began as a student and was employed as an early years practitioner on completing her level 3. Saira considers the children's centre team to be committed to the same vision and ethos, wanting positive outcomes for all children and families who access the centre.

Saira's professional life was disrupted when she moved into a new building that has recently been added to the children's centre. Her work contract changed, and Saira is now required to work additional weeks in the year and on a shift rota. This had an impact on her family commitments and childcare arrangements. Saira started her degree at about the same time, so she found this a very challenging time. The children's centre team expanded and new staff were employed with higher level qualifications but less experience than Saira. New staff wanted to change practice, in Saira's view, because of lack of understanding of the philosophy and pedagogy that informed existing practice. In a supervision meeting, the centre manager suggested to Saira that she should not resist changes, but Saira applied theoretical learning and reflective practice models from her degree programme to assert the rationale for the approach taken to promote children's learning with new colleagues. She communicated the rationale for pedagogical practice in a staff meeting, and used research, readings and ideas to inform the materials that she had prepared. Saira also drew on the support from fellow students on the programme, as discussions in module sessions had focused on the analysis of critical incidents. Students had been willing to share equivalent dilemmas as well as achievements, and group examination had resulted in their identification of strategies in response.

Saira has recently been offered a new role at the children's centre as a team-leader, working specifically with families with babies and very young children. She is looking forward to the challenges of being a team-leader, and considers that her recent professional development (from her degree, from her colleagues and from her experiences in the setting as it went through the transition to a children's centre) has placed her in a position of preparedness for the role. This has been confirmed by her manager in recent supervision meetings. Saira will be leading a team of four staff with varying levels of qualification and experience.

Working with children, young people and families

Activity

Outline what have been, and what will be, the key challenges for Saira. You may want to consider some of the points in the chapter, such as: communities of learning, communities of practice and legitimate peripheral participation; the role of mentors and supervisors; and change and models of reflective practice.

Are there any aspects of management, organisation or development that could have been done differently in order to improve the outcomes for Saira as described here?

Conclusion

If practitioners wish to develop themselves, then we suggest that it is the articulation of aspirations for themselves and their clients that is critical as well as the means and resources to achieve those aspirations. Herein lies the challenge. Informed, reflective practitioners understand the power of their own agency, and how this influences professional practice as the route to improved outcomes for children, young people and families. What this chapter has attempted to do is suggest themes to promote debate and enhance practice, so readers can consider what might assist their continuing development. At the same time, there is acknowledgement of the reality of working in a sector that is often under scrutiny, criticism and significant change.

Further reading

Some of the books below have been written as a result of research undertaken with practitioners working in different contexts, but all with children, young people or families. Because they are research-based, they provide a real-world context for current dilemmas facing those working with children, young people and families. The texts include debates arising from first-hand experiences and research that relates to ways in which workers are able to develop their professional selves. Others develop models, theories and ideas related to reflective practice in health and education sectors.

Anning, A., Cottrell, D., Frost, N., Green, J. and Robinson, M. (2006) *Developing Multi-professional Teamwork for Integrated Children's Services*. Maidenhead: Open University Press.

Bolton, G. (2001) *Reflective Practice*. London: Paul Chapman Publishing.

Ghaye, T. and Lillyman, S. (1997) *Learning Journals and Critical Incidents*. Wiltshire: Quay Books.

Petrie, P., Boddy, J., Cameron, C., Wigfall, V. and Simon, A. (2006) *Working with Chidren in Care*. Maidenhead: McGraw Hill.

Weinberger, J., Pickstone, C. and Hannon, P. (2005) *Learning from Sure Start*. Maidenhead: Open University Press.

12

Where are we going?

Graham Brotherton and Gill McGillivray

The aims of this chapter are to:

- Reflect on and highlight issues and debates considered in previous chapters
- Offer concluding thoughts on future directions and challenges.

We hope the chapters in this book have promoted reflection and prompted you to consider new perspectives on working with children, young people and families. In order to offer a summary of possible perspectives, but at the same time acknowledging that there is no 'future-proofing' or certainty in this field of work, the following points are intended to provoke further debate.

It could be argued that we need to take an introspective interrogation of ourselves, and our personal and professional positions before we are able to then position ourselves within our work or study. Ways in which we can de-construct (a notion proposed by Derrida, see Sim, 1999) ourselves as we undertake work with children, young people and families can allow us to examine personal values first, before articulating professional values. Inevitably, the communities in which we work and learn are critically influential in this context. Again, positions will change and evolve, as our trajectories lead us in various professional directions. We need to cut through the rhetoric of 'effective practice', 'well-being' and 'outcomes' so we are not perpetuating dominant discourses, but de-constructing (and possibly re-constructing) them in order to strengthen our positions as advocates for each other as well as the children, young people and families that we work with.

We have already exposed within the chapters of the book how competing demands, multiple identities, expectations of others, changing roles and responsibilities and uncertainty impact on our work. The next activity is intended to stimulate some consideration of these.

What do you consider to be significant challenges for you at this stage of your study/work career? If you were to arrange the following in any particular order, how would you rank them? Do peers/colleagues agree? If there is difference, why might this be?

- Working alongside other professionals
- Accessing the professional development you wish to
- Local government and national government policy initiatives
- The needs of the children, young people and families you work with, and your ability to meet them
- The demands made on you on a day-to-day basis due to your work role, responsibilities and context
- Others.

The value we place on our work, our learning and those whom we work with is a foundation stone for what we do, as well as the knowledge we have, and the judgements we make along the way. So what is needed to illuminate the future pathway for work in the sector? What kind of practitioner is needed to work 'effectively' with children, young people and families? How would you articulate the ideal: agentive; anticipatory; sensitive; responsive; informed? Indeed, does the concept of 'ideal' obscure what we need to start with?

What of policy relating to the children, young people and families whom we work with, and the uncertainty at the time of writing regarding the stance of the party who will be in government from June 2010? The economic recession of 2008 to 2009 has exacerbated difficulties for families in terms of unemployment, debt, housing and the cost of living. At the same time, rumours of unsustainable public spending on Sure Start and workforce reform, for example, mean that the future is uncertain.

As we conclude this book then, we now seek to pull together some of its main themes, review key issues and consider what this means for practitioners. Since the election of New Labour in 1997 there has been a whole range of changes which taken together are often referred to as the 'Every Child Matters' agenda. The key elements of this agenda are summarised below:

- A move from a reactive emphasis on child protection to a much more proactive emphasis on 'safeguarding' children and young people
- Linked to this, an emphasis on early identification and intervention
- Increased emphasis on the development of multi-agency and inter-agency approaches to working with children, young people and their families
- Development of targeted services to work with particular groups of children and young people and their families (e.g. Care Matters or Sure Start)

- An emphasis on services which promote parental employment, whether through the provision of child care or education
- An emphasis on bringing private and voluntary sector organisations into the provision of services.

These changes taken together represent fundamental changes in the overall pattern of services in terms of the extent of provision, the roles of practitioners and the relationship between practitioners and the children, young people and families that they work with. At the time of writing this book there seems to be a broad political consensus about the changes, though within this there are clear differences in emphasis, for example the Conservative Party have on a number of occasions highlighted the centrality of the health visitor's role and suggested that there is a need for an increased number of health visitors.

Nonetheless a number of key debates remain in terms of future direction. As has already been suggested, the issue of financial resources has to be seen as a key issue. In the current rhetoric about future spending there seems little doubt that the real terms increases in spending on services for children, young people and families will not be sustained in the medium term and that there is a real possibility of actual cuts in some areas, though it is by no means clear which these are likely to be.

At this point it is worth returning to the ideological context within which practice takes place. In looking at the overview of the current policy framework presented earlier in this chapter it is possible to argue that a particular model of service characterised by a market-led approach to both the provision and consumption of services has become dominant. In terms of the provision of services this means much greater emphasis on contracted services from a range of organisations and greater use of multi-agency approaches to the commissioning of services. For 'service users', be they children, young people or their families, thus may mean a number of things some positive (e.g. the ability to make genuine choices between a range of possible options (school choice, choice of care providers)) and some negative, (e.g. falling through the net in a context of tightly defined and targeted, contracted services). For parents the issue of being held accountable for decisions made as a consumer of services is also likely to be significant, especially in the context of a more surveillance-driven approach (as noted in earlier chapters).

For practitioners, the future is likely to be complex and perhaps less certain, but also one in which there are possibilities, but we would argue that to maximise these possibilities requires an ethical approach to practice which acknowledges the existence of value positions which reflect dominant discourses, especially policy discourses. To give a couple of specific examples; as we discussed in Chapter 5 on health, the absence of certain discourses, in that particular context, about the impact of relative inequalities, can lead to limited, partial and we would argue insufficient or inappropriate responses. A second example relates to the increasing requirement not just to make professional judgements but also to formally record them in documents which may be shared between agencies (e.g. through

Working with children, young people and families

the Common Assessment process) which have implications in terms of both professional accountability and the potential to label.

Activity

Having read our arguments throughout this book, are you convinced by the idea that working with children, young people and families has an inherent moral (and therefore in the broad sense of the word 'political') dimension which we are required to address as practitioners? For example, is it a requirement of good practice that we seek to advocate for a more equal society as argued by Wilkinson and Pickett (2009)(see Chapter 5) or is our role to simply seek to provide the best possible service for the people we work with?

In concluding a book such as this we would seek to avoid giving an over simple and platitudinous answer to this question (especially as in practice it is clear that both are important). Nonetheless it is clearly the case that our ability to open up possibilities for all children, young people and their families does require us to acknowledge that opportunities are not currently equally divided. The Milburn Report (produced by an all-party group of MPs chaired by the former Labour minister Alan Milburn) on access to the 'professions' was published as this chapter was being written and a quote from the introduction to this is helpful here:

> And because we believe that social mobility will not advance if we think it is only wealth that is unevenly distributed in our society we make proposals that are about redistributing power.
>
> If Britain is to get moving again socially, people need to be able not just to get a job or training or childcare but also to enjoy greater control and to have a bigger say in how they lead their lives. Unlocking our country so that it is open to aspiration and effort requires a new drive to fundamentally change how power is distributed in our society. (The Cabinet Office, 2009: 5).

However, the solutions proposed in the report are, in the authors' opinion, selective, and represent only a limited start in addressing the fundamental differences in opportunity that remain. The report further reinforces the continuing centrality of the inequality debate for all practitioners and that it requires us to continue to develop constructively critical perspectives on both policy and practice.

Where are we going?

References

Able-Smith, B. and Townsend, P. (1965) *The Poor and the Poorest*. Occasional Papers in Social Administration No. 17. London: Bell & Co.

Abrahams, N., Casey, K. and Daro, D. (1992) 'Teachers' knowledge, attitudes and beliefs about child abuse and its prevention', *Child Abuse and Neglect* 16: 229–238.

Action for Children (2008) *As Long as it Takes: A New Politics for Children*. Available at: www.actionforchildren.org.uk (accessed January 2009).

Alcock, P. (2006) *Understanding Poverty*, 3rd edn. Basingstoke: Palgrave Macmillan.

Alderson, P. (2004) 'Ethics', in S. Fraser, V. Lewis, S. Ding, M. Kellett and C. Robinson (eds) *Doing Research with Children and Young People*. London: Sage Publications.

Alderson, P. (2005) 'Designing ethical research with children', in A. Farrell (ed.) *Ethical Research with Children*. Maidenhead: Open University Press.

Aldgate, J. and Tunstill, J. (1995) 'Making sense of section 17: implementing services for children in need within the 1989 Children Act', in Department of Health (2001) *The Children Act 1989 Now: Messages from Research*. London: The Stationary Office. pp. 154–6.

Anderson, R., Brady, I., Dowly, T., Inglesant, P., Heath, W. and Sasse, A. (2009) *Database State*. York: The Joseph Rowntree Reform Trust Ltd. Available at http://www.jrrt.org.uk/uploads/database-state.pdf

Annas, G.J. and Grodin, M.A. (1992) *The Nazi Doctors and the Nuremburg Code*. Oxford: Oxford University Press.

Anning, A., Cottrell, D., Frost, N., Green, J. and Robinson, M. (2006) *Developing Multi-professional Teamwork for Integrated Children's Services*. Maidenhead: Open University Press.

Arber, S. and Cooper, H. (2000) 'Gender and inequalities in health across the lifecourse', in Annandale L. and Hunt K. (eds) *Gender Inequalities in Health*. Buckingham: Open University Press. pp. 123–50.

Ariès, P. (1962) *Centuries of Childhood*. London: Jonathan Cape.

Arthur, J., Grainger, T. and Wray, D. (2006) *Learning to Teach in the Primary School*. London: Routledge.

Ashley, J. (2004) 'Britain needs the nanny state now more than ever', available at: http://www.guardian.co.uk/society/2004/jan/01/futureforpublicservices.comment (date accessed 06/11/09).

Audit Commission (1994) *Seen But Not Heard: Co-ordinating Community Child Health and Social Services for Children in Need*. London: HMSO.

Bakker, J. and Denessen, E. (2007) 'The concept of parent involvement. Some theoretical and empirical considerations', *International Journal about Parents in Education*, 1(0): 188–99, available at: http://www.ernape.net/ejournal/index.php/IJPE/article/view/42/32

Ball, S.J. (1990) *Politics and Policy making in Education*. London: Routledge.

Ball, S.J. (2008) *The Education Debate*. Dorchester: Henry Ling Ltd.

Balloch, S. and Jones, B. (1990) *Poverty and Anti-poverty Strategy: The Local Government Response*. London: Association of Metropolitan Authorities.

Baltes, P.B. (1987) 'Theoretical propositions of life-span developmental psychology: on the dynamics of growth and decline', *Developmental Psychology*, 23: 611–26.

Baltes, P.B., Lindenberger, U. and Strandinger, U. (1998) 'Life-span theory in developmental psychology', in W. Damon (ed.) *Handbook of Child Psychology, Volume 1*. New York: Wiley.

Bambra, C. (2004) 'The worlds of welfare: illusory and gender blind?', *Social Policy and Society*, 3: 201–12.

Baraitser, L. (2009) *Maternal Encounters: The Ethics of Interruption*. London: Routledge.

Barker, R. (ed.) (2009) *Making Sense of Every Child Matters: Multi-Professional Practice Guidance*. Bristol: The Policy Press.

Barron, I. (2005) 'Understanding development in early childhood', in L. Jones, R. Holmes and J. Powell (eds) *Early Childhood Studies: A Multi-Professional Perspective*. Maidenhead: Open University Press.

Barron, I., Holmes, R., MacLure, M. and Runswick-Cole, K. (2007) *Primary Schools and Other Agencies* (Primary Review Research Survey 8/2). Cambridge: University of Cambridge Faculty of Education.

Bauman, Z. (1992) *Intimations of Postmodernity*. London: Routledge.

Bauman, Z. (1993) *Postmodern Ethics*. Oxford: Blackwell.

Beck, H.P., Levinson, S. and Irons, G. (2009) 'Finding little Albert: a journey to John B. Watson's infant laboratory', *American Psychologist*, 64(7): 605–14.

Beck, K.A., Ogloff, J.R.P. and Corbishley, A. (1994) 'Knowledge, compliance and attitudes of teachers towards mandatory child abuse and reporting in British Columbia', *Canadian Journal of Education*, 19(1): 15–29.

Beckett, C. (2007) *Child Protection: An Introduction*, 2nd edn. London: Sage.

Belsky, J. and Melhuish, E. (2007) 'Impact on Sure Start local programmes on children and families', in J. Belsky, J. Barnes and E. Melhuish (eds) *The National Evaluation of Sure Start: Does Area-based Early Intervention Work?* Bristol: The Policy Press, pp. 133–54.

Beveridge, W. (1942) *Social Insurance and Allied Services*. London: Macmillan.

Black, D. (1992) *The Black Report*. London: Penguin.

Bolton, G. (2001) *Reflective Practice*. London: Paul Chapman Publishing.

Boud, D., Keough, R. and Walker, D. (1985) *Reflection: Turning Experience into Learning*. London: Kogan Page.

Bourdieu, P. (1997) 'The forms of capital', in A. Halsey, H. Lauder, P. Brown and A. Wells (eds) *Education, Culture, Economy and Society*. Oxford: Oxford University Press.

Bowlby, J. (1951) *Maternal Care and Mental Health*. Geneva: World Health Organization.

Bowlby, J. (1969) *Attachment and Loss, Volume 1: Attachment*. London: Hogarth.

Bowlby, J. (1973) *Attachment and Loss, Volume 2: Separation*. London: Hogarth.

Bowlby, J. (1980) *Attachment and Loss, Volume 3: Loss*. London: Hogarth.

Bowlby, J. (1988) *A Secure Base: Clinical Applications of Attachment Theory*. London: Routledge.

Brandon, M., Thoburn, J., Lewis, A. and Way, A. (2001) 'Safeguarding children with the Children Act 1989', in Department of Health (2001) *The Children Act 1989 Now: Messages from Research*. London: The Stationary Office. pp. 165–8.

Broadbent, D. (1958) *Perception and Communication*. London: Pergamon.

Bronfenbrenner, U. (1979) *The Ecology of Human Development: Experiments by Nature and Design*. Cambridge, MA: Harvard University Press.

Bronfenbrenner, U. (2005) *Making Human Beings Human: Bioecological Perspectives on Human Development*. Newbury Park, CA: Sage.

Brooker, L. (2002) *Starting School*. Buckingham: Open University Press.

Brown, A.P. (2004) 'Anti-social behaviour, crime control and social control', *Howard Journal of Criminal Justice*, 43(2) May: 203–11.

Browne, N. (2008) 'Children's social and emotional development', in A. Paige-Smith and A. Craft (eds) *Developing Reflective Practice in the Early Years*. Maidenhead: McGraw Hill.

Buckingham, D. (2000) *After the Death of Childhood: Growing up in the Age of Electronic Media*. Cambridge: Polity Press.

References

Burman, E. (2008) *Deconstructing Developmental Psychology*. Hove: Routledge.

Burns, G.E. and Lake, D.E. (1983) 'A sociological perspective on implementing child abuse legislation in education', *Interchange*, 14(2): 33–53, The Ontario Institute for Studies in Education.

Burrows, R. and Loader, L. (1994) *Towards a Post-Fordist Welfare State?* London Routledge.

Cajkler, W., Sage, R., Tennant, G., Tiknas, Y., Tucker, S. and Taylor, C. (2007) *A Systematic Literature Review on the Perceptions of Ways in which Teaching Assistants Work to Support Pupils' Social and Academic Engagement in Secondary Schools (1988–2005)*, in Research Evidence in Education Library. London: EPPI-Centre, Social Science Research Unit, Institute of Education, University of London.

CAMHS (2008) *Children and Young People in Mind: The Final Report of the CAMHS Review*. Available at: http://www.dcsf.gov.uk/CAMHSreview (accessed 7/04/09).

Capacity and Esmee Fairbairn Foundation (2007) *Children's Centres: Ensuring that Families Most in Need Benefit*. Teddington: Beechgrove Press.

Catholic Bishops' Conference (1999) *Foundations For Excellence: Catholic Primary Schools in Urban Poverty Areas*. London: Catholic Bishops' Conference of England and Wales.

CESI (Centre for Economic and Social Inclusion) (2009) *Child Poverty. Children in Low Income Families*. Available at: http://www.cesi.org.uk/research/completed_projects/child_poverty/8236_endchildpoverty.htm (accessed 2/10/09).

Chamorro-Premuzic, T. (2007) *Personality and Individual Differences*. Oxford: BPS Blackwell.

Children Act 1989. London: HMSO.

Chomsky, N. (1959) '*Review of Verbal Behavior* by B.F. Skinner', *Language*, 35: 26–58.

Christensen, P. and James, A. (eds) (2003) *Research with Children: Perspectives and Practices*. London: Routledge Falmer.

Clark, A. and Moss, P. (2008) *Spaces to Play*. London: National Children's Bureau.

Claxton, G. (2000) 'The anatomy of intuition', in T. Atkinson and G. Claxton (eds) *The Intuitive Practitioner*. Maidenhead: Open University.

Coates, K. and Silburn, R. (1973) *Poverty: The Forgotten Englishmen*. London: Pelican.

Coates, K. and Silburn, R. (2006) *Poverty: The Forgotten Englishmen*, 3rd edn. London: Pelican.

Cohen, B., Moss, P., Petrie, P. and Wallace, J. (2004) *A New Deal for Children?* Bristol: Policy Press.

Cohen, S. (2002) *Folk Devils and Moral Panics*, 3rd edn. London: Routledge.

Cohen, L., Manion, L. and Morrison, K. (2007) *Research Methods in Education*, 6th edn. Abingdon: Routledge.

Coles, C. (2002) 'Developing professional judgment', *Journal of Continuing Education in the Health Professions*, 22 (1): 3–10.

Collin, K. and Tynjala, P. (2003) 'Integrating theory and practice? Employees' and students' experiences of learning at work', *Journal of Workplace Learning*, 15(7/8): 338–44.

Commission for Social Justice (1994) *Social Justice: Strategies for National Renewal*. London: Vintage.

Connors, C. and Stalker, K. (2003) *The Views and Experiences of Disabled Children and Their Siblings*. London: Jessica Kingsley Publishers.

Cree, V.E., Kay, H. and Tisdall, K. (2002) 'Research with children: sharing the dilemmas', *Child and Family Social Work*, 7: 47–56.

Crick, B. (1998) *Education for Citizenship and the Teaching of Democracy in Schools: Final Report of Advisory Group on Citizenship*. London: QCA.

Cunningham, H. (2006) *The Invention of Childhood*. London: BBC Books.

Cummings, C., Dyson, A., Muijs, D., Papps, I. et al. (2007) *Evaluation of the Full Service Extended Schools Initiative: Final Report*. Nottingham: DfES.

Cuskelly, M. (2005) 'Ethical inclusion of children with disabilities in research', in A. Farrell (ed.) *Ethical Research with Children*. Maidenhead: Open University Press.

Working with children, young people and families

Dahlberg, G. and Moss, P. (2005) *Ethics and Politics in Early Childhood Education.* Abingdon: Routledge Falmer.

Danby, S. and Farrell, A. (2005) 'Opening the research conversation', in A. Farrell (ed.) *Ethical Research with Children.* Maidenhead: Open University Press.

Daniel, B. and Wassell, S. (2002) *Adolescence: Assessing and Promoting Resilience in Vulnerable Children.* London: Jessica Kingsley.

Daniels, H., Cole, M. and Wertsch, J.V. (eds) (2007) *The Cambridge Companion to Vygotsky.* Cambridge: Cambridge University Press.

Darwin, C. (1877) 'A biographical sketch of an infant', *Mind*, 2: 285–94.

David, T., Goouch, K., Powell, S. and Abbott, L. (2002) *Review of the Literature to Support Birth to Three Matters.* London: DfES.

Davies, L. and Yamashita, H. (2007) *School Councils – School Improvement. The London Secondary School Councils Action Research Project.* Birmingham: Centre for International Education and Research.

DCSF (2007a) *The Children's Plan: Building Brighter Futures.* Norwich: HMSO.

DCSF (2007b) *Children and Young People Today: Evidence to Support the Development of the Children's Plan.* Available at: http://publications.dcsf.gov.uk/eOrderingDownload/ Children&young_people_today.pdf (accessed 13/06/09).

DCSF (2008a) *What is a Children's Trust.* Available at: http://www.governornet.co.uk/ linkAttachments/ACF9F3F.pdf (accessed 25/07/09).

DCSF (2008b) *National Foundation for Educational Research: Citizenship Educational Longitudinal Study, 6th Report.* London: DCSF.

DCSF (2009a) Contactpoint. Available at: http://www.everychildmatters.gov.uk/contactpoint (accessed 7/05/09).

DCSF (2009b) *2020 Children and Young People's Workforce Strategy.* London: DCSF.

DCSF (2009c) *Next Steps for Early Learning and Childcare.* London: DCSF.

Denscombe, M. (2003) *The Good Research Guide for Small-scale Social Research Projects*, 2nd edn. Maidenhead: Open University Press.

Department of Health (1995) *Child Protection: Messages from Research.* London: HMSO.

Department of Health (1998) *Independent Inquiry into Inequalities in Health Report. Chairman: Sir Donald Acheson.* Available at: http://www.archive.official-documents. co.uk/document/doh/ih/ih.htm (accessed 14/06/09).

Department of Health (2000) *Children in Need in England: First Results of a Survey of Activity and Expenditure by Local Authority Social Services Children and Families Teams for a Survey Week in February 2000.* London: Department of Health.

Department of Health (2001) *The Children Act 1989 Now: Messages from Research.* London: The Stationary Office.

Department of Health (2002) *Safeguarding Children: A Joint Chief Inspectors' Report on Arrangements to Safeguard Children.* London: Department of Health Publications.

Department of Health (2003) *The Victoria Climbié Inquiry Report by Lord Laming.* London: HMSO.

Department of Health (2004) *Choosing Health.* London: DoH.

Department of Health and Department for Education and Employment (1999) *The Quality Protects Programme: Transforming Children's Services 2000/1.* Health Service Circular (HSC(99)237), Local Authority Circular (LAC(99)33) and DfEE Circular No. 18/99. London: Department of Health.

Department of Health and Social Services (1974) *Non-Accidental Injury to Children* (Com 3/74). London: DHSS.

Department of Health, Department for Education and Employment and Home Office (2000) *Framework for the Assessment of Children in Need and their Families.* London: The Stationary Office.

References

Department of Health, Home Office, Department for Education and Employment (1999) *Working Together to Safeguard Children: A Guide to Inter-agency Working to Safeguard and Promote the Welfare of Children*. London: The Stationary Office.

Department of Work and Pensions (2007) *Working for Children*. London: DWP.

Desforges, C. and Abouchaar, A. (2003) *The Impact of Parental Involvement, Parental Support and Family Education On Pupil Achievement and Adjustment: A Literature Review*. London: Department for Education and Skills.

Dewey, J. (1933) *How We Think*. Chicago: Henrey Regney.

DfEE (1999) *The National Curriculum: Handbook for Primary Teachers in England*. London: QCA.

DfEE (2001) *Schools: Building on Success* (Green Paper). Norwich: HMSO.

DfES (2001a) *The Special Educational Needs Code of Practice*. London: DfES.

DfES (2001b) *Schools Achieving Success* (White Paper). Annesley: DFES.

DfES (2002) *Citizenship: A Scheme of Work for Key Stage 3. Teacher's Guide*. London: DfES.

DfES (2003a) *Excellence and Enjoyment – A Strategy for Primary Schools*. London: DfES.

DfES (2003b) *Every Child Matters*. London: DFES.

DfES (2004a) *Engaging Fathers: Involving Parents, Raising Achievement*. London: DfES. Available at: www.teachernet.gov.uk

DfES (2004b) *Every Child Matters: Change for Children in Schools*. London DfES.

DfES (2004c) *Every Child Matters – Change for Children*. London: DfES.

DfES (2005a) *The Common Core of Skills and Knowledge for the Children's Workforce*. London: DfES.

DfES (2005b) *Children's Workforce Strategy*. London: DfES.

DfES (2007) *Every Parent Matters*. Annesley: HMSO.

Dixon, R.A. and Lerner, R.M. (1992) 'History and systems in developmental psychology', in M.H. Bornstein and M.E. Lamb (eds) *Developmental Psychology: An Advanced Textbook*, 3rd edn. Mahwah, NJ: Lawrence Erlbaum.

Dockrell, J., Lewis, A. and Lindsay, G. (2000) 'Researching children's perspective: a psychological dimension', in A. Lewis and G. Lindsay (eds) *Researching Children's Perspectives*. Buckingham: Open University Press.

Dreyfus, H.L. and Dreyfus, S.E. (1986) *Mind Over Machine*. Oxford: Basil Blackwell.

Eagle, M. (1997) 'Contributions of Erik Erikson', *Psychoanalytic Review*, 84: 337–47.

Early Years Commission (2008) *Breakthrough Britain: The Next Generation*. London: The Centre for Social Justice.

Eraut, M. (1994) *Developing Professional Knowledge and Competence*. London: Routledge Falmer.

Eraut, M., Maillardet, F.J., Miller, C., Steadman, S., Ali, S., Blackman, C. and Furner, J. (2004) 'Early career learning at work', paper presented at the TLRP Conference, Cardiff. Available at: http://www.tlrp.org/dspace/retrieve/253/Eraut+CardiffTLRPpaper Nov2004.doc

Erickson, F. and Schultz, J. (1992) 'Students experience in the curriculum', in P. Jackson (ed.) *Handbook of Research on Curriculum*. New York: Macmillan. pp. 464–85.

Erikson, E. (1950) *Childhood and Society*. New York: W. W. Norton.

Erikson, E. (1959) 'Identity and the life cycle', *Psychological Issues*, 1, New York: International Universities Press.

Erikson, E. (1963) *Childhood and Society*. New York: Norton.

Esping-Andersen, G. (1990) *The Three Worlds of Welfare Capitalism*. Cambridge: Polity Press.

Ethnicity and Health (2007) Available at: http://www.parliament.uk/documents/upload/postpn276.pdf (accessed 12/05/09)

Etzioni, A. (1993) *The Spirit of Community*. New York: Crown Publishing.

Evans, G. (2006) *Educational Failure and Working Class White Children in Britain*. London: Palgrave Macmillan.

Working with children, young people and families

Farrell, A. (2005) 'Ethics and research with children', in A. Farrell (ed.) *Ethical Research with Children*. Maidenhead: Open University Press.

Fealey, G. (2004) '"The good nurse": visions and values in images of the nurse', *Journal of Advanced Nursing*, 46(6): 649–56.

Ferguson, B. et al. (2006) *Indications of Public Health in the English Regions: 5. Child Health*. London: APHO.

Feyerabend, P. (1975) *Against Method*. London: New Left Books.

Flaherty, J., Veit-Wilson, J. and Dornan, P. (2007) *Poverty: The Facts*. London: Child Poverty Action Group.

Flavell, J.H., Miller, P.H. and Miller, S.A. (2002) *Cognitive Development*. Englewood Cliffs: Prentice-Hall.

Foucault, M. (1980) *Power/Knowledge: Selected Interviews and Other Writings, 1972–1977*. Ed. C. Gordon. London: Harvester Wheatsheaf.

Foucault, M. (1982) 'The subject and power. Afterword', in H.L. Dreyfus and P. Rabinow (eds) *Michel Foucault: Beyond Structuralism and Hermeneutics*. Hemel Hempstead: Harvester Wheatsheaf.

Fox Harding, H. (1996) *Family, State and Social Policy*. Basingstoke: Macmillan.

Fraser, S. (2004) 'Situating empirical research', in S. Fraser, V. Lewis, S. Ding, M. Kellett and C. Robinson (eds) *Doing Research with Children and Young People*. London: Sage Publications.

Freud, A. (1965) 'The assessment of normality in childhood', in *Normality and Pathology in Childhood*. New York: International University Press.

Freud, S. (1920/1955) 'Beyond the pleasure principle', *The Standard Edition of the Complete Psychological Works of Sigmund Freud*, 18. London: Hogarth. pp. 1–64.

Frost, N., Robinson, M. and Anning, A. (2005) 'Social workers in multi-disciplinary teams: issues and dilemmas for professional practice', *Child and Family Social Work*, 10: 187–96.

Gewirtz, S. (2001) 'Cloning the Blairs: New Labour's programme for the re-socialization of working-class parents', *Journal of Education Policy*, 16(4): 365–78.

Ghaye, A. and Ghaye, K. (1998) *Teaching and Learning through Critical Reflective Practice*. London: David Fulton Publishers.

Giddens, A. (2009) *Sociology*. Cambridge: Polity.

Gilligan, C. (1982) *In a Different Voice: Psychological Theory and Women's Development*. Cambridge, MA: Harvard University Press.

Gillis, J.R. (1981) *Youth and History*. Academic Press: New York.

Glennerster, H., Hills, J., Plachaud, D. and Webb, J. (2004) *One Hundred Years of Poverty and Policy*. York: Joseph Rowntree Foundation.

Glenny, G. and Roaf, G. (2008) *Multiprofessional Education Making Systems Work for Children*. Maidenhead: Open University Press/McGraw-Hill Education.

Goldman, R. (2005) *Fathers' Involvement in their Children's Education*. London: NFPI.

Goleman, D. (1995) *Emotional Intelligence*. New York: Bantam.

Goleman, D. (1998) *Working with Emotional Intelligence*. London: Bloomsbury Publishing.

Gordon, D. and Townsend, P. (n.d.) *Measuring the Poverty Line*. Available at: http://www.radstats.org.uk/no047/gordontownsend.pdf (accessed 21/04/09).

Greene, S. and Hill, M. (2005) 'Researching children's experience: methods and methodological issues', in S. Greene and D. Hogan (eds) *Researching Children's Experiences: Approaches and Methods*. London: Sage Publications.

Griffin, C. (1993) *Representations of Youth: The Study of Adolescence in Britain and America*. Cambridge: Polity Press.

Griffiths, L. (2004) 'Becoming a person', in J. Willan, R. Parker-Rees and J. Savage (eds) *Early Childhood Studies*. Exeter: Learning Matters.

Griggs, J. and Walker, R. (2008) *The Costs of Child Poverty for Individuals and Society: A Literature Review*. York: Joseph Rowntree Foundation.

References

Group of Eight (2009) G8. Available at: http://en.wikipedia.org/wiki/G8 (accessed 2/10/09).

Hall, P. (1976) *Reforming the Welfare*. London: Heinemann.

Hansen, K. and Joshi, H. (eds) (2007) *Millennium Cohort Study: Second Survey*. London: Institute of Education.

Harker, L. (2006a) *Chance of a Lifetime: The Impact of Bad Housing on Children's Lives*. London: Shelter.

Harker, L. (2006b) *Delivering on Child Poverty: What Would it Take? A Report of the Department of Work and Pensions*. London: The Stationery Office.

Harris, B. (1979) 'Whatever happened to Little Albert?', *American Psychologist*, 34: 2: 151–60, available at: http://htpprints.yorku.ca/archive/00000198/01/BHARRIS.HTM

Harris, M. (2008) *Exploring Developmental Psychology: Understanding Theory and Methods*. London: Sage.

Harris, M. and Butterworth, G. (2002) *Developmental Psychology: A Student's Handbook*. Hove: Psychology Press.

Hart, R. (1992) *Children's Participation from Tokenism to Citizenship*. Florence, Italy: UNICEF.

Harwood, R.L., Miler, J.G. and Irizarry, N.L. (1995) *Culture and Attachment*. New York: The Guildford Press.

Harvey, A. (1960) *Casualties of the Welfare State*. London: The Fabian Society.

Hendrick, H. (2003) *Child Welfare, Historical Dimensions, Contemporary Debate*. Bristol: The Policy Press.

Hill, M.J. (2005) *The Public Policy Process*. Harlow: Pearson Longman.

Hill, M. (2006) 'Ethical considerations in researching children's experiences', in S. Greene and D. Hogan (eds) *Researching Children's Experiences: Approaches and Methods*. London: Sage Publications.

HMSO (2004) *Child Poverty Review*. Norwich: The Stationary Office. Available at: http://www.hm-treasury.gov.uk/d/childpoverty_annexes_290704.pdf (accessed 2/10/09).

Holdsworth, R. (2001) 'Youth participation, charting the course', ACT and SE NSW Regional Youth Services Conference, October 2001.

Holmes, J. (1993) *John Bowlby and Attachment Theory*. London: Routledge.

Horwath, J. (2007) *Child Neglect*. London: Palgrave Macmillan.

Hoyle, D. (2008) 'Problematizing Every Child Matters', *the encyclopaedia of informal education*. Available at: www.infed.org/socialwork/every_child_matters_a_critique.htm (accessed 27/04/09).

Illingworth, R.S. (1987) *The Development of the Infant and Young Child: Normal and Abnormal*. Edinburgh: Churchill Livingstone.

Isles-Buck, E. and Newstead, S. (2003) *Essential Skills for Managers of Child-Centred Settings*. London: David Fulton Publishers.

Jagger, G. (2008) *Judith Butler: Sexual Politics, Social Change and the Power of the Performative*. London: Routledge.

James, A., Jenks, C. and Prout, A. (1998) *Theorising Childhood*. Cambridge: Polity Press.

Jenks, C. (2005) *Childhood*, 2nd edn. Abingdon: Routledge.

Jones, A. (2004) 'Involving children and young people as researchers', in S. Fraser, V. Lewis, S. Ding, M. Kellett and C. Robinson (eds) *Doing Research with Children and Young People*. London: Sage Publications.

Jones, C. and Leverett, S. (2008) 'Policy into practice: assessment, evaluation and multi-agency working with children', in P. Foley and A. Rixon (eds) *Changing Children's Services: Working and Learning Together*. Bristol: The Policy Press and The Open University.

Kavka, J. (1984) 'Wordsworth on teaching a child to lie: some thoughts on creative fiction-alism', *The Annual of Psychoanalysis*, 12: 395–414.

Working with children, young people and families

Kelly, B. (2007) 'Methodological issues for qualitative research with learning disabled children', *International Journal of Social Research Methodology*, 10(1): 21–35.

Kenny, M.C. (2001) 'Child abuse reporting: teachers' perceived deterrents', *Child Abuse and Neglect*, 25: 81–92.

Klein, J. (1993) *Our Need for Others and its Roots in Infancy*. London: Routledge.

Kuhn, T.S. (1962) *The Structure of Scientific Revolutions*. Chicago: University of Chicago Press.

Labour Party Autumn Conference (2008) 'Gordon Brown MP, Prime Minister and Leader of the Labour Party speaks to conference', available at: http://www.labour.org.uk/gordon_brown_conference (accessed 2/11/09).

Lacan, J. (2007) *Ecrits*. New York: Norton.

Laming, H. (2003) *The Victoria Climbié Inquiry Summary Report*. Norwich: HMSO.

Laming, H. (2009) *The Protection of Children in England: A Progress Report*. Norwich: The Stationery Office.

Landsdowe, G. (1994) *UK Agenda for Children: A Systematic Analysis of the Extent to which Law, Policy and Practice in the UK Complies with the Principles and Standards of the UN Convention on the Rights of the Child*. London: Children's Rights.

Layard, R. and Dunn, J. (2009) *A Good Childhood*. London: Penguin.

Lepper, J. (2009) 'Social care – social pedagogy demystified', *Children and Young People Now*, 2 April.

Lewis, M., Feiring, C. and Rosenthal, S. (2000) 'Attachment over time', *Child Development*, 71: 707–20.

Lipsky, M. (1980) *Street-level Bureaucracy: Dilemmas of the Individual in Public Services*. New York: Russell Sage Foundation.

Lister, R. (2004) *Poverty*. Cambridge: Polity Press.

Lister, S. (2009) 'Baby P would have lived if anyone had gone beyond the call of duty', in *TimesOnline*, available at: http://www.timesonline.co.uk/tol/life_and_style/health/child_health/article6276087.ece (accessed 18/05/09).

Lobstein, T., Baur, L. and Uavy, L. (2004) 'Obesity in children and young people: a crisis in public health', in *Obesity Reviews*, 5(1): 4–85.

Locke, J. (1693) *Some Thoughts Concerning Education*. London: A. and J. Churchill.

Lonne, B., Parton, N., Thomson, J. and Harries, M. (2009) *Reforming Child Protection*. Abingdon: Routledge.

Lyotard, J-F. (1984) *The Post-modern Condition: A Report on Knowledge*. Manchester: Manchester University Press.

MacBeath, J., Demetriou, H. and Rudduck, J. (2003) *Ways of Consulting Pupils: Tools of Schools*. Cambridge: Pearson Publishing Company.

MacNaughton, G. and Smith, K. (2005) 'Transforming research ethics: the choices and challenges of researching with children', in A. Farrell (ed.) *Ethical Research with Children*. Maidenhead: Open University Press.

Mahler, M.S., Pine, F. and Bergman, A. (2000) *The Psychological Birth of the Human Infant: Symbiosis and Individuation*. New York: Basic Books.

Malin, N. and Morrow, G. (2008) *Evaluating Sure Start*. London: Whiting and Birch.

Mayall, B. (2001) 'Conversations with children: working with generational issues', in P. Christensen and A. James (eds) *Research with Children: Perspectives and Practices*. London: Routledge Falmer.

Mayall, B. (2002) *Towards a Sociology of Childhood*. Maidenhead: Open University Press.

McGillivray, G. (2007) 'England', in M. Clark and T. Waller (eds) *Early Childhood Education and Care*. London: Sage Publications.

McGillivray, G. (2008) 'Nannies, nursery nurses and early years professionals: constructions of professional identity in the early years workforce in England', *European Early Childhood Education Research Journal*, 16(2): 242–54.

References

McGillivray, G. and Davies, H. (forthcoming) 'Skills for placement learning', in G. Brotherton and S. Parker (ed.) *Work-based Learning and Practice Placement: A Textbook for Health and Social Care Students.* Devon: Reflect Press Ltd.

McIntyre, D., Pedder, D. and Rudduck, J. (2005) 'Pupil voice: comfortable and uncomfortable learnings for teachers', *Research Papers in Education*, 20(2): 149–68 (University of Cambridge).

Miller, P.H. (2002) *Theories of Developmental Psychology.* New York: Worth.

Moon, J. (2008) *Critical Thinking: An Exploration of Theory and Practice.* Abingdon: Routledge.

Moran, P., Jacobs, C., Bunn, A. and Bifulco, A. (2007) 'Multi-agency working: implications for an early-intervention social work team', *Child and Family Social Work*, 12: 143–51.

Morrow, V. (2005) 'Ethical issues in collaborative research with children', in A. Farrell (ed.) *Ethical Research with Children.* Maidenhead: Open University Press.

Mortiboys, A. (2005) *Teaching with Emotional Intelligence.* Abingdon: Routledge.

Moss, P. and Petrie, P. (2002) *From Children's Services to Children's Spaces.* Abingdon: Routledge Falmer.

Moylett, H. (2003) 'Early years education and care', in S. Bartlett and D. Burton (eds) *Education Studies: Essential Issues.* London: Sage.

Munro, E. (1998) *Understanding Social Work: An Empirical Approach.* London: The Athlone Press.

Munro, E. (2005) 'Improving practice: child protection as a systems problem', *Children and Youth Services Review*, 27: 375–91.

Munro, E. (2007) 'Confidentiality in a preventive child welfare system', *Ethics and Social Welfare*, 1(1) April: 41–55.

Munro, E. (2008) 'Lessons learned, boxes ticked, families ignored', *The Independent* 10 May, available at: http://www.independent.co.uk/opinion/commentators/eileen-munro-lessons-learnt-boxes-ticked-families-ignored-1020508.html (accessed 2/07/09).

Murray, L., Adams, G., Patterson, P. and Goodyer, I.M. (2006) 'Socioemotional development in adolescents at risk for depression: the role of maternal depression and attachment style', *Development and Psychopathology* 18(2): 489–516.

National Children's Bureau (NCB)(2003) *Guidelines for Research.* Available at: http://www.ncb.org.uk/dotpdf/open%20access%20-%20phase%201%20only/research_guidelines_200604.pdf

National Evaluation of Sure Start (2007) *Sure Start and Black and Minority Ethnic Populations.* London: HMSO.

National Youth Agency (2009) *Hear by Right.* Available at http://hbronya.org.uk/ Accessed November 2009.

Nazroo, J.Y. (1997) *The Health of Britain's Ethnic Minorities.* London: PSI.

Neill, A.S. (1998) *Summerhill School.* New York: St Martins Press.

Neubauer, P.B. (1984) 'Anna Frued's concept of developmental lines', *Psychoanalytic Study of the Child*, 39: 15–27.

Newman, T. and Blackburn, S. (2002) *Transitions in the Lives of Children and Young People: Resilience Factors.* Barnardo's Policy, Research and Influencing Unit. Edinburgh: Scottish Executive Education Department.

Newson, J. (1982) 'Dialogue and development', in M. Braham (ed.) *Aspects of Education.* London: Wiley.

Nickell, S.J. (2004) 'Poverty and worklessness in Britain', *Economic Journal*, 114 (494) March 2004: C1–C25.

Nickerson, R.S. (1999) 'Enhancing creativity', in R.J. Sternberg (ed.) *Handbook of Creativity.* Cambridge: Cambridge University Press.

Nieuwenhuys, O. (2004) 'Participatory action research in the majority world', in S. Fraser, V. Lewis, S. Ding, M. Kellett and C. Robinson (eds) *Doing Research with Children and Young People.* London: Sage Publications.

Working with children, young people and families

Nixon, J., Martin, J., McKeown, P.O. and Ranson, S. (1996) *Encouraging Learning: Towards a Theory of the Learning School*. Buckingham: Open University Press.

Noddings, N. (1995) *Philosophy of Education*. Boulder, CO: Westview Press.

NSPCC (2003) *Learning to Protect*. London: NSPCC.

Ofsted (2008) *How Well Are They Doing? The Impact of Children's Centres and Extended Schools*. London: Crown Publications.

O'Neill, O. (2002) *A Question of Trust*. Cambridge: Cambridge University Press.

Osgood, J. (2006) 'Professionalism and performativity: the feminist challenge facing early years practitioners', *Early Years*, 26(2): 187–99.

Pain, R., Grundy, S., Gill, S., Towner, E., Sparkes, G. and Hughes, K. (2005) '"So long as I take my mobile": mobile phones, urban life and geographies of young peoples' safety', *International Journal of Urban and Regional Research*, 29(4): 814–30.

Parke, R.D. and Gauvin, M. (2009) *Child Psychology: A Contemporary Viewpoint*. Boston: McGraw Hill.

Parker, S. (2007) 'Work based learning and reflective practice', in G. Brotherton and S. Parker (2007) *Your Foundation in Health and Social Care*. London: Sage.

Parton, N. (2006) *Safeguarding Childhood: Early Intervention and Surveillance in a Late Modern Society*. Basingstoke: Palgrave.

Parton, N. and Thomas, T. (1983) 'Child abuse and citizenship', in B. Jordan and N. Parton (eds) *The Political Dimensions of Social Work*. Oxford: Basil Blackwell.

Pavlov, I.P. (1928) *Lectures on Conditioned Reflexes. Twenty-Five Years of Objective Study of the Higher Nervous Activity (Behaviour) of Animals*. Trans. by W.H. Grant and G. Volborth. New York: International Publishers.

Payne, S. (n.d.) *Poverty, Social Exclusion and Mental Health: Findings from the 1999 PSE Survey*. Available at: http://www.bris.ac.uk/poverty/pse/99PSE-WP15.doc (accessed 20/05/09).

Payne, L. (2008) *Legislation for Sure Start Children's Centres*. London: National Children's Bureau.

Penn, H. (2005) *Understanding Early Childhood*. Maidenhead: Open University Press.

Percy-Smith, J. (2000) *Policy Responses to Social Exclusion: Towards Inclusion* Buckingham: OUP.

Petrie, P., Boddy, J., Cameron, C., Wigfall, V. and Simon, A. (2006) *Working with Children in Care*. Maidenhead: McGraw Hill.

Petrie, P., Boddy, J., Cameron, C., Heptinstall, E., McQuail, S., Simon, A. and Wigfall, V. (2008) *Pedagogy – A Holistic, Personal Approach to Work with Children and Young People Across Services: European Models for Practice, Training, Education and Qualification*. Thomas Coram Research Unit: Briefing Update. Available at: http://eprints.ioe.ac. uk/58/1/Pedagogy_briefing_paper.pdf

Piaget, J. (1970) *Genetic Epistemology*. New York: Columbia University Press.

Piaget, J. (1985) *The Equilibration of Cognitive Structures*. Chicago: University of Chicago Press.

Popper, K. (1963) *Conjectures and Refutations*. London: Routledge.

Postman, N. (1994) *The Disappearance of Childhood*. New York: Random House.

Pratt, J. (2006) 'Citizenship, social solidarity and social policy', in M. Lavalette and A. Pratt (eds) *Social Policy: Theories, Concepts and Issues*, 3rd edn. London: Sage Publications.

Prout, A. (2005) *The Future of Childhood*. London: Routledge Falmer.

Putnam, R. (2000) *Bowling Alone*. New York: Simon and Schuster.

Pykett, J. (2008) 'Making citizens governable? The Crick Report as governmental technology', *Journal of Education Policy*, 22(3): 301–20.

QCA (2000) *Citizenship: Key Stage 3: Teacher's Guide*. London: Qualifications and Curriculum Authority.

Randhawa, G. (2007) *Tackling Health Inequalities for Minority Ethnic Groups: Challenges and Opportunities*. London: Race Equality Foundation.

References

Rayner, E., Joyce, A., Rose, J. and Twyman, M. (2005) *Human Development: An Introduction to the Psychodynamics of Growth, Maturity and Aging*. London: Routledge.

Reading, R. and Reynolds, S. (2001) 'Debt, social disadvantage and maternal depression', *Social Sciences and Medicine*, 53(4): 441–53.

Reid, B. (1993) 'But we're doing it already! Exploring a response to the concept of reflective practice in order to improve its facilitation', *Nurse Education Today*, 13: 305–9.

Reid, K. (2005) 'The implications of Every Child Maters and the Children Act for schools', *Pastoral Care in Education*, 23: 12–18.

Ritchie, J. (2003) 'The applications of qualitative methods to social research', in J. Ritchie and J. Lewis (eds) *Qualitative Research Practice: A Guide for Social Science Students and Researchers*. London: Sage Publications.

Roberts, H. (2004) 'Health and social care', in S. Fraser, V. Lewis, S. Ding, M. Kellett and C. Robinson (eds) *Doing Research with Children and Young People*. London: Sage Publications.

Robinson, C. and Kellett, M. (2004) 'Power', in S. Fraser, V. Lewis, S. Ding, M. Kellett and C. Robinson (eds) *Doing Research with Children and Young People*. London: Sage Publications.

Rodd, J. (2006) *Leadership in Early Childhood*, 3rd edn. Maidenhead: Open University Press.

Rousseau, J.J. (1979) *Emil, or on Education*. Trans. Allan Bloom. New York: Basic Books.

Rudduck, J. (2003) *Pupil Voice and Citizenship Education – A Report for the QCA Citizenship and PHSE Team*. University of Cambridge.

Rutter, M. (2008) 'Implications of attachment theory and research for child care policies', in J. Cassidy and P.R. Shaver (eds) *Handbook of Attachment: Theory, Research and Clinical Applications*. London: Guilford Press. pp. 958–74.

Rutter, M. and Rutter, M. (1992) *Developing Minds. Challenge and Continuity Across the Life Span*. London: Penguin.

Schaffer, H.R. (2006) *Key Concepts in Developmental Psychology*. London: Sage.

Schön, D. (1983) *The Reflective Practitioner: How Professionals Think in Action*. New York: Basic Books.

Scott, J. (2000) 'Children as respondents: the challenge for quantitative methods', in P. Christensen and A. James (eds) *Research with Children: Perspectives and Practices*. London: Routledge Falmer.

Scott, S. and Hayden, D. (2005) *Barnardo's Statement of Ethical Research Practice*. Barnardos' Policy and Research Unit.

Seaman, P., Turner, K., Hill, M., Stafford, A. and Walker, M. (2006) *Parents and Children's Resilience in Disadvantaged Communities*. Available at: http://www.jrf.org.uk/publications/parenting-and-childrens-resilience-disadvantaged-communities (accessed 7/04/09).

Secretary of State for Social Services (1974) *Report of the Inquiry into the Care and Supervision Provided in Relation to Maria Colwell*. London: HMSO.

Secretary of State for Social Services (1988) *Report of the Inquiry into Child Abuse in Cleveland* (Cm 412). London: HMSO.

Shah, A. (2009) 'Global issues', available at: http://www.globalissues.org/article/26/poverty-facts-and-stats (accessed 2/10/09).

Shaw, M., Dorling, D., Gordon, D. and Davey Smith, G. (1999) *The Widening Gap: Health Inequalities and Policy in Britain*. Bristol: Policy Press.

Shelter (2006) *Against the Odds*. London: Shelter.

Siegler, R.S. (1998) *Children's Thinking*. Upper Saddle River, NJ: Prentice-Hall.

Sim, S. (1999) *Derrida and the End of History*. Cambridge: Icon Books.

Simon, A. (2007) *The Involvement of Children and Young People from Black and Minority Ethnic Communities as Advocates in their own Health Care*. Birmingham and The Black Country Strategic Health Authority and Newman College of Higher Education. Available at: http://www.newman.ac.uk/courses/SC_PD/esf_reports/Health%20Care%20Report%20%28New%20Coll%29.pdf

Working with children, young people and families

Skelton, T. (2008) 'Research with children and young people: exploring the tensions between ethics, competence and participation', *Children's Geographies*, 6(1): 21–36.

Skinner, B.F. (1938) *The Behavior of Organisms*. New York: Appleton, Century, Crofts.

Skinner, B.F. (1948) *Walden Two*. New York: Macmillan.

Skinner, B.F. (1953) *Science and Human Behavior*. New York: Macmillan.

Skinner, B.F. (1971) *Beyond Freedom and Dignity*. New York: Knopf.

Skinner, B.F. (1974) *About Behaviorism*. New York: Vintage.

Slater, A. and Bremner, G. (eds) (2003) *An Introduction to Developmental Psychology*. Oxford: Blackwell.

Smidt, S. (2008) *Introducing Vygotsky*. London: Routledge.

Smith, J. and Baltes, P.B. (1999) 'Life-span perspectives on development', in M.H. Bornstein and M.E. Lamb (eds) *Developmental Psychology: An Advanced Textbook*. Mahwah. NJ: Erlbaum.

Socialist Health Association (2009) *Poverty and Inequality in Health*. Available at: http://www.sochealth.co.uk/news/poverty.htm (accessed: 12/05/09).

Speake, J. (2004) *The Oxford Book of Proverbs*, 4th edn. Oxford: Oxford University Press. Available at: http://www.highbeam.com/doc/1O90-CHILDRENandfoolstllthtrth.html (accessed 02/12/09).

Staudt, M. and Kemp Powell, K. (1996) 'Serving children and adolescents in the school: can social work meet the challenge?', *Child and Adolescent Social Work Journal*, 13(5): 433–46.

Stone, B. and Rixon, A. (2008) 'Towards integrated working', in P. Foley and A. Rixon (eds) *Changing Children's Services*. Bristol: Policy Press.

Stroobants, J., Chambers, P. and Clarke, B. (2008) *Reflective Journeys*. Rome: Leonardo da Vinci Reflect Project.

Sugarman, L. (2001) *Life-Span Development: Frameworks, Accounts and Strategies*. Hove: Psychology Press.

Sure Start Local Programmes (2006) Available at: http://www.everychildmatters.gov.uk/earlyyears/Sure Start/local/ (accessed 13/05/09).

Tett, L. (2001) 'Parents as problems or parents as people? Parental involvement programmes, schools and adult educators', *International Journal of Lifelong Education*, 20(3): 188–98.

The Cabinet Office (2009) *Unleashing Aspiration: The Final Report of the Panel on Fair Access to the Professions (The Milburn Report)*. Available at: http://news.bbc.co.uk/1/shared/bsp/hi/pdfs/21_07_09_fair_access.pdf (accessed 27/07/09).

The Poverty Site (2009) Available at: http://www.poverty.org.uk/61/index.shtml?2 (accessed 12/05/09).

Thoburn, J., Wilding, J. and Watson, J. (2001) 'Family support in cases of emotional mal-treatment and neglect', in Department of Health (2001) *The Children Act 1989 Now: Messages from Research*. London: The Stationary Office. pp. 231–4.

Thomas, D. (2007) *Breaking Through the Sound Barrier: Difficulties of Voiced Research in Schools Uncommitted to Public Voice*. University of Nottingham: BERA.

Thompson, D. (ed.) (1995) *The Concise Oxford Dictionary*, 9th edn. Oxford: Clarendon Press.

Thorndike, E.L. (1911) *Animal Intelligence: Experimental Studies*. New York: Macmillan. Available at: http://psychclassics.yorku.ca/Thorndike/Animal/chap5.htm

Tite, R. (1993) 'How teachers define and respond to child abuse: the distinction between theoretical and reportable cases', *Child Abuse and Neglect*, 17: 591–603.

Townsend, P. (1979) *Poverty in the United Kingdom: A Survey of Household Resources and Standards of Living*. London: Penguin.

Tucker, S. (2004) 'Youth working: professional identities given, received or contested?', in J. Roche, S. Tucker, R. Thomson and R. Flynn (eds) *Youth in Society*, 2nd edn. London: Sage Publications.

References

Turing, A.M. (1950) 'Computing machinery and intelligence', *Mind*, 59: 433–60, available at: http://www.loebner.net/Prizef/TuringArticle.html

UK School Councils Network (2002) *School Councils Network Newsletter*. London: UK School Council.

UNICEF (2007) *Report Card 7, Child Poverty in Perspective: An Overview of Child Well-being in Rich Countries*. UNICEF Innocenti Research Centre, Florence.

United Nations Conventions on the Rights of the Child (UNCRC) (1989) *UN General Assembly Resolution 44/25*.

Unwin, L. and Fuller, A. (2003) *Expanding Learning in the Workplace*, NIACE Policy Discussion Paper. Leicester: NIACE.

Urban, M. (2008) 'Dealing with uncertainty: challenges and possibilities for the early childhood profession', *European Early Childhood Education Research Journal*, 16(2): 135–52.

Vaillant, G.E. (2003) *Aging Well: Guideposts to a Happier Life*. Boston: Little Brown.

Vygotsky, L.S. (1978) *Mind in Society: The Development of Higher Psychological Processes*. Cambridge, MA: Harvard University Press.

Waldman, J. (2007) *Narrowing the Gap in Outcomes for Vulnerable Groups*. Slough: NFER.

Waters, E., Weinfield, N. and Hamilton, C. (2000) 'The stability of attachment security from infancy to adolescence and early adulthood: general discussion', *Child Development*, 71(3): 703–6.

Watson, J.B. (1928) *Psychological Care of Infant and Child*. New York: Norton.

Watson, J.B. (1930) *Behaviorism*. Norton: New York.

Watson, J.B. and Rayner, R. (1920) 'Conditioned emotional reactions', *Journal of Experimental Psychology*, 3: 1–14, available at: http://psychclassics.yorku.ca/Watson/emotion.htm

Weber, S. and Mitchell, C. (1995) *'That's Funny, You Don't Look Like a Teacher'*. London: The Falmer Press.

Wedderburn, D. (1963) *Poverty in Britain Today – The Evidence*. Cambridge: University of Cambridge. Reprint Series No. 196.

Welsh, E., Buchanan, A., Flouri, E. and Lewis, J. (2004) *'Involved' Fathering and Child Well-being: Fathers' Involvement with Secondary School Age Children*. York: Joseph Rowntree Foundation. Available at: www.jrf.org.uk

Wenger, E. (1998) *Communities of Practice*. Cambridge: Cambridge University Press.

Whitehead, M. (1992) *The Health Divide*. London: Penguin.

Whitty, G. and Wisby, E. (2007) *Real Decision Making? School Councils in Action*. London: DCSF.

Wilce, H. (2008) 'How the Government's plans to end child poverty were botched', *The Independent*, 8 May. Available at: http://www.independent.co.uk/news/education/schools/how-the-governments-plans-to-end-child-poverty-were-botched-822521.html (accessed June 2009).

Wilkinson, R. (1996) *Unhealthy Societies*. London: Routledge.

Wilkinson, R. and Pickett, K. (2009) *The Spirit Level*. London: Allen Lane.

Winnicott, D.W. (1952) 'Anxiety associated with insecurity', in *Through Paediatrics to Psychoanalysis: Collected Papers*. London: Hogarth, 1975. pp. 97–100.

Woodhead, M. and Faulkner, D. (2000) 'Subjects or participants? Dilemmas of psychological research with children', in P. Christensen and A. James (eds) *Research with Children: Perspectives and Practices*. London: Routledge Falmer.

Wordsworth, W. (1802) 'My heart leaps up when I behold', in *The Complete Poetical Works*. London: Macmillan, 1888.

Wyness, M. (2006) *Childhood and Society*. Basingstoke: Palgrave.

Working with children, young people and families

Index

Working with children, young people and families

Index

Working with children, young people and families